WORKBOOK

AAT Foundation NVQ/SVQ Level 2 in Accounting

UNIT 30 : WORKBOOK

British Library Cataloguing-in-Publication Data

A catalogue record for this book is available from the British Library.

Published by
Kaplan Publishing
Unit 2 The Business Centre
Molly Millars Lane
Wokingham
Berkshire
RG41 2QZ

ISBN 978-1-84710-334-5

© FTC Kaplan Limited, May 2007

Printed and bound in Great Britain.

We are grateful to the Association of Accounting Technicians for permission to reproduce past assessment materials. The solutions have been prepared by Kaplan Publishing.

All rights reserved. No part of this publication may be reproduced, stored in a retrieval system, or transmitted, in any form or by any means, electronic, mechanical, photocopying, recording or otherwise, without the prior written permission of Kaplan Publishing.

CONTENTS

Preface ix

		Questions	Answers

Key Techniques Question Bank

Textbook chapters

		Questions	Answers
1	Double entry bookkeeping – introduction	2	272
2	Ledger accounting	3	275
3	Balancing the ledger accounts	5	280
4	Credit sales – discounts and VAT	7	282
5	The sales day book – main and subsidiary ledgers	8	285
6	The analysed cash receipts book	16	289
7	Credit purchases – discounts and VAT	18	292
8	The purchases day book – main and subsidiary ledgers	18	293
9	The analysed cash payments book	29	296

CONTENTS

		Questions	Answers
10	Credit sales: documents	33	299
11	The banking system	37	301
12	Checking receipts	41	302
13	Banking receipts	46	303
14	Debtors' statements	72	313
15	Accounting for sales – summary	84	320
16	Credit purchases: documents	100	329
17	Making payments	109	330
18	Payroll procedures	116	333
19	Accounting for purchases – summary	124	338
20	Petty cash systems	132	342

CONTENTS

		Questions	Answers
21	Bank reconciliations	147	348
22	Ledger balances and control accounts	161	356
23	Drafting an initial trial balance	165	362

	Questions	Answer Booklet	Answers
Mock Simulation 1	175	229	369
Mock Simulation 2	191	247	387
Mock Simulation 3	199	263	401

	Questions	Answers
Specimen Examination	207	411

PREFACE

WORKBOOK

This workbook has been specifically written for Unit 30.

It is designed to complement the single study text which covers Unit 30.

The Workbook has the following features.

A section of 'Key Techniques' which reinforce the main competencies which students must acquire to succeed at these units. The questions are grouped following the order of the textbook chapters for ease of access.

The questions in the key techniques question bank are a mixture of short questions which reinforce specific techniques and longer 'mini-scenario' questions which reinforce students' understanding of the topics.

The specimen examination at the end of the book will help prepare students for the examination.

KEY TECHNIQUES QUESTIONS

UNIT 30 : WORKBOOK

Chapter 1
Double entry bookkeeping - introduction

▷ **ACTIVITY 1**

Bertie Wooster started a business as an antique dealer on 1 July 20X7.

Required

Show the accounting equation which results from each of the following transactions made during Bertie's first two weeks of trading.
(a) Started the business with £5,000 in cash as opening capital.
(b) Bought an Edwardian desk for £500 cash.
(c) Bought five art deco table lamps for £200 each, on credit from Roderick Spode.
(d) Sold the desk for £750 cash.
(e) Sold four of the table lamps for £300 each on credit to his Uncle Tom.
(f) Paid rent of £250 cash.
(g) Drew £100 in cash out of the business for living expenses.
(h) Earned £50 for writing a magazine article, but had not yet been paid for it.
(i) Paid Roderick Spode £500 on account.
(j) Received £1,200 from Uncle Tom in full settlement of the amount due.
(k) Bought a van for use in the business for £4,000 cash.
(l) Received a telephone bill for £150 but did not pay it yet.

Note: Each transaction follows on from the one before.

▷ **ACTIVITY 2**

On 1 January 20X6 Esmond Haddock inherited £3,000 from an aunt and decided to open his own sports equipment shop. During January the following transactions took place.

01 January	Paid the £3,000 into a bank account
02 January	Paid one month's rent of £100 for the shop premises
10 January	Bought stock of sports equipment for £1,000 cash
14 January	Paid £50 for display equipment
30 January	Drew out £150 for his own use
31 January	Bought sports equipment on credit for £1,500

During the month he sold for £830 half of the equipment he purchased on 10 January. £800 was received in cash and £30 was owed to him by one customer.

Required

Show the accounting equation of the business at 31 January 20X6.

Note: Profit will be the balancing figure.

KEY TECHNIQUES : QUESTIONS

Chapter 2
Ledger accounting

▷ **ACTIVITY 3**   ▷▷▷▷

Z has the following transactions:
(a) Pays £4,000 into the bank as capital.
(b) Buys a computer for £1,000.
(c) Pays rent of £400.
(d) Earns £800 for consultancy services.

Write up the ledger accounts for the above.

▷ **ACTIVITY 4**   ▷▷▷▷

Using the information in question 3 above, fill in the following table to explain the dual nature of each transaction. The first one is done to explain what to do.

		Debit		Credit
Transaction	Account	Reason	Account	Reason
(a) £4,000 capital	Bank	Cash paid into the bank – an asset	Capital	Cash paid in by owner - a liability
(b) 1,000 comp				
(c) 400 Rent				
(d) 800 consult				

▷ **ACTIVITY 5**   ▷▷▷▷

A makes the following cash transactions:
(a) Pays £5,000 into the bank as capital.
(b) Buys goods for £800.
(c) Pays rent of £500.
(d) Buys a van for £2,000.
(e) Sells some of the goods for £600.
(f) Sells some more of the goods for £700.
(g) Buys goods for £1,000.
(h) Buys stationery for £200.
(i) Takes £500 out of the bank as drawings.

Write up the ledger accounts for the above.

KAPLAN PUBLISHING

UNIT 30 : WORKBOOK

▷ ACTIVITY 6

B makes the following cash transactions:
(a) Pays £4,000 into the bank as capital.
(b) Buys goods for £700.
(c) Buys champagne to entertain the staff for £300.
(d) Purchases three computers for £3,000.
(e) Sells goods for £1,500.
(f) Draws £500 cash.
(g) Purchases goods for £1,200.
(h) Pays telephone bill of £600.
(i) Receives telephone bill rebate of £200.
(j) Buys stationery for £157.

Write up the ledger accounts for the above.

▷ ACTIVITY 7

C makes the following cash transactions:
(a) Pays £2,000 into the bank as capital.
(b) Purchases goods for £1,000.
(c) Buys a van costing £900.
(d) Sells goods for £2,500.
(e) Receives £3,000 for consultancy services.
(f) Purchases goods for £1,000.
(g) Buys stationery for £260.
(h) Pays rent of £750.
(i) Pays staff wages of £600.
(j) Receives £100 for returned stationery.

Write up the ledger accounts for the above.

▷ ACTIVITY 8

A sells books to B for £1,000 on credit.

A also sells books to C for £90 credit.

B pays £500 and C pays £90.

Write up these transactions in the ledger accounts of A.

▷ ACTIVITY 9

X purchases £600 of goods from Y and £750 of goods from Z on credit.

X pays Y £300 and Z £500.

Write up these transactions in the ledger accounts of X.

Chapter 3
Balancing the ledger accounts

▷ ACTIVITY 10

The following cash book has been written up for the month of May 20X4. There was no opening balance.

Bank

	£		£
Capital	10,000	Computer	1,000
Sales	2,000	Telephone	567
Sales	3,000	Rent	1,500
Sales	2,000	Rates	125
		Stationery	247
		Petrol	49
		Purchases	2,500
		Drawings	500
		Petrol	42

Bring down the balance on the account.

▷ ACTIVITY 11

The following bank account has been written up during May 20X4. There was no brought forward balance.

Bank

	£		£
Capital	5,000	Purchases	850
Sales	1,000	Fixtures	560
Sales	876	Van	1,500
Rent rebate	560	Rent	1,300
Sales	1,370	Rates	360
		Telephone	220
		Stationery	120
		Petrol	48
		Car repairs	167

Bring down the balance on the account.

UNIT 30 : WORKBOOK

▷ ACTIVITY 12

The following bank account has been written up during June 20X4.

Bank

	£		£
Balance b/f	23,700	Drawings	4,000
Sales	2,300	Rent	570
Sales	1,700	Purchases	6,000
Debtors	4,700	Rates	500
		Salaries	3,600
		Car expenses	460
		Petrol	49
		Petrol	38
		Electricity	210
		Stationery	89

Bring down the balance on the account.

▷ ACTIVITY 13

X Ltd has analysed its sales in a matrix as follows.

	North	South	East	West	Total
Garden plants	253,865	27,598	315,634	109,521	
Garden equipment	2,734,384	274,393	382,726	3,726,125	
Consultancy	2,438,549	374,385	3,728,398	37,261	
TOTAL					

Cast and cross-cast the matrix.

ACTIVITY 14

The following is the analysed cash paid book of Y Ltd.

Date	Narrative	Folio	Total	Creditors	Stationery	Rent	Telephone	Postage	Fixed assets	Sundry
				23,894	678	4,563	5,675	456	456	78
				6,743					55,433	467
				56,432	654	675				786
				5,643	564		786	78	564	786
				675	89			675	765	8,943
				6,754	675		785	78	897	98
TOTAL										

Cast and cross-cast the cash book.

Chapter 4
Credit sales – discounts and VAT

ACTIVITY 15

Calculate the VAT on the following sales:
(a) A sale for £140.00 plus VAT.
(b) A sale for £560.00 plus VAT.
(c) A sale for £780.00 including VAT.
(d) A sale for £970.00 including VAT.

ACTIVITY 16

Calculate the VAT on the following sales:
(a) A sale for £280.00 plus VAT where a settlement discount of 2% is offered.
(b) A sale for £480.00 plus VAT where a settlement discount of 3% is offered.
(c) A sale for £800.00 plus VAT where a settlement discount of 5% is offered but not taken.
(d) A sale of £650.00 plus VAT where a settlement discount of 4% is offered but not taken.

ACTIVITY 17

A sells £600 of goods to B. VAT has to be added and A offers B a settlement discount of 3%. Calculate the amount that B will pay A if:
(a) B takes the settlement discount; and
(b) B does not take the settlement discount.

ACTIVITY 18

A sells £700 of goods to C net of VAT. A offers C a settlement discount of 5%. Enter the sale and payment for the sale in the ledger accounts assuming:
(a) C takes the settlement discount; and
(b) C does not take the settlement discount.

Chapter 5
The sales day book – main and subsidiary ledgers

ACTIVITY 19

You work in the accounts department of D F Engineering and one of your tasks is to write up the day books. In your organisation there is no separate sales returns day book and therefore any credit notes are entered as negative amounts in the sales day book.

Given below are the details of the sales invoices and credit notes that have been issued this week. D F Engineering does not offer trade or settlement discounts but is registered for VAT and all sales are of standard rated goods.

Invoices sent out:

		Code	£		Invoice number
20X1					
1 May	Fraser & Co	SL14	128.68	plus VAT	03466
	Letterhead Ltd	SL03	257.90	plus VAT	03467
2 May	Jeliteen Traders	SL15	96.58	plus VAT	03468
3 May	Harper Bros	SL22	268.15	plus VAT	03469
	Juniper Ltd	SL17	105.38	plus VAT	03470
4 May	H G Frank	SL30	294.67	plus VAT	03471
5 May	Keller Assocs	SL07	110.58	plus VAT	03472

Credit notes sent out:

		Code	£		Credit note number
20X1					
2 May	Garner & Co	SL12	68.70	plus VAT	0746
4 May	Hill Traders	SL26	117.68	plus VAT	0747

Required

Write up the sales day book given for the week ending 5 May 20X1 and total all of the columns.

KEY TECHNIQUES : QUESTIONS

Sales day book						
Date	Invoice No	Customer name	Code	Total £	VAT £	Net £

▷ ACTIVITY 20 ▷ ▷ ▷ ▷

You work in the accounts department of Keyboard Supplies, a supplier of a wide range of electronic keyboards to a variety of music shops on credit. Given below are three sales invoices that you have just sent out to customers and these are to be written up into the sales day book given below.

Sales of four different types of keyboard are made and the sales are analysed into each of these four types and coded as follows:

Atol keyboards   01
Bento keyboards   02
Garland keyboards   03
Zanni keyboards   04

Required

Write up the analysed sales day book and total each of the columns.

INVOICE

Invoice to:
B Z S Music
42 Westhill
Nutford TN11 3PQ

Deliver to:
As above

Keyboard Supplies
Trench Park Estate
Fieldham
Sussex TN21 4AF
Tel: 01829 654545
Fax: 01829 654646

Invoice no:	06116
Tax point:	18 April 20X1
VAT reg no:	466 1128 30
Your reference:	SL01
Purchase order no:	77121

Code	Description	Quantity	VAT rate %	Unit price £	Amount exclusive of VAT £
B4012	Bento Keyboard	3	17.5	180.00	540.00
Z2060	Zanni Keyboard	6	17.5	164.00	984.00
					1,524.00
Trade discount 20%					304.80
					1,219.20
VAT at 17.5%					206.95
Total amount payable					1,426.15

Deduct discount of 3% if paid within 10 days, net 30 days

INVOICE

Invoice to:
M T Retail
Fraser House
Perley TN7 8QT

Deliver to:
As above

Keyboard Supplies
Trench Park Estate
Fieldham
Sussex TN21 4AF
Tel: 01829 654545
Fax: 01829 654646

Invoice no:	06117
Tax point:	18 April 20X1
VAT reg no:	466 1128 30
Your reference:	SL29
Purchase order no:	P04648

Code	Description	Quantity	VAT rate %	Unit price £	Amount exclusive of VAT £
A6060	Atol Keyboard	1	17.5	210.00	210.00
Z4080	Zanni Keyboard	1	17.5	325.00	325.00
					535.00
VAT at 17.5%					93.62
Total amount payable					628.62

Net 30 days

KEY TECHNIQUES : QUESTIONS

INVOICE

Invoice to:
Harmer & Co
1 Acre Street
Nutford TN11 6HA

Deliver to:
As above

Keyboard Supplies
Trench Park Estate
Fieldham
Sussex TN21 4AF
Tel: 01829 654545
Fax: 01829 654646

Invoice no:	06118
Tax point:	18 April 20X1
VAT reg no:	466 1128 30
Your reference:	SL17
Purchase order no:	047721

Code	Description	Quantity	VAT rate %	Unit price £	Amount exclusive of VAT £
G4326	Garland Keyboard	3	17.5	98.00	294.00
B2040	Bento Keyboard	5	17.5	115.00	575.00
					869.00
VAT at 17.5%					147.51
Total amount payable					1,016.51

Deduct discount of 3% if paid within 10 days, net 30 days

Sales day book

Date	Invoice No	Customer name	Code	Total £	VAT £	01 £	02 £	03 £	04 £

UNIT 30 : WORKBOOK

▷ ACTIVITY 21

Graham Haddow runs a buildings maintenance and decorating business and sends out invoices for the work that he has done. He analyses his sales between the maintenance work and decorating work. You are given three sales invoices that he sent out last week.

Required

Enter the sales invoice details into the analysed sales day book given and total all of the columns.

INVOICE

Invoice to:
Portman & Co
Portman House
Tonbridge TN1 4LL

Graham Haddow
59 East Street
Medford
MF6 7TL
Tel: 0122 280496

Invoice no:	07891
Tax point:	1 May 20X1
VAT reg no:	431 7992 06
Your reference:	P2

	Amount exclusive of VAT £
Repair of window	66.00
Clearing of guttering	73.00
	139.00
VAT at 17.5%	23.83
Total amount payable	162.83

Deduct discount of 2% if paid within 14 days, net 30 days

INVOICE

Invoice to:
Stanton Associates
323 Main Road
Tonbridge TN1 6EL

Graham Haddow
59 East Street
Medford
MF6 7TL
Tel: 0122 280496

Invoice no:	07892
Tax point:	3 May 20X1
VAT reg no:	431 7992 06
Your reference:	S3

	Amount exclusive of VAT £
Decoration of meeting room	1,100.00
VAT at 17.5%	188.65
Total amount payable	1,288.65

Deduct discount of 2% if paid within 14 days, net 30 days

INVOICE

Invoice to:
Boreham Bros
50/54 Hill Drive
Medford MF2 8AT

Graham Haddow
59 East Street
Medford
MF6 7TL
Tel: 0122 280496

Invoice no:	07893
Tax point:	5 May 20X1
VAT reg no:	431 7992 06
Your reference:	B7

	Amount exclusive of VAT £
Repair of door frames	106.00
Re-decorating of door frames	130.00
	236.00
VAT at 17.5%	41.30
Total amount payable	277.30

UNIT 30 : WORKBOOK

Sales day book							
Date	Invoice No	Customer name	Code	Total £	VAT £	Maintenance £	Decorating £

▷ **ACTIVITY 22**

Given below is an analysed sales day book.

Required

Total the sales day book and check that the totals cross-cast; post the totals to the main ledger accounts; and post the individual entries to the subsidiary ledger accounts.

Sales day book							
Date	Invoice No	Customer name	Code	Total £	VAT £	Group 01 £	Group 02 £
20X0							
1 Feb	61612	Worker Ltd	SL11	217.37	32.37	68.90	116.10
4 Feb	61613	P T Associates	SL04	122.38	18.22		104.16
5 Feb	61614	Paul Bros	SL13	289.27	43.08	106.19	140.00
8 Feb	61615	S D Partners	SL07	109.54	16.31	72.40	20.83
9 Feb	61616	Harper Ltd	SL08	399.97	59.57	160.18	180.22
11 Feb	C241	P T Associates	SL04	(23.68)	(3.52)		(20.16)
15 Feb	61617	Worker Ltd	SL11	144.26	21.48	50.60	72.18
17 Feb	61618	P T Associates	SL04	201.67	30.03	60.41	111.23
18 Feb	61619	Harper Ltd	SL08	345.15	51.40	110.15	183.60
22 Feb	C242	Paul Bros	SL13	(35.72)	(5.32)	(10.18)	(20.22)
25 Feb	61620	P T Associates	SL04	129.01	19.21	62.17	47.63
26 Feb	61621	S D Partners	SL07	56.58	8.42	48.16	

KEY TECHNIQUES: **QUESTIONS**

▷ ACTIVITY 23

Given below is an analysed sales returns day book for the month of April.

Required

Post the totals to the main ledger accounts; and post the individual entries to the subsidiary ledger accounts.

\multicolumn{9}{c	}{Sales returns day book}
Date	Credit note No	Customer name	Code	Total £	VAT £	01 £	02 £	03 £
20X1								
7/4	2114	Gerard & Co	G01	34.36	5.11	16.80		12.45
15/4	2115	Filmer Ltd	F02	44.92	6.69	20.41	17.82	
20/4	2116	T Harrison	H04	24.44	3.64			20.80
28/4	2117	Rolls Ltd	R01	36.47	5.43	16.80	14.24	
				140.19	20.87	54.01	32.06	33.25

KAPLAN PUBLISHING

15

UNIT 30 : WORKBOOK

Chapter 6
The analysed cash receipts book

▷ ACTIVITY 24

Your organisation receives a number of cheques from debtors through the post each day and these are listed on the cheque listing. It also makes some cash sales each day which include VAT at the standard rate.

Today's date is 28 April 20X1 and the cash sales today were £265.08. The cheque listing for the day is given below:

Cheque listing 28 April 20X1

G Heilbron	£108.45
L Tessa	£110.57 – settlement discount of £3.31 taken
J Dent	£210.98 – settlement discount of £6.32 taken
F Trainer	£ 97.60
A Winter	£105.60 – settlement discount of £3.16 taken

An extract from the customer file shows the following:

Customer	Sales ledger code
J Dent	SL17
G Heilbron	SL04
L Tessa	SL15
F Trainer	SL21
A Winter	SL09

Required

(a) Write up the cash receipts book given below; total each of the columns of the cash receipts book and check that they cross-cast
(b) Post the totals of the cash receipts book to the main ledger accounts.
(c) Post the individual receipts to the subsidiary ledger, the sales ledger.

Cash receipts book							
Date	Narrative	SL Code	Total £	VAT £	Debtors £	Cash sales £	Discount £

KEY TECHNIQUES : **QUESTIONS**

▷ ACTIVITY 25

Given below is the cheque listing for your organisation showing all of the cheques received in the week ending 15 May 20X1.

Customer	Sales ledger code	£	Discount taken £
McCaul & Partners	M04	147.56	2.95
Dunn Associates	D02	264.08	
P Martin	M02	167.45	
F Little	L03	265.89	7.97
D Raine	R01	158.02	3.95

There were also cash sales of £446.50 including standard rate VAT during the week.

Required

(a) Write up the cash receipts book given for the week; total the columns of the cash receipts book and check that they cross-cast
(b) Post the totals to the main ledger accounts.
(c) Post the individual receipts to the subsidiary ledger accounts in the sales ledger.

Cash receipts book							
Date	Narrative	SL Code	Total £	VAT £	Debtors £	Cash sales £	Discount £

Chapter 7
Credit purchases – discounts and VAT

▷ ACTIVITY 26

Calculate the VAT for the following:
(a) X purchases £400 goods from Y net of VAT.
(b) X purchases £650 goods from Y net of VAT.
(c) X purchases £425 goods from Y including VAT.
(d) X purchases £77 goods from Y including VAT.

▷ ACTIVITY 27

Calculate the VAT on the following:
(a) X purchases £850 goods from Y and takes the 3% settlement discount offered.
(b) X purchases £600 goods from Y and takes the 5% settlement discount offered.
(c) X purchases £325 goods from Y and does not take the 2% settlement discount offered.
(d) X purchases £57 goods from Y and does not take the 4% settlement discount offered.

▷ ACTIVITY 28

Z buys £600 of goods net of VAT from A and takes the 3% settlement discount offered.

Post these transactions in the ledger accounts of Z.

Chapter 8
The purchases day book – main and subsidiary ledgers

▷ ACTIVITY 29

Curtain Decor is a business that makes curtains and blinds to order. Its purchases are analysed between fabric purchases, header tape purchases and others. A separate purchases returns day book is not kept so any credit notes received are recorded as negative amounts in the purchases day book. The business only has five credit suppliers and they are as follows:

Mainstream Fabrics	PL01
C R Thorne	PL02
Fabric Supplies Ltd	PL03
Lillian Fisher	PL04
Headstream & Co	PL05

Today's date is 12 April 20X1 and given below are three invoices and a credit note. These are to be entered into the analysed purchases day book and each column is to be totalled.

KEY TECHNIQUES : **QUESTIONS**

INVOICE

Invoice to:
Curtain Decor
Field House
Warren Lane
Hawkhurst   TN23 1AT

Deliver to:

As above

Fabric Supplies Ltd
12/14 Tike Road
Wadfield
TN11 4ZP
Tel: 01882 467111
Fax: 01882 467112

Invoice no: 06738
Tax point: 7 April 20X1
VAT reg no: 532 6741 09

Code	Description	Quantity	VAT rate %	Unit price £	Amount exclusive of VAT £
B116-14	Header Tape 14cm	30 m	17.5	4.62	138.60
P480-G	Fabric – Green	56 m	17.5	14.25	798.00
					936.60
VAT at 17.5%					160.62
Total amount payable					1,097.22

Deduct discount of 2% if paid within 10 days

INVOICE

Invoice to:
Curtain Decor
Field House
Warren Lane
Hawkhurst   TN23 1AT

Deliver to:

As above

Lillian Fisher
61 Park Crescent
Hawkhurst
TN23 8GF
Tel: 01868 463501
Fax: 01868 463502

Invoice no: 0328
Tax point: 6 April 20X1
VAT reg no: 469 7153 20

Code	Description	Quantity	VAT rate %	Unit price £	Amount exclusive of VAT £
TB06	Tie Back Cord – Yellow	10 m	17.5	6.55	65.50
TB09	Tie Back Cord – Green	4 m	17.5	6.55	26.20
					91.70
VAT at 17.5%					16.04
Total amount payable					107.74

UNIT 30 : WORKBOOK

CREDIT NOTE

Credit note to:
Curtain Decor
Field House
Warren Lane
Hawkhurst   TN23 1AT

Headstream & Co
140 Myrtle Place
Fenham
TN16 4SJ
Tel: 01842 303136
Fax: 01842 303137

Credit note no: CN0477
Tax point: 7 April 20X1
VAT reg no: 663 4892 77

Code	Description	Quantity	VAT rate %	Unit price £	Amount exclusive of VAT £
HT479	Header Tape 11 cm	2 m	17.5	8.30	16.60
CCF614Y	CC Fabric – Yellow	4 m	17.5	12.85	51.40
					68.00
VAT at 17.5%					11.90
Total credit					79.90

INVOICE

Invoice to:
Curtain Decor
Field House
Warren Lane
Hawkhurst   TN23 1AT

Deliver to:
As above

Mainstream Fabrics
Tree Tops House
Farm Road
Tonbridge
TN2 4XT
Tel: 01883 214121
Fax: 01883 214122

Invoice no: 07359
Tax point: 8 April 20X1
VAT reg no: 379 4612 04

Code	Description	Quantity	VAT rate %	Unit price £	Amount exclusive of VAT £
DG4167F	Design Guild Fabric – Fuchsia	23 m	17.5	13.60	312.80
					312.80
Trade discount 10%					31.28
					281.52
VAT at 17.5%					48.52
Total amount payable					330.04

Deduct discount of 1½% if paid within 14 days

KEY TECHNIQUES : QUESTIONS

Purchases day book								
Date	Invoice No	Code	Supplier	Total	VAT	Fabric	Header Tape	Other

▷ ACTIVITY 30

Nethan Builders analyse their purchases into wood, bricks and cement, and small consumables such as nails and screws. You are given three purchase invoices, recently received, to enter into the purchases day book given.

An extract from the purchase ledger coding manual is given:

Supplier	Purchase ledger code
A J Broom & Co Ltd	PL08
Jenson Ltd	PL13
Magnum Supplies	PL16

Today's date is 3 May 20X1.

Enter the invoices into the analysed purchases day book and total each of the columns.

UNIT 30 : WORKBOOK

INVOICE

Invoice to:
Nethan Builders
Brecon House
Stamford Road
Manchester
M16 4PL

Magnum Supplies
140/150 Park Estate
Manchester
M20 6EG
Tel: 0161 561 3202
Fax: 0161 561 3200

Deliver to:

As above

Invoice no:	077401
Tax point:	1 May 20X1
VAT reg no:	611 4337 90

Code	Description	Quantity	VAT rate %	Unit price £	Amount exclusive of VAT £
BH47732	House Bricks – Red	400	17.5	1.24	496.00
					496.00
Trade discount 15%					74.40
					421.60
VAT at 17.5%					72.30
Total amount payable					493.90

Deduct discount of 2% if paid within 10 days

INVOICE

Invoice to:
Nethan Builders
Brecon House
Stamford Road
Manchester
M16 4PL

A J Broom & Company Limited
59 Parkway
Manchester
M2 6EG
Tel: 0161 560 3392
Fax: 0161 560 5322

Deliver to:

As above

Invoice no:	046193
Tax point:	1 May 20X1
VAT reg no:	661 2359 07

Code	Description	Quantity	VAT rate %	Unit price £	Amount exclusive of VAT £
DGT472	SDGS Softwood 47 x 225 mm	11.2 m	17.5	8.44	94.53
NBD021	Oval Wire Nails 100 mm	7 boxes	17.5	2.50	17.50
					112.03
Trade discount 10%					11.20
					100.83
VAT at 17.5%					17.64
Total amount payable					118.47

KEY TECHNIQUES : **QUESTIONS**

INVOICE

Invoice to:
Nethan Builders
Brecon House
Stamford Road
Manchester
M16 4PL

Deliver to:
As above

Jenson Ltd
30 Longfield Park
Kingsway
M45 2TP
Tel: 0161 511 4666
Fax: 0161 511 4777

Invoice no:	47823
Tax point:	1 May 20X1
VAT reg no:	641 3229 45
Purchase order no:	7211

Code	Description	Quantity	VAT rate %	Unit price £	Amount exclusive of VAT £
PLY8FU	Plywood Hardboard	16 sheets	17.5	17.80	284.80
BU611	Ventilator Brick	10	17.5	8.60	86.00
					370.80
VAT at 17.5%					62.94
Total amount payable					433.74

Deduct discount of 3% if paid within 14 days

Purchases day book								
Date	Invoice No	Code	Supplier	Total	VAT	Wood	Bricks/ Cement	Consumables

▷ ACTIVITY 31

Nethan Builders have recently received the three credit notes given. They are to be recorded in the analysed purchases returns day book given.

An extract from the purchase ledger coding manual shows:

Supplier	Purchase ledger code	Settlement discount on original purchase
Jenson Ltd	PL13	3%
Haddow Bros	PL03	2%
Magnum Supplies	PL16	2%

Today's date is 3 May 20X1.

You are required to enter the credit notes into the analysed purchases returns day book and to total each of the columns.

UNIT 30 : WORKBOOK

CREDIT NOTE

Credit note to:
Nethan Builders
Brecon House
Stamford Road
Manchester
M16 4PL

Jenson Ltd
30 Longfield Park
Kingsway
M45 2TP
Tel: 0161 511 4666
Fax: 0161 511 4777

Credit note no: CN06113
Tax point: 28 April 20X1
VAT reg no: 641 3229 45
Sales invoice no: 47792

Code	Description	Quantity	VAT rate %	Unit price £	Amount exclusive of VAT £
PL432115	Door Lining Set – Wood 32 x 115 mm	1	17.5	30.25	30.25
					30.25
Trade discount 15%					4.54
					25.71
VAT at 17.5%					4.36
Total amount payable					30.07

CREDIT NOTE

Credit note to:
Nethan Builders
Brecon House
Stamford Road
Manchester
M16 4PL

Haddow Bros
The White House
Standing Way
Manchester
M13 6FH
Tel: 0161 560 3140
Fax: 0161 560 6140

Credit note no: 06132
Tax point: 27 April 20X1
VAT reg no: 460 3559 71

Code	Description	Quantity	VAT rate %	Unit price £	Amount exclusive of VAT £
PLY8FE1	Plywood Hardwood 2440 x 1220 mm	2	17.5	17.80	35.60
					35.60
VAT at 17.5%					6.10
Total amount of credit					41.70

KEY TECHNIQUES : QUESTIONS

CREDIT NOTE

Credit note to:
Nethan Builders
Brecon House
Stamford Road
Manchester
M16 4PL

Magnum Supplies
140/150 Park Estate
Manchester
M20 6EG
Tel: 0161 561 3202
Fax: 0161 561 3200

Credit note no: C4163
Tax point: 30 April 20X1
VAT reg no: 611 4337 90

Code	Description	Quantity	VAT rate %	Unit price £	Amount exclusive of VAT £
BU1628	Ventilator Brick	5	17.5	9.20	46.00
					46.00
Trade discount 15%					6.90
					39.10
VAT at 17.5%					6.70
Total amount of credit					45.80

Purchases returns day book								
Date	Credit note no	Code	Supplier	Total	VAT	Wood	Bricks/ Cement	Consumables

▷ ACTIVITY 32

Given below is a purchases returns day book.

You are required to:
· post the totals to the main ledger accounts;
· post the individual entries to the subsidiary ledger accounts.

UNIT 30 : WORKBOOK

Purchases returns day book									
Date	Credit note	Code	Supplier	Total £	VAT £	01 £	02 £	03 £	04 £
15/4/X1	C0179	PL16	J D Withers	27.49	4.09		23.40		
18/4/X1	C4772	PL06	F Williams	164.50	24.50	32.00		108.00	
19/4/X1	06638	PL13	K Bartlett	53.11	7.91	28.40			16.80
				245.10	36.50	60.40	23.40	108.00	16.80

Main ledger

Purchases ledger control account

	£			£
		12/4	Balance b/f	12,678.57

VAT account

	£			£
		12/4	Balance b/f	1,023.90

Purchases returns – 01 account

	£			£
		12/4	Balance b/f	337.60

Purchases returns – 02 account

	£			£
		12/4	Balance b/f	228.59

Purchases returns – 03 account

	£			£
		12/4	Balance b/f	889.46

Purchases returns – 04 account

	£			£
		12/4	Balance b/f	362.78

Subsidiary ledger

F Williams PL06

£			£
	12/4	Balance b/f	673.47

K Bartlett PL13

£			£
	12/4	Balance b/f	421.36

J D Withers PL16

£			£
	12/4	Balance b/f	446.37

▷ ACTIVITY 33

Given below is the purchases day book for a business.

Purchases day book						
Date	Invoice no	Code	Supplier	Total £	VAT £	Net £
20X1						
1 May	36558	PL03	L Jameson	393.91	58.66	335.25
1 May	102785	PL07	K Davison	124.96	18.61	106.35
3 May	92544	PL02	H Samuels	109.79	16.35	93.44
4 May	03542	PL04	G Rails	180.93	26.94	153.99
5 May	002633	PL01	T Ives	192.98	28.74	164.24
				1,002.57	149.30	853.27

You are required to:
- post the totals of the purchases day book to the main ledger accounts given;
- post the individual invoices to the creditors' accounts in the subsidiary ledger given.

Main ledger

Purchases ledger control account

	£			£
		1 May	Balance b/d	3,104.67

VAT account

	£			£
		1 May	Balance b/d	723.56

Purchases account

		£		£
1 May	Balance b/d	24,367.48		

Subsidiary ledger

T Ives — PL01

	£			£
		1 May	Balance b/d	332.56

H Samuels — PL02

	£			£
		1 May	Balance b/d	286.90

L Jameson — PL03

	£			£
		1 May	Balance b/d	623.89

G Rails — PL04

	£			£
		1 May	Balance b/d	68.97

K Davison — PL07

	£			£
		1 May	Balance b/d	125.47

Chapter 9
The analysed cash payments book

▷ ACTIVITY 34

Given below is the cheque listing for a business for the week ending 12 March 20X1.

Cheque payment listing

Supplier	Code	Cheque number	Cheque amount £	Discount taken £
Homer Ltd	PL12	03648	168.70	5.06
Forker & Co	PL07	03649	179.45	5.38
Cash purchases		03650	334.87	
Print Associates	PL08	03651	190.45	
ABG Ltd	PL02	03652	220.67	6.62
Cash purchases		03653	193.87	
G Greg	PL19	03654	67.89	

You are required to:
- enter the payments into the cash payments book and total each of the columns;
- post the totals to the main ledger accounts given;
- post the individual entries to the subsidiary ledger accounts given.

Cash payments book									
Date	Details	Cheque no	Code	Total	VAT	Purchases ledger	Cash purchases	Other	Discounts received
				£	£	£	£	£	£

UNIT 30 : WORKBOOK

Main ledger

Purchases ledger control account

	£			£
		5/3	Balance b/d	4,136.24

VAT account

	£			£
		5/3	Balance b/d	1,372.56

Purchases account

		£		£
5/3	Balance b/d	20,465.88		

Discounts received account

	£			£
		5/3	Balance b/d	784.56

Subsidiary ledger

ABG Ltd — PL02

	£			£
		5/3	Balance b/d	486.90

Forker & Co — PL07

	£			£
		5/3	Balance b/d	503.78

Print Associates — PL08

	£			£
		5/3	Balance b/d	229.56

Homer Ltd — PL12

	£			£
		5/3	Balance b/d	734.90

G Greg — PL19

	£			£
		5/3	Balance b/d	67.89

KEY TECHNIQUES : QUESTIONS

▷ ACTIVITY 35

Given below is the cheque listing for Nethan Builders for the week ended 30 May 20X1.

Cheque listing

Supplier	Code	Cheque number	Cheque amount £	Discount taken £
J M Bond	PL01	200572	247.56	
Magnum Supplies	PL16	200573	662.36	13.25
A J Broom Ltd	PL08	200574	153.57	
Jenson Ltd	PL13	200575	336.57	6.73
KKL Traders	PL20	200576	442.78	8.85
Cash purchases		200577	108.66	

The figure for cash purchases includes VAT at 17.5%.

You are required to:
- enter these amounts in the cash payments book provided and to total each of the columns;
- post the totals to the main ledger accounts given;
- post the individual entries to the subsidiary ledger accounts given.

Cash payments book									
Date	Details	Cheque no	Code	Total	VAT	Purchases ledger	Cash purchases	Other	Discounts received
				£	£	£	£	£	£

Main ledger

Purchases ledger control account

	£		£
		23 May Balance b/d	5,328.46

VAT account

	£		£
		23 May Balance b/d	1,365.35

Purchases account

	£		£
23 May Balance b/d	36,785.90		

Discounts received account

	£		£
		23 May Balance b/d	1,573.56

Subsidiary ledger

J M Bond   *PL01*

	£		£
		23 May Balance b/d	247.56

A J Broom Ltd   *PL08*

	£		£
		23 May Balance b/d	524.36

Jenson Ltd   *PL13*

	£		£
		23 May Balance b/d	512.36

Magnum Supplies   *PL16*

	£		£
		23 May Balance b/d	675.61

KKL Traders   *PL20*

	£		£
		23 May Balance b/d	612.46

Chapter 10
Credit sales: documents

▷ ACTIVITY 36

You have been given details of goods that have been returned to Keyboard Supplies. The return has been checked and authorised and you are now to prepare the credit note.

Return from: H H Music SL 09
 Tenant House Trade discount 15%
 Perley TN7 8ER

Goods returned: 1 Bento keyboard Code B3060 Unit price (before VAT and discount) £126.00

Reason for return: Goods not ordered

Today's date is 17 April 20X1 and the last credit note to have been issued was CN 0336.

Required

Prepare the credit note on the blank credit note given below

CREDIT NOTE

Credit note to:

Keyboard Supplies
Trench Park Estate
Fieldham
Sussex TN21 4AF
Tel: 01829 654545
Fax: 01829 654646

Credit Note no:
Tax point:
VAT reg no: 466 1128 30
Your reference:
Purchase order no:

Code	Description	Quantity	VAT rate %	Unit price £	Amount exclusive of VAT £

Trade discount   %

VAT at 17.5%

Total amount

UNIT 30 : WORKBOOK

▷ ACTIVITY 37

You work in the accounts department of Keyboard Supplies, a supplier of a wide range of electronic keyboards to a variety of music shops on credit. Given below are three purchase orders for goods which are due to be despatched today.

You also have an extract from the customer master file:

Customer	Sales ledger code	Trade discount	Settlement discount
F T Music Supplies	SL23	15%	–
Musicolor Ltd	SL06	10%	3% – 10 days
Newford Music	SL18	20%	3% – 10 days

Today's date is 17 April 20X1 and the last sales invoice to be sent out was invoice number 06112. Normal credit terms are 30 days although some customers are offered a settlement discount. The business is registered for VAT and all of the goods are standard rated.

Required

Complete the sales invoices for these sales on the blank invoices supplied.

PURCHASE ORDER

Musicolor Ltd
23 High Street
Nutford
Sussex TN11 4TZ
Tel: 01826 434111
Fax: 01826 434112
Date: 12 April 20X1
Purchase order no: 04318

To: **Keyboard Supplies**
Trench Park Estate
Fieldham
Sussex TN21 4AF

Delivery address
(If different from above)

Invoice address
(If different from above)

Code	Quantity	Description	Unit price (exclusive of VAT and discounts) £
Z4600	2	Zanni Keyboard	185.00
A4802	3	Atol Keyboard	130.00

PURCHASE ORDER

Newford Music
32/34 Main Street
Welland
Sussex TN4 6BD
Tel: 01760 437711
Fax: 01760 436204
Date: 10 April 20X1
Purchase order no: 47115

To: Keyboard Supplies
Trench Park Estate
Fieldham
Sussex TN21 4AF

Delivery address
(If different from above)

Invoice address
(If different from above)

Code	Quantity	Description	Unit price (exclusive of VAT and discounts) £
Z4406	4	Zanni Keyboard	165.00

PURCHASE ORDER

F T Music Supplies
The Barn
Nutford
Sussex TN11 7AJ
Tel: 01826 431799
Fax: 01826 431800
Date: 13 April 20X1
Purchase order no: 71143

To: Keyboard Supplies
Trench Park Estate
Fieldham
Sussex TN21 4AF

Invoice address
(If different from above)

Invoice address
(If different from above)

Code	Quantity	Description	Unit price (exclusive of VAT and discounts) £
B2010	2	Bento Keyboard	148.00
G4706	3	Garland Keyboard	96.00

UNIT 30 : WORKBOOK

INVOICE

Invoice to:

Deliver to:

Keyboard Supplies
Trench Park Estate
Fieldham
Sussex TN21 4AF
Tel: 01829 654545
Fax: 01829 654646

Invoice no:
Tax point:
VAT reg no: 466 1128 30
Your reference:
Purchase order no:

Code	Description	Quantity	VAT rate %	Unit price £	Amount exclusive of VAT £

Trade discount   %

VAT at 17.5%

Total amount payable

INVOICE

Invoice to:

Deliver to:

Keyboard Supplies
Trench Park Estate
Fieldham
Sussex TN21 4AF
Tel: 01829 654545
Fax: 01829 654646

Invoice no:
Tax point:
VAT reg no: 466 1128 30
Your reference:
Purchase order no:

Code	Description	Quantity	VAT rate %	Unit price £	Amount exclusive of VAT £

Trade discount   %

VAT at 17.5%

Total amount payable

KEY TECHNIQUES : QUESTIONS

INVOICE

Invoice to:

Keyboard Supplies
Trench Park Estate
Fieldham
Sussex TN21 4AF
Tel: 01829 654545
Fax: 01829 654646

Deliver to:

Invoice no:
Tax point:
VAT reg no: 466 1128 30
Your reference:
Purchase order no:

Code	Description	Quantity	VAT rate %	Unit price £	Amount exclusive of VAT £

Trade discount   %

VAT at 17.5%

Total amount payable

Chapter 11
The banking system

▷ ACTIVITY 38

Simon Harris is a self-employed accountant who has a number of clients who all pay by cheque. Today's date is 5 May 20X1 and in the last week he has received the following cheques.

Required

Inspect each one carefully to ensure that it is valid and make a note of any problems that you find.

UNIT 30 : WORKBOOK

NATIONAL BANK PLC
18 Coventry Road
Birmingham
B13 2TU

19–14–60

30 April 20 X1

Pay S Harris

or order

One hundred and three pounds

and 80 pence

Account payee

£ 103.80

P DUNSTER

P Dunster

200550   19–14–60   50731247

WESTERN BANK PLC
20 Hill Place
Bristol
BR2 4XY

20-15-60

28 April 20 X1

Pay Simon Harris

or order

Fifty pounds only

Account payee

£ 50.00

J Kline

J Kline

401061   20-15-60   43215287

NORTHERN BANK PLC
68 Main Road
Warwick
B15 2KP

21-18-40

15 April 20 X1

Pay S Harris

or order

Forty eight pounds

and 20 pence

Account payee

£ 48.20

K T LOPEZ

461002   21-18-40   39761114

CENTRAL BANK PLC
44 Warwick Road
Birmingham
B6 4LK

16-20-30

1 May 20 X1

Pay   S Harris   or order

One hundred and eighteen pounds   £ 118.50

and 50 pence -----------------------

                                                              A RANKIN

                                                              A Rankin

610400   16-20-30   32146921

NATIONAL BANK PLC
18 Coventry Road
Birmingham
B13 2TU

19-14-60

12 May 20 X1

Pay   S Harris   or order

Two hundred and one pounds   £ 201.67

and 67 pence---------------------

                                                              L GARRY

                                                              L Garry

201640   19-14-60   43012004

CENTRAL BANK PLC
44 Warwick Road
Birmingham
B6 4LK

16-20-30

1 May 20 X1

Pay   S Harper   or order

Sixty two pounds   £ 62.50

and 50 pence ---------------------

                                                              L BARRETT

                                                              L Barrett

100417   16-20-30   31426107

UNIT 30 : WORKBOOK

NATIONAL BANK PLC
18 Coventry Road
Birmingham
B13 2TU

19-14-60

12 April 20 X1

Pay   S Harris   or order

Forty eight pounds   £ 48.60

and 60 pence ----------------------

Account payee

F DELAWARE

F Delaware

389152   19-14-60   61298432

FIRST NATIONAL BANK PLC
Trent Park
Leeds
LS4 6OL

23-16-40

21 Oct 20 X0

Pay   S Harris   or order

One hundred and thirty-seven pounds   £ 137.40

and 40 pence ----------------------

Account payee

P IBBOTT

P Ibbott

001071   23-16-40   71294684

NATIONAL BANK PLC
18 Coventry Road
Birmingham
B13 2TU

19-14-60

28 April 20 X1

Pay   S Harris   or order

One hundred and thirty five pounds   £ 153.80

and 80 pence ----------------------

Account payee

J LOVELL

J Lovell

041261   19-14-60   32114687

KEY TECHNIQUES : QUESTIONS

CENTRAL BANK PLC
44 Warwick Road
Birmingham
B6 4LK

16-20-30

1 May 20 X1

Pay   S Harris   or order

Eighty pounds   £ 80.60

and 60 pence --------------------------

                                                         G L ELLIS

                                                         G L Ellis

104010   16-20-30   40162174

Chapter 12
Checking receipts

▷ ACTIVITY 39

Today's date is 12 May 20X1 and the following five cheques have arrived in this morning's post. You have found the invoices that these payments relate to – these are also given.

Required

Check that each receipt is correct and make a note of any problems that you find.

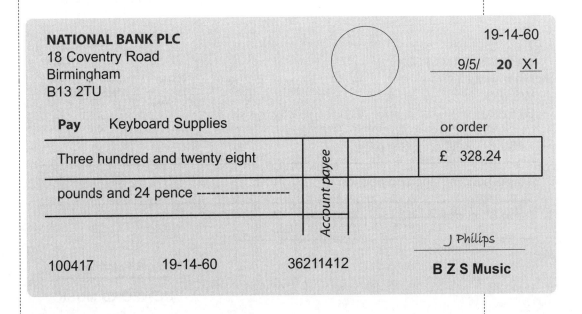

NATIONAL BANK PLC
18 Coventry Road
Birmingham
B13 2TU

19-14-60

9/5/ 20 X1

Pay   Keyboard Supplies   or order

Three hundred and twenty eight   £ 328.24

pounds and 24 pence --------------------

                                                         J Philips

100417   19-14-60   36211412   **B Z S Music**

41
KAPLAN PUBLISHING

UNIT 30 : WORKBOOK

CENTRAL BANK PLC
14 High Street
Nutford
TN11 4AC

20-40-16

9/5   20   X1

Pay   Keyboard Supplies   or order

Eight hundred and thirty six pounds   £ 836.01

and 01 pence

Account payee

P Taylor
F Simms

007112   20-40-16   43612978   **MUSICOLOR LTD**

NATIONAL BANK PLC
18 Coventry Road
Birmingham
B13 2TU

19-14-60

10/5/   20   X1

Pay   Keyboard Supplies   or order

Three hundred and thirty five pounds   £ 335.08

and 8 pence

Account payee

J T Harmer

040611   19-14-60   38664943   **HARMER & CO**

WESTERN BANK PLC
Mace House
Warwick
B15 8KJ

15-20-40

9/5   20   X1

Pay   Keyboard Supplies   or order

Nine hundred and two pounds   £ 902.68

and 68 pence

Account payee

SJ Newford

004128   15-20-40   82823937   **NEWFORD MUSIC**

KEY TECHNIQUES : **QUESTIONS**

FIRST NATIONAL BANK PLC
Main Square
Nottingham
NT2 4XJ

20-14-60

10/5/ 20 X1

Pay   Keyboard Supplies   or order

Four hundred and twenty eight pounds   £ 428.89

and 89 pence ---------------------------

Account payee

T Gilchrist

201067   20-14-60   67112604   **Trent Music**

INVOICE

Invoice to:

B Z S Music
42 Westhill
Nutford TN11 3PQ

Deliver to:

Keyboard Supplies
Trench Park Estate
Fieldham
Sussex TN21 4AF
Tel: 01829 654545
Fax: 01829 654646

Invoice no:	06180
Tax point:	3 May 20X1
VAT reg no:	466 1128 30
Your reference:	SL01
Purchase order no:	77147

Code	Description	Quantity	VAT rate %	Unit price £	Amount exclusive of VAT £
B4012	Bento Keyboard	2	17.5	180.00	360.00
					360.00
Trade discount 20%					72.00
					288.00
VAT at 17.5%					48.88
Total amount payable					336.88

Deduct discount of 3% if paid within 10 days, net 30 days

INVOICE

Invoice to:

Musicolor Ltd
23 High Street
Nutford TN11 4TZ

Deliver to:

As above

Keyboard Supplies
Trench Park Estate
Fieldham
Sussex TN21 4AF
Tel: 01829 654545
Fax: 01829 654646

Invoice no:	06176
Tax point:	1 May 20X1
VAT reg no:	466 1128 30
Your reference:	SL06
Purchase order no:	6362

Code	Description	Quantity	VAT rate %	Unit price £	Amount exclusive of VAT £
Z4600	Zanni Keyboard	3	17.5	185.00	555.00
A4802	Atol Keyboard	2	17.5	130.00	260.00
					815.00
Trade discount 10%					81.50
					733.50
VAT at 17.5%					124.51
Total amount payable					858.01

Deduct discount of 3% if paid within 10 days, net 30 days

INVOICE

Invoice to:

Harmer & Co
1 Acre Street
Nutford TN11 0HA

Deliver to:

As above

Keyboard Supplies
Trench Park Estate
Fieldham
Sussex TN21 4AF
Tel: 01829 654545
Fax: 01829 654646

Invoice no:	06183
Tax point:	3 May 20X1
VAT reg no:	466 1128 30
Your reference:	SL17
Purchase order no:	047786

Code	Description	Quantity	VAT rate %	Unit price £	Amount exclusive of VAT £
G4326	Garland Keyboard	3	17.5	98.00	294.00
					294.00
VAT at 17.5%					49.90
Total amount payable					343.90

Deduct discount of 3% if paid within 10 days, net 30 days

INVOICE

Invoice to:
Newford Music
32/34 Main Street
Welland
Sussex TN4 6BD

Deliver to:
As above

Keyboard Supplies
Trench Park Estate
Fieldham
Sussex TN21 4AF
Tel: 01829 654545
Fax: 01829 654646

Invoice no:	06171
Tax point:	30 April 20X1
VAT reg no:	466 1128 30
Your reference:	SL18
Purchase order no:	47202

Code	Description	Quantity	VAT rate %	Unit price £	Amount exclusive of VAT £
Z4406	Zanni Keyboard	6	17.5	165.00	990.00
					990.00
Trade discount 20%					198.00
					792.00
VAT at 17.5%					134.44
Total amount payable					926.44

Deduct discount of 3% if paid within 10 days, net 30 days

INVOICE

Invoice to:
Trent Music
Trent House
Main Street
Fieldham TN21 6ZF

Deliver to:
As above

Keyboard Supplies
Trench Park Estate
Fieldham
Sussex TN21 4AF
Tel: 01829 654545
Fax: 01829 654646

Invoice no:	06184
Tax point:	3 May 20X1
VAT reg no:	466 1128 30
Your reference:	SL41
Purchase order no:	93754

Code	Description	Quantity	VAT rate %	Unit price £	Amount exclusive of VAT £
G4030	Garland Keyboard	4	17.5	105.00	420.00
					420.00
Trade discount 10%					42.00
					378.00
VAT at 17.5%					64.16
Total amount payable					442.16

Deduct discount of 3% if paid within 10 days, net 30 days

UNIT 30 : WORKBOOK

Chapter 13
Banking receipts

▷ ACTIVITY 40

You are responsible for paying monies received each day by your business into the bank. Today's date is 4 May 20X1 and you are to pay into the bank the following cash and cheques:

Cash

Notes/coins	Quantity
£10	2
£5	11
£2	3
£1	15
50p	17
20p	9
10p	13
5p	16
2p	12
1p	8

Cheque listing 4 May 20X1

K Fisher	£135.49
J Gilman	£225.78
S David	£174.67
L Craig	£258.34

Required

Complete the paying-in slip given for the cash and cheques that are to be paid in to the bank, as far as you are able.

KEY TECHNIQUES : **QUESTIONS**

```
                                                    To be retained by receiving bank
For the credit of _____
Cheques etc for collection to be included in total credit of £_____ paid in_____ 20____.
```

	£	Brought forward	£	Brought forward	£
Carried forward	£	Carried forward	£	Total cheques etc	£

Date _____
Cashier's stamp and initials   £50 Notes

56 - 28 - 48

FINANCIAL BANK PLC
EXETER HIGH STREET

£20 Notes
£10 Notes
£5 Notes
£2 Coins
£1 Coins
50p
20p
Silver
Bronze
Total Cash
Cheques, POs etc

Fee | No Chqs | Paid in by _____

Address/Ref No. _____   TOTAL   £

▷ ACTIVITY 41

The cash, cheques and credit card vouchers received by your organisation today are listed below:

Cash

Notes/coins	Quantity
£20	3
£10	15
£5	17
£2	5
£1	9
50p	13
20p	11
10p	6
5p	7
2p	18
1p	14

UNIT 30 : WORKBOOK

Cheque listing

K Tenterton	£258.70
H Ollie	£117.58
E Edwards	£274.51
P Trench	£330.24
C Beale	£264.67

Credit card vouchers

P Reardon	£59.79
L Duncan	£69.99
H Fellows	£58.70
K Vintner	£89.45

Today's date is 10 April 20X0.

Required

Fill out the paying-in slip and credit card summary voucher given below, as far as you are able.

To be retained by receiving bank

For the credit of _____

Cheques etc for collection to be included in total credit of £_____ paid in_____20____.

	£	Brought forward	£	Brought forward	£
Carried forward	£	Carried forward	£	Total cheques etc	£

Date _____

Cashier's stamp and initials

56 - 28 - 48

FINANCIAL BANK PLC
EXETER HIGH STREET

Cheques,
Paid in by _____

Address/Ref No. _____

| Fee | No Chqs |

£50 Notes		
£20 Notes		
£10 Notes		
£5 Notes		
£2 Coins		
£1 Coins		
50p		
20p		
Silver		
Bronze		
Total Cash		
POs etc		
TOTAL £		

KEY TECHNIQUES : **QUESTIONS**

Have you imprinted the summary with your Retailer's Card?
Bank processing copy of Summary with your Vouchers in correct order:
1 Summary
2 Sales Vouchers
3 Refund Vouchers
Keep Retailer's copy and
        Retailer's Duplicate copy
No more than 200 Vouchers to each Summary
Do not use Staples, Pins, Paper Clips

	Items	Amount	
Sales vouchers			
Less Refund Vouchers			
			:

Retailer's Copy

Retailer Summary

_____
Retailer's Signature

Retailer Summary

Complete this summary for every Deposit of Sales Vouchers and enter the Total on your normal Current Account paying-in slip

UNIT 30 : WORKBOOK

		£	p
Please do not pin or staple this voucher as this will affect the machine processing.	1		
	2		
	3		
All sales vouchers must be deposited within three banking days of the dates shown on them.	4		
	5		
	6		
	7		
If you are submitting more than 26 vouchers please enclose a separate listing.	8		
	9		
	10		
If a voucher contravenes the terms of the retailer agreement then the amount shown on the voucher may be charged back to your bank account, either direct or via your paying in branch.	11		
	12		
	13		
	14		
	15		
	16		
Similarly, if the total amount shown on the Retail Voucher Summary does not balance with our total of vouchers, the difference will be credited (or debited) to your bank account.	17		
	18		
	19		
	20		
	21		
	22		
	23		
	24		
	25		
	26		
SALES VOUCHERS	TOTAL		

		£	p
	1		
	2		
	3		
	4		
	5		
	6		
	7		
REFUND VOUCHERS	TOTAL		

KEY TECHNIQUES : **QUESTIONS**

▷ ACTIVITY 42

Today is 6 April 20X1.

You are required to deal with the following transactions which have taken place in George Jones Scrapmerchants, the business where you are employed as an accounts assistant.

Task 1   Ensure that cheques received are correctly completed.

Any items with errors must not be banked. They must be placed to one side. A 2% discount is offered on all invoices which are paid within 30 days of the invoice date. If the discount taken is wrong, but everything else is correct, the item can still be accepted.

Task 2   Check the cheques received against remittance advices.

If you find any discrepancies you must alter the remittance advice.

Task 3   You have received cash as follows:

	Sale 1	Sale 2	Sale 3
£10 notes	2		1
£5 notes	1	1	
£1 coins	2	3	1
50p coins	1		1
20p coins		2	2
5p coins	1	1	

Sale 1   Arthur Denton
           17 Bury New Road
           Bolton
           BL4 6FG

Sale 2   Steel Associates
           Copper Mill
           Copper Street
           Oldham
           OL6 2YJ

Sale 3   A J Palmer & Co Ltd
           89 Store Street
           Manchester
           M17 3SD

Issue receipts for the three cash sales.

Task 4   List all monies received on the remittance list.

Task 5   Prepare the paying-in slip for that day.

UNIT 30 : WORKBOOK

REMITTANCE ADVICE

Norman Charles
390 Windmill Street
Denton
MANCHESTER M18 0SA

Invoice No.	Date	Amount	Discount
920	19 / 3 / X1	£210.16	£4.20

STERLING BANK

19 Corporation Street, M2 0WK

- ## -

1 April 20X1

Pay George Jones Scrapmerchant   or order

Two hundred and five pounds 96   £ 205 - 96

N R CHARLES

Norman Charles

- ## - ##

REMITTANCE ADVICE

Proctor and Proctor
366 New Earth Street
Lees
Oldham
OL4 8BE

Invoice No.	Date	Amount	Discount
899	11 / 3 / X1	£258.40	£5.17

KEY TECHNIQUES : **QUESTIONS**

MONEY CITY BANK
Cross Street Branch
598 Cross Street, M1 5HP

- ## -
2 April   20X1

Pay   George Jones Scrapmerchant   or order

Two hundred and fifty three pounds 23 pence   £ 253 - 23

PROCTOR AND PROCTOR

J Proctor

- ## - ##

REMITTANCE ADVICE

Terrence James & Co Ltd
35 Fleet Road
Beswich
Manchester
M28 6EW

Invoice No.	Date	Amount	Discount
880	08 / 3 / X1	£86.67	£1.73

MONEY CITY BANK
Cross Street Branch
598 Cross Street, M1 5HP

- ## -
5 April   20X1

Pay   George Jones Scrapmerchant   or order

Eighty four pounds and 94 pence only   £ 84 - 94

TERRENCE JAMES & CO LTD

T James

- ## - ##

UNIT 30 : WORKBOOK

REMITTANCE ADVICE

Sid Pearl Scrapmerchants
48 Canal Walk
Newton Heath
Manchester
M3 7BJ

Invoice No.	Date	Amount	Discount
820	01 / 3 / X1	£56.47	£1.12

STERLING BANK

George House 27 Broad Lane
Newton Heath M3 3AW

- ## -
1 April   20X1

Pay   George Jones Scrapmerchant   or order

Fifty five pounds and 35 pence   £ 55 - 35

Sid Pearl

- ## - ##

REMITTANCE ADVICE

Palatine Supplies
404 Palatine Road
Withington
Manchester
M20

Invoice No.	Date	Amount	Discount
855	03 / 3 / X1	£345.64	

KEY TECHNIQUES : **QUESTIONS**

MIDWESTERN BANK

19 Union Street, Oldham OL1 2GH
Union Street Oldham Branch

- ## -

7 April 20X1

Pay George Jones and Co Ltd   or order

Three hundred and forty five pounds 64 pence

£ 345 - 64

George Fox

G. Fox

- ## - ##

SOUTHERN BANK PLC

29 Union Street, Oldham OL1 2GJ
Union Street Oldham Branch

- ## -

5 April 20X1

Pay George Jones Scrap Merchant   or order

Sixty-six pounds and 23 pence

£ 66 - 23

J R Berry

J.R. Berry

- ## - ##

REMITTANCE ADVICE

Foster Brothers
409 Edgware Street
Newton Heath
Manchester
M3 4ED

Invoice No.	Date	Amount	Discount
822	01 / 3 / X1	£20.00	

KAPLAN PUBLISHING

55

UNIT 30 : WORKBOOK

NOT NEGOTIABLE   ###### #####
£20   **BRITISH POSTAL ORDER**
              SENDER MUST FILL IN PAYEE'S NAME IN INK
                        PLEASE PAY

George Jones Scrapmerchants   **£20**

              TWENTY POUNDS
                    AT POST OFFICE

                    RECEIVED/SIGNATURE

              POSTAGE STAMPS
              One or two postage stamps may
              be added to a maximum of ninety-
              nine pence

Paying Office Date Stamp   *Paying Office Date Stamp*

REMITTANCE ADVICE

Acme Scrap
Horseshoe Lane
Overton
Preston
PR5 3RF

Invoice No.	Date	Amount	Discount
865	05 / 3 / X1	£7.00	

KEY TECHNIQUES : QUESTIONS

```
          NOT NEGOTIABLE                    ###### #####
    £7           BRITISH POSTAL ORDER
              SENDER MUST FILL IN PAYEE'S NAME IN INK
                         PLEASE PAY
                                                      £7
             _George Jones Scrapmerchants_

                    SEVEN POUNDS
                       AT POST OFFICE
                    _____
                       RECEIVED/SIGNATURE

                    ┌────────────────────────┐
                    │    POSTAGE STAMPS      │
                    │ One or two postage     │
                    │ stamps may be added    │
                    │ to a maximum of        │
                    │ ninety-nine pence      │
                    └────────────────────────┘
```

Blank receipts for Task 3

```
                                                    123
   George Jones Scrapmerchants
   34 Coppice Street
   Oldham
   OL6 3RT

   Date _____

   Customer _____
   _____
                              £  _____
              Received with thanks
```

```
                                                    124
   George Jones Scrapmerchants
   34 Coppice Street
   Oldham
   OL6 3RT

   Date _____

   Customer _____
   _____
                              £  _____
              Received with thanks
```

UNIT 30 : WORKBOOK

                                                                125
George Jones Scrapmerchants
34 Coppice Street
Oldham
OL6 3RT

Date _____

Customer _____
_____
                                          £ _____
                   Received with thanks

Remittance List for Task 4

Date _____

Customer	Receipt no	Invoice no	£	Discount allowed
		TOTAL		

Analysis   Cash
           Cheques
           Postal order   _____
                          ══════

KEY TECHNIQUES : **QUESTIONS**

```
                                                 To be retained by receiving bank
For the credit of George Jones Scrapmerchants_____
Cheques etc for collection to be included in total credit of £_____ paid in_____20____.
```

	£	Brought forward	£	Brought forward	£
Carried forward	£	Carried forward	£	Total cheques etc	£

Date _____
Cashier's stamp and initials   £50 Notes

                                                            £20 Notes
                    25-45-67   £10 Notes
                                                            £5 Notes
                                                            £2 Coins
                                                            £1 Coins
              MIDWESTERN BANK   50p
              UNION STREET   20p
              OLDHAM   Silver
                                                            Bronze
                                                            Total Cash
           Credit George Jones Scrapmerchants   Cheques,
    Fee   No   Paid in by _____   POs etc
           Chqs
                   Address/Ref No. _____   TOTAL £

▷ ACTIVITY 43   ▷ ▷ ▷ ▷

Today is 25 June 20X1. It is afternoon. You are the accounts assistant at T-S Designs Ltd and are currently dealing with payments received in today's post and credit card payments received by telephone today.

Task 1 Check all orders and cheques received in today's post. Also check all telephone orders and credit card payments. List all discrepancies found. Make short notes on how you would deal with each error.

Task 2 List all valid payments received on the monies received listing.

Task 3 Prepare the paying-in slip and credit card retail voucher summary.

UNIT 30 : WORKBOOK

To: T-S Designs Limited, Unit 4, Cobbold Industrial Estate, Cobbold Road, Shepherd's Bush, London W12 9RE

PLEASE SEND ME (NUMBER)   Please complete in BLOCK LETTERS

RAINBOW	__extra large	__large	__medium	__small	
PEGASUS	✓ extra large	__large	__medium	__small	
CLOUDS	__extra large	✓ large	__medium	__small	
MOUNTAIN	__extra large	__large	__medium	__small	
Total no	1 extra large	1 large	__medium	__small	
	@£10	@£9	@£8	@£7	

Name   J.FISHER
Address 23 GREENBAM RD
         DARTFORD
Postcode DA8 LBR

__I enclose ~~my own~~ design and a deposit of ~~£20~~

Total £   [10]   [9]   [ ]   [ ]

__I wish to purchase the items shown which total £ 19

__I enclose a cheque for £ 19

Please make cheques payable to T-S Designs Limited.

MONEY CITY BANK   ## - ## - ##

DARTFORD BRANCH   20/6   20X1
34 HIGH STREET, DARTFORD DA1 1ED

Pay   T-S Designs Limited   or order

Nineteen pounds only   £ 19 - 00

                                          J D FISHER

                                          J.D. Fisher

- ## - ##

To: T-S Designs Limited, Unit 4, Cobbold Industrial Estate, Cobbold Road, Shepherd's Bush, London W12 9RE

PLEASE SEND ME (NUMBER)   Please complete in BLOCK LETTERS

RAINBOW	__extra large	__large	__medium	__small	
PEGASUS	__extra large	__large	__medium	__small	
CLOUDS	__extra large	__large	__medium	__small	
MOUNTAIN	__extra large	__large	__medium	1 small	
Total no	__extra large	__large	__medium	1 small	
	@£10	@£9	@£8	@£7	

Name   G. KWONG
Address 22 HYDE PARK AV
         DARTFORD
Postcode LEEDS

__I enclose ~~my own~~ design and a deposit of ~~£20~~

Total £   [ ]   [ ]   [ ]   [7]

__I wish to purchase the items shown which total £ 7

__I enclose a cheque for £ 7

Please make cheques payable to T-S Designs Limited.

KEY TECHNIQUES : **QUESTIONS**

MIDWESTERN BANK
57 BRIGGATE LEEDS LS1 3TY

- ## -
20/6   20X1

Pay   T-S Designs Limited

or order

Seven pounds only   £ 7 - 00

G KWONG

G Kwong

- ## - ##

To: T-S Designs Limited, Unit 4, Cobbold Industrial Estate, Cobbold Road, Shepherd's Bush, London W12 9RE

PLEASE SEND ME (NUMBER)   Please complete in BLOCK LETTERS

RAINBOW	1 extra large	__large	__medium	__small	
PEGASUS	__extra large	__large	__medium	__small	
CLOUDS	1 extra large	__large	__medium	__small	
MOUNTAIN	__extra large	__large	__medium	__small	
Total no	2 extra large	__large	__medium	__small	
	@£10	@£9	@£8	@£7	

Name   JASBAR MAHAL
Address 17 RAILWAY CUTINGS
         BRISTOL
Postcode BS1 FX

__ I enclose my own design and a deposit of £20

✓ I wish to purchase the items shown which total £ 20

__ I enclose a cheque for £ 20

Total £   20

Please make cheques payable to T-S Designs Limited.

SOUTHERN BANK PLC
98 BROAD STREET BRISTOL BS1 2EY

- ## -
22/6   20X1

Pay   T-S Designs Limited

or order

Twenty pounds only   £ 20 - 00

Ms J. MAHAL

J. Mahal

- ## - ##

UNIT 30 : WORKBOOK

To: T-S Designs Limited, Unit 4, Cobbold Industrial Estate, Cobbold Road, Shepherd's Bush, London W12 9RE

PLEASE SEND ME (NUMBER)   Please complete in BLOCK LETTERS

RAINBOW   __extra large ___large ___medium ___small   Name   MS FLETCHER
PEGASUS   __extra large ___large ___medium ___small   Address   29 COLD HARBOUR LANE
CLOUDS   __extra large ___large ___medium ___small   LONDON
MOUNTAIN __extra large ___large   1 medium ___small   Postcode SW9 8LF

Total no __extra large ___large   1 medium ___small   __I enclose my own design and a
          @£10   @£9   @£8   @£7   deposit of £20

Total £   [   ]   [   ]   [8]   [   ]   ✓ I wish to purchase the items shown
                                                           which total £ 8.00

                                                           __I enclose a cheque for £ 8.00
          Please make cheques payable to T-S Designs Limited.

FINANCIAL BANK PLC   fb   ## - ## - ##

98 HOLLAND PARK AVENUE LONDON W11 7UT   20/6   20X1

Pay   T-S Designs Limited   or order

       Eight pounds only   £ 18 - 00

                                                    Ms P FLETCHER

                                                    Petra Fletcher

       ######   ## - ## - ##   ########

To: T-S Designs Limited, Unit 4, Cobbold Industrial Estate, Cobbold Road, Shepherd's Bush, London W12 9RE

PLEASE SEND ME (NUMBER)   Please complete in BLOCK LETTERS

RAINBOW   1 extra large ___large ___medium ___small   Name   CHERYL DODGSON
PEGASUS   __extra large   ___large ___medium ___small   Address   58 BRUDENHALL RD
CLOUDS   __extra large   ___large ___medium ___small   LONDON
MOUNTAIN   1 extra large ___large   1 medium ___small   Postcode SW3 5PK

Total no   2 extra large ___large   1 medium ___small   __I enclose my own design and a
           @£10   @£9   @£8   @£7   deposit of £20

Total £   [20]   [   ]   [   ]   [   ]   ✓ I wish to purchase the items shown
                                                           which total £ 20

                                                           __I enclose a cheque for £ 20
          Please make cheques payable to T-S Designs Limited.

KEY TECHNIQUES : QUESTIONS

SOUTHERN BANK PLC
61 PAUL'S STREET LEEDS LS1 2TE

- ## -
20/6 20X1

Pay T-S Designs Limited or order
Twenty pounds only   £ 20 - 00
             Miss C Dodgson
             Cheryl Dodgson

- ## - ##

To: T-S Designs Limited, Unit 4, Cobbold Industrial Estate, Cobbold Road, Shepherd's Bush, London W12 9RE

PLEASE SEND ME (NUMBER)   Please complete in BLOCK LETTERS

	extra large	large	medium	small		
RAINBOW	__	__	__	42	Name	TREVOR PATRICK
PEGASUS	__	__	__	__	Address	MOFFATS PASSAGE
CLOUDS	__	__	__	__		SOUTHAMPTON
MOUNTAIN	__	__	__	3	Postcode	SO2 0BX

Total no   __extra large   __large   __medium   45 small
           @£10   @£9   @£8   @£7

__ I enclose my own design and a deposit of £20

Total £ [   ]   [   ]   [   ]   215

✓ I wish to purchase the items shown which total £ 215

__ I enclose a cheque for £ 215

Please make cheques payable to T-S Designs Limited.

FINANCIAL BANK PLC
98 HOLLAND PARK AVENUE LONDON W11 7UT

- ## -
24/6 20X1

Pay T-S Designs Limited or order
Two hundred and fifteen pounds only   £ 215.00
             MR T PATRICK
             T Patrick

- ## - ##

UNIT 30 : WORKBOOK

To: T-S Designs Limited, Unit 4, Cobbold Industrial Estate, Cobbold Road, Shepherd's Bush, London W12 9RE

PLEASE SEND ME (NUMBER)   Please complete in BLOCK LETTERS

RAINBOW	__extra large	__large	__medium	__small	Name: MR R GROSSMAN
PEGASUS	1 extra large	__large	__medium	__small	Address: 2 CHARLOTTE AV.
CLOUDS	__extra large	__large	__medium	__small	BROCKLEY
MOUNTAIN	__extra large	__large	__medium	__small	Postcode: SE4 1PY

Total no   1 extra large   __large   __medium   __small   __I enclose my own design and a
             @£10   @£9   @£8   @£7   deposit of £20

Total £   [10]   [   ]   [   ]   [   ]   ✔ I wish to purchase the items shown
                                                                    which total £ 10

                                                                    __I enclose a cheque for £ 10

Please make cheques payable to T-S Designs Limited.

FINANCIAL BANK PLC
98 HOLLAND PARK AVENUE LONDON W11 7UT

fb

- ## -
20/6   20X1

Pay   T-S Designs Limited   or order

Ten pounds only   £ 10.00

                                             MR R GROSSMAN

                                             R GROSSMAN

- ## - ##

To: T-S Designs Limited, Unit 4, Cobbold Industrial Estate, Cobbold Road, Shepherd's Bush, London W12 9RE

PLEASE SEND ME (NUMBER)   Please complete in BLOCK LETTERS

RAINBOW	__extra large	__large	1 medium	__small	Name: JANET REARDON
PEGASUS	__extra large	__large	__medium	__small	Address: 16 SALISBURY ROAD
CLOUDS	__extra large	__large	__medium	__small	CHISLEHURST
MOUNTAIN	__extra large	__large	__medium	__small	Postcode: BR7 6AL

Total no   __extra large   __large   1 medium   __small   __I enclose my own design and a
             @£10   @£9   @£8   @£7   deposit of £20

Total £   [   ]   [   ]   [8]   [   ]   ✔ I wish to purchase the items shown
                                                                    which total £ 8

                                                                    __I enclose a cheque for £ 8

Please make cheques payable to T-S Designs Limited.

FINANCIAL BANK PLC
22 GREEN PARK LONDON W1 4DT

- ## -
21/6   20X1

Pay   T-S Designs Limited   or order

Eight pounds only   £ 8.00

                                         JANET REARDON
                                         J Reardon

- ## - ##

TELEPHONE ORDER

Date 25 / 6 / X1

RAINBOW   __extra large   __large   ___medium   ___small   Name   T DANIELSON
PEGASUS   1_extra large   1_large   ___medium   ___small   Address   16 RYDAL AV
CLOUDS   __extra large   __large   ___medium   ___small   OLDHAM
MOUNTAIN __extra large   __large   ___medium   ___small   Postcode   OL9 5ST

Total no   1_extra large 1_large   ___medium   ___small   CREDIT CARD___ EXPRESS___ GLOBAL _✓_
           @£10   @£9   @£8   @£7   NUMBER 3553 9004 6525 1122

Total £ | 10 | | 9 | | | | | EXPIRY DATE 10/X2
                                                             TOTAL AMOUNT £ 19.00

Please make cheques payable to T-S Designs Limited.

UNIT 30 : WORKBOOK

3553 9004 6525 1122
10 / X2
T DANIELSON
16 RYDAL AVENUE
OLDHAM OL9 5ST
EXPRESS

EXPRESS

234 5768
T-S DESIGNS LTD

CARDHOLDER'S SIGNATURE

Telephone order.

CARDHOLDER'S DECLARATION:
I promise to pay the total amount shown as payable together with any charge sthereon subject to the rules of issue.

DAY	MONTH	YEAR	DEPT	SALES NO	INITIALS
2 5	0 6	X 1			AB

DESCRIPTION	Amount
T shirts	19.00

AUTHORISATION CODE

TOTAL POUNDS PENCE

| | | | | | | 1 | 9 | : | 0 | 0 |

CARDHOLDER COPY

SALES VOUCHER
Please keep this copy for your records

TELEPHONE ORDER

Date 25 / 6 / XI

RAINBOW	__extra large	__large	__medium	__small
PEGASUS	1 extra large	__large	__medium	__small
CLOUDS	__extra large	1 large	1 medium	__small
MOUNTAIN	__extra large	__large	__medium	__small

Name A TORQUIST
Address 16 BRYANT STREET
         HAMMERSMITH, LONDON
Postcode W6 0P7

Total no	1 extra large	1 large	1 medium	__small
	@£10	@£9	@£8	@£7

CREDIT CARD __ EXPRESS __ GL~~OBAL~~ __
NUMBER 3553 8612 3474 0111

| Total £ | 10 | 9 | 8 | |

EXPIRY DATE 12/X1
TOTAL AMOUNT £ 27.00

Please make cheques payable to T-S Designs Limited.

KEY TECHNIQUES : **QUESTIONS**

3553 8612 3474 0111
12 / X1
A TORQUIST
16 BRYANT STREET
HAMMERSMITH
LONDON W6 0P7

EXPRESS

234 5768
T-S DESIGNS LTD

CARDHOLDER'S SIGNATURE

Telephone order.

CARDHOLDER'S DECLARATION:
I promise to pay the total amount shown as payable together with any charge sthere-on subject to the rules of issue.

DAY	MONTH	YEAR	DEPT	SALES NO	INITIALS
2 5	0 6	X 1			AB

DESCRIPTION	Amount
T shirts	27.00

AUTHORISATION CODE

TOTAL POUNDS PENCE

| | | | 2 | 7 : 0 | 0 |

CARDHOLDER COPY

SALES VOUCHER
Please keep this copy for your records

TELEPHONE ORDER

Date 25 / 6 / XI

RAINBOW __extra large __large ___medium ___small
PEGASUS 1 extra large __large ___medium ___small
CLOUDS   __extra large __large 1 medium ___small
MOUNTAIN __extra large __large ___medium ___small

Total no   1 extra large __large 1 medium ___small
           @£10   @£9   @£8   @£7

Total £ | 10 | | | 8 | |

Name   N METZGER
Address 151 NEEDHAM ROAD
        FULHAM, LONDON
Postcode SW6 6PN

CREDIT CARD __ EXPRESS __ GLOBAL __
NUMBER 3553 8111 2344 3113

EXPIRY DATE 5/X1
TOTAL AMOUNT £ 18.00

Please make cheques payable to T-S Designs Limited.

3553 8111 2344 3113
5 / X1
N METZGER
151 NEEDHAM ROAD
SW6 6PN

EXPRESS

234 5768
T-S DESIGNS LTD

CARDHOLDER'S SIGNATURE						
Telephone order.						

CARDHOLDER'S DECLARATION:
I promise to pay the total amount shown as payable together with any charge sthereon subject to the rules of issue.

DAY	MONTH	YEAR	DEPT	SALES NO	INITIALS
2 5	0 6	X 1			AB
DESCRIPTION				Amount	
T shirts				18.00	

AUTHORISATION CODE	TOTAL POUNDS PENCE
	1 8 : 0 0

CARDHOLDER COPY

SALES VOUCHER
Please keep this copy for your records

Customer name	Order No	Deposit/balance	Cheque £	Postal order	Express £	Global £	Discount allowed £
Total							

UNIT 30 : WORKBOOK

	£	Brought forward	£	Brought forward	£
Carried forward	£	Carried forward	£	Total cheques etc	£

To be retained by receiving bank
For the credit of <u>T-S Designs Limited</u>
Cheques etc for collection to be included in total credit of £_____ paid in_____ 20____.

Date _____

Cashier's stamp and initials

45 - 67 - 17

SOUTHERN BANK PLC
SHEPHERD'S BUSH GREEN

£50 Notes	
£20 Notes	
£10 Notes	
£5 Notes	
£2 Coins	
£1 Coins	
50p	
20p	
Silver	
Bronze	
Total Cash	
Cheques, POs etc	
TOTAL £	

Fee | No Chqs

Credit T-S DESIGNS
    Paid in by _____

    Address/Ref No. _____

KEY TECHNIQUES : **QUESTIONS**

	£ p
Please do not pin or staple this voucher as this will affect the machine processing.	1 _____ 2 _____ 3 _____
All sales vouchers must be deposited within three banking days of the dates shown on them.	4 _____ 5 _____ 6 _____ 7 _____
If you are submitting more than 26 vouchers please enclose a separate listing.	8 _____ 9 _____ 10 _____
If a voucher contravenes the terms of the retailer agreement then the amount shown on the voucher may be charged back to your bank account, either direct or via your paying in branch.	11 _____ 12 _____ 13 _____ 14 _____ 15 _____
Similarly, if the total amount shown on the Retail Voucher Summary does not balance with our total of vouchers, the difference will be credited (or debited) to your bank account.	16 _____ 17 _____ 18 _____ 19 _____ 20 _____ 21 _____ 22 _____ 23 _____ 24 _____ 25 _____ 26 _____

SALES VOUCHERS   TOTAL

	£ p
	1 _____ 2 _____ 3 _____ 4 _____ 5 _____ 6 _____ 7 _____

REFUND VOUCHERS   TOTAL   _____

UNIT 30 : WORKBOOK

```
                          EXPRESS

PLEASE WRIE FIRMLY WITH A
BALLPOINT PEN

                          DAY MONTH YEAR    RETAILER NUMBER

RETAIL VOUCHER SUMMARY
                          DESCRIPTION            Amount
   RETAILER NAME          NO OF VOUCHERS
                          SALES VOUCHERS
                          REFUND VOUCHERS

VOUCHERS ARE ACCEPTED SUB-
JECT TO VERIFICATION AND TO
TERMS AND CONDITIONS OF
THE MERCHANT AGREEMENT    AUTHORISATION     TOTAL POUNDS PENCE
                          CODE
KEEP COPIES 1 & 2 AND REMIT
COPIES 3 & 4 WITH YOUR SALES
VOUCHERS
PLEASE COMPLETE THIS SUMMARY QUOTING YOUR CURRENT RETAILER NUMBER
                                                    RETAILER COPY
```

Chapter 14
Debtors' statements

▷ ACTIVITY 44

You work in the accounts department of Farmhouse Pickles Ltd and given below are two debtors' accounts from the subsidiary sales ledger.

Grant & Co   **SL07**

		£			£
1 April	Balance b/d	337.69	12 April	SRDB - 0335	38.70
4 April	SDB 32656	150.58	20 April	CRB	330.94
18 April	SDB 32671	179.52	20 April	CRB - discount	6.75
25 April	SDB 32689	94.36	24 April	SRDB - 0346	17.65

Mitchell Partners   **SL10**

		£			£
1 April	Balance b/d	180.46	12 April	SRDB - 0344	66.89
7 April	SDB 32662	441.57	21 April	CRB	613.58
20 April	SDB 32669	274.57	21 April	CRB - discount	8.45

KEY TECHNIQUES : QUESTIONS

Required

Prepare statements to be sent to each of these customers at the end of April 20X1 on the blank statements provided.

FARMHOUSE PICKLES LTD

To:

225 School Lane
Weymouth
Dorset
WE36 5NR
Tel: 0261 480444
Fax: 0261 480555
Date:

STATEMENT

Date	Transaction	Debit £	Credit £	Balance £

May we remind you that our credit terms are 30 days

UNIT 30 : WORKBOOK

FARMHOUSE PICKLES LTD

To:

225 School Lane
Weymouth
Dorset
WE36 5NR

Tel: 0261 480444
Fax: 0261 480555
Date:

STATEMENT

Date	Transaction	Debit £	Credit £	Balance £

May we remind you that our credit terms are 30 days

▷ ACTIVITY 45 ▷▷▷▷

Today is 4 December 20X1. You are the sales ledger clerk at Toybox Games Ltd, a manufacturer of board games supplied to the toy market.

Cash received during the previous week has already been posted to the main ledger and the subsidiary (sales) ledger.

You have just received the sales day book from the accounts assistant, Andrew Donnelly. He has already prepared a journal entry.

Task 1 Check the journal entry form and correct it if necessary.

Task 2 Post the totals for the week ending 30 November 20X1 to the correct main ledger accounts.

Task 3 Post the individual transactions to the correct debtors accounts in the subsidiary (sales) ledger.

Task 4 You now turn your attention to the sales returns day book. Total the sales returns day book.

Task 5 Prepare the journal entry required to post the sales returns day book.

Task 6 Post the totals of the sales returns day book to the correct main ledger accounts.

Task 7 Post the individual transactions from the sales returns day book to the correct debtors accounts in the subsidiary (sales) ledger.

Task 8 Prepare statements to send to Daisychains and Jubilee Games & Toys.

Sales Day Book

Date	Code	Customer	Invoice	Total £	01 £	02 £	03 £	04 £	VAT £
26/11/X1	D2	Daisychains	2205	1,661.63	205.25			1,208.90	247.48
	J2	Jubilee Games	2206	4,325.30		3,681.11			644.19
27/11/X1	M3	Mirabelle Leisure	2207	954.04				811.95	142.09
	A2	Arnold Toys	2208	456.19	388.25				67.94
	H3	Highlight Ltd	2209	260.98			222.11		38.87
28/11/X1	L1	Lighthouse Products	2210	7,069.34		2,065.18	3,951.28		1,052.88
	D2	Daisychains	2211	2,057.17	580.33		459.27	711.18	306.39
29/11/X1	G4	Gameboard Ltd	2212	2,657.24		1,538.98	722.50		395.76
	M3	Mirabelle Leisure	2213	946.82	221.95	381.55	202.30		141.02
30/11/X1	B2	Gerald Blythe	2214	629.68				535.90	93.78
		Total		21,018.39	1,395.78	7,666.82	5,557.46	3,267.93	3,130.40

Sales returns day book									
Date	Code	Customer	CN	Total £	01 £	02 £	03 £	04 £	VAT £
26/11/X1	B2	Gerald Blythe	C461	190.11				161.80	28.31
30/11/X1	H3	Highlight Ltd	C462	47.70			40.60		7.10
30/11/X1	L1	Lighthouse Products	C463	228.37		111.16	83.20		34.01

SUBSIDIARY (SALES) LEDGER ACCOUNTS

Customer name	Arnold Toys	Account number	A2
Customer address	57 Gray Street Bath BA1 2NT
Telephone	01225 633112

Dr   Cr

Date	Transaction	£		Date	Transaction	£	
19/11	Invoice 2195	118	08	20/11	CR 2198	323	60
20/11	Invoice 2198	2,201	95		c/f	1,996	43
		2,320	03			2,320	03
23/11	b/f	1,996	43	27/11	Cash	118	08
				29/11	Cash	118	08

Customer name	Gerald Blythe & Sons	Account number	B2
Customer address	121 St John's Road Cambridge CB2 3AH
Telephone	01223 461922

Dr   Cr

Date	Transaction	£		Date	Transaction	£	
12/11	Invoice 2186	325	11	20/11	Cash	325	11
22/11	Invoice 2203	119	80		c/f	119	80
		444	91			444	91
23/11	b/f	119	80				

SUBSIDIARY (SALES) LEDGER ACCOUNTS

Customer name   Daisychains   Account number   D2
Customer address 111 George Street Crawley RH10 1HL
Telephone   01293 811566

Dr   Cr

Date	Transaction	£		Date	Transaction	£	
13/9	Invoice 2103	3,115	11				
27/09	Invoice 2122	211	55		c/f	3,326	66
		3,326	66			3,326	66
28/09	b/f	3,326	66	19/10	Cash	3,115	11
16/10	Invoice 2150	501	30		c/f	712	85
		3,827	96			3,827	96
19/10	b/f	712	85				
23/10	Invoice 2157	871	07		c/f	1,583	92
		1,583	92			1,583	92
26/10	b/f	1,583	92				

Customer name   Gameboard Ltd   Account number   G4
Customer address 15 Park Street Woking GU21 1BY
Telephone   01483 757442

Dr   Cr

Date	Transaction	£		Date	Transaction	£	
2/11	b/f	3	09	8/11	Cr	3	09
14/11	Invoice 2187	115	83	16/11	Contra	86	94
					c/f	28	89
		115	83			115	83
16/11	b/f	28	89	20/11	Cash	28	89

UNIT 30 : WORKBOOK

SUBSIDIARY (SALES) LEDGER ACCOUNTS

Customer name   Highlight Ltd   Account number   H3
Customer address   10 Station Road St Albans AL4 3EH
Telephone   01727 46737

Dr							Cr
Date	Transaction	£		Date	Transaction	£	
2/11	Invoice 2173	202	95 ✓	14/9	b/f	33	75 ✓
					c/f	169	20
		202	95			202	95
2/11	b/f	169	20	16/11	Cash	169	20 ✓
14/11	Invoice 2185	311	87 ✓		c/f	311	87
		481	07			481	07
16/11	b/f	311	87	22/11	Cash	311	87 ✓

Customer name   Jubilee Games & Toys   Account number   J2
Customer address   3 Bourne Avenue Bracknell RG12 1AR
Telephone   01344 678222

Dr							Cr
Date	Transaction	£		Date	Transaction	£	
23/10	Invoice 2159	86	90	13/11	Cash	73	20

KEY TECHNIQUES : QUESTIONS

Customer name	Lighthouse Products		Account number		L1	
Customer address	135 Chapel Road Windsor S14 1UL					
Telephone	01753 828688					
Dr						Cr
Date	Transaction	£		Date	Transaction	£	
13/11	Invoice 2188	326	11	20/11	CONTRA	44	22
	c/f	44	22	21/11	Cash	326	11
		370	33			370	33
				23/11	b/f	44	22

Customer name	Mirabelle Leisure		Account number		M3	
Customer address	19 Masons Hill Brighton BN1 8RT					
Telephone	01273 207146					
Dr						Cr
Date	Transaction	£		Date	Transaction	£	
14/11	Invoice 2189	411	38				
15/11	Invoice 2190	83	91		c/f	495	29
		495	29			495	29
16/11	b/f	495	29	20/11	Cash	459	29
					c/f	36	00
		495	29			495	29
23/11	b/f	36	00				

MAIN LEDGER

Account name Sales ledger control **Account no** 01 06 10 00

23/11/X1 b/f	3,705.63	27/11/X1 Cash	118.08
		29/11/X1 Cash	118.08

Account name Sales – Product 01 **Account no** 03 70 10 01

		23/11/X1 b/f	34,875.94

Account name Sales – Product 02 **Account no** 03 70 10 02

		23/11/X1 b/f	175,311.50

Account name Sales – Product 03 **Account no** 03 70 10 03

		23/11/X1 b/f	123,844.73

Account name Sales – Product 04 **Account no** 03 70 10 04

		23/11/X1 b/f	78,914.90

Account name VAT control **Account no** 02 08 90 00

		23/11/X1 b/f	20,935.86

KEY TECHNIQUES : **QUESTIONS**

MAIN LEDGER

| **Account name** | Sales returns – Product 01 | **Account no** | 04 60 10 01 |

| 23/11/X1 | b/f | 3,105.89 | |

| **Account name** | Sales returns – Product 02 | **Account no** | 04 60 10 02 |

| 23/11/X1 | b/f | 15,222.75 | |

| **Account name** | Sales returns – Product 03 | **Account no** | 04 60 10 03 |

| 23/11/X1 | b/f | 10,413.67 | |

| **Account name** | Sales returns – Product 04 | **Account no** | 04 60 10 04 |

| 23/11/X1 | b/f | 6,116.70 | |

UNIT 30 : WORKBOOK

JOURNAL SALES DAY BOOK POSTINGS		NO 3347
Prepared by A Donnelly	Week ending	30/11/X1
Authorised by		
Account	Debit	Credit
Sales ledger control	21,018.39	
Sales product 01		1,395.78
Sales product 02		7,666.82
Sales product 03		5,557.46
Sales product 04		3,267.93
VAT		3,130.40
TOTALS	21,018.39	21,018.39

JOURNAL SALES DAY BOOK POSTINGS		NO 3348
Prepared by	Week ending	30/11/X1
Authorised by		
Account	Debit	Credit
VAT		
TOTALS		

KEY TECHNIQUES : QUESTIONS

TOYBOX GAMES LTD						
125 Finchley Way Bristol BS1 4PL Tel: 01272 200299						
STATEMENT OF ACCOUNT						
Customer name				**Customer account no**		
Customer address						
Statement date		Dr		Cr		Balance
Date	Transaction	£	p	£	p	£	p

TOYBOX GAMES LTD						
125 Finchley Way Bristol BS1 4PL Tel: 01272 200299						
STATEMENT OF ACCOUNT						
Customer name				**Customer account no**		
Customer address						
Statement date		Dr		Cr		Balance
Date	Transaction	£	p	£	p	£	p

UNIT 30 : Workbook

Chapter 15
Accounting for sales – summary

▷ **ACTIVITY 46**   ▷▷▷▷

Today is 16 May 20X0. You are a ledger clerk in Elliott Brook Associates, a business providing temporary catering staff to hotels on the south coast of England. You have been sent the memorandum reproduced below, from Andrew Brook, the chief accountant.

Task 1   Check the following batch of invoices prepared by the sales ledger clerk as clerically accurate. Show any corrections needed on the face of the invoice.

Task 2   Enter the (corrected) invoices in the sales day book provided.

Task 3   Check the following batch of credit notes prepared by the sales ledger clerk for authorisation, and note any errors.

Task 4   Enter the (corrected) credit notes in the credit notes day book provided. (This is the same as a sales returns day book but 'returns' are not relevant to a service industry.)

MEMORANDUM

To: A Student   cc: A N Other
From: Andrew Brook
Subject: Rates and discounts   Date: 20 March 20X0

Please note the following new rates and discounts (with effect from 25 March 20X0).

Grade	Rate per hour £
A	7.50 plus VAT
B	6.25 plus VAT
C	4.00 plus VAT
D	3.00 plus VAT

Invoice equal to or over £	Discount %
300.00	10
500.00	20

Please also note that no credit notes should be issued unless I have authorised them in writing on the face of the credit note.

KEY TECHNIQUES : QUESTIONS

SALES INVOICE

ELLIOTT BROOK ASSOCIATES

39114

Address
25 Eaton Terrace Telephone 01323 866755
Eastbourne BN16 3RS Fax 01323 995655
VAT Reg No 544 2900 17 **Tax point** **16 May 20X0**

Hire of staff
FAO Catering Manager
Imperial Hotel
45 The Promenade
Eastbourne
Client code IMP 23

Name	Start	Finish	Hours	Grade	Rate £	Total excl VAT £
Wilson	7/5/X0	13/5/X0	40	A	7.50	300.00
			Discount			30.00
						270.00
			VAT at 17.5%			47.25
						317.25 : £317.25

SALES INVOICE

ELLIOTT BROOK ASSOCIATES

39115

Address
25 Eaton Terrace Telephone 01323 866755
Eastbourne BN16 3RS Fax 01323 995655
VAT Reg No 544 2900 17 **Tax point** **16 May 20X0**

Hire of staff
FAO Catering Manager
Rosetree Hotel
355 The Promenade
Eastbourne
Client code ROS 10

Name	Start	Finish	Hours	Grade	Rate £	Total excl VAT £
Stewart	11/5/X0	15/5/X0	11	B	6.25	68.75
Brightwell	7/5/X0	14/5/X0	32	C	4.00	128.00
						196.75
			Discount			0
						196.75
			VAT at 17.5%			34.43
						231.18 : £231.18

SALES INVOICE
ELLIOTT BROOK ASSOCIATES

39116

Address
25 Eaton Terrace Telephone 01323 866755
Eastbourne BN16 3RS Fax 01323 995655
VAT Reg No 544 2900 17 Tax point 16 May 20X0

Hire of staff
FAO The Manager
West Bay Hotel
67 Western Drive
Eastbourne
Client code WST 02

Name	Start	Finish	Hours	Grade	Rate £	Total excl VAT £
Brown	15/5/X0	15/5/X0	5	B	6.25	31.25
Robinson	8/5/X0	13/5/X0	37	C	4.00	148.00
						179.25
			Discount			0
						179.25
			VAT at 17.5%			31.37
						210.62 : £210.62

SALES INVOICE
ELLIOTT BROOK ASSOCIATES

39118

Address
25 Eaton Terrace Telephone 01323 866755
Eastbourne BN16 3RS Fax 01323 995655
VAT Reg No 544 2900 17 Tax point 16 May 20X0

Hire of staff
FAO The Manager
Kenmare Hotel
73 East Sands Way
Eastbourne
Client code KEN 11

Name	Start	Finish	Hours	Grade	Rate £	Total excl VAT £
Price	10/5/X0	13/5/X0	12	D	3.00	36.00
Haines	11/5/X0	13/5/X0	16	C	4.00	64.00
Peters	7/5/X0	12/5/X0	30	B	6.25	97.50
						197.50
			Discount			0
						197.50
			VAT at 17.5%			34.56
						232.06 : £232.06

SALES INVOICE
ELLIOTT BROOK ASSOCIATES

39119

Address
25 Eaton Terrace
Eastbourne BN16 3RS
VAT Reg No 544 2900 17

Telephone 01323 866755
Fax   01323 995655
Tax point 16 May 20X0

Hire of staff
FAO Trina Watts
Seaview Hotel
173 East Sands Way
Eastbourne
Client code SEA 05

Name	Start	Finish	Hours	Grade	Rate £	Total excl VAT £
Clark	9/5/X0	13/5/X0	16	A	7.50	120.00
Frost	10/5/X0	13/5/X0	20	D	3.00	60.00
						180.00
			Discount			0
						180.00
			VAT at 17.5%			31.50
						211.50 : £211.50

SALES INVOICE
ELLIOTT BROOK ASSOCIATES

39120

Address
25 Eaton Terrace
Eastbourne BN16 3RS
VAT Reg No 544 2900 17

Telephone 01323 866755
Fax   01323 995655
Tax point 16 May 20X0

Hire of staff
FAO Services Manager
Royal Hotel
Royal View
Eastbourne
Client code ROY 05

Name	Start	Finish	Hours	Grade	Rate £	Total excl VAT £
Clarke	7/5/X0	8/5/X0	15	A	7.50	112.50
Hartley	9/5/X0	13/5/X0	40	A	7.50	300.00
						412.50
			Discount			0
						412.50
			VAT at 17.5%			72.19
						484.69 : £484.69

SALES INVOICE
ELLIOTT BROOK ASSOCIATES

39121

Address
25 Eaton Terrace
Eastbourne BN16 3RS
VAT Reg No 544 2900 17

Telephone 01323 866755
Fax 01323 995655
Tax point **16 May 20X0**

Hire of staff
FAO Sheila Green
Crown and Anchor
Royal View
Eastbourne
Client code CRO 12

Name	Start	Finish	Hours	Grade	Rate £	Total excl VAT £
Chadwick	11/5/X0	13/5/X0	10	D	3.00	30.00
						30.00
			Discount			0
						30.00
			VAT at 17.5%			5.25
						35.25 : £35.25

CREDIT NOTE
ELLIOTT BROOK ASSOCIATES

12233

Address
25 Eaton Terrace
Eastbourne BN16 3RS
VAT Reg No 544 2900 17

Telephone 01323 866755
Fax 01323 995655
Tax point **16 May 20X0**

Reason for credit Clerical error on invoice 38999

FAO Services Manager
Royal Hotel
Royal View
Eastbourne

Client code ROY 05

Name	Start	Finish	Hours	Grade	Rate £	Total excl VAT £
Clarke						12.90
			VAT at 17.5%			2.26
						15.16

A Brook (signature)

CREDIT NOTE
ELLIOTT BROOK ASSOCIATES

12235

Address
25 Eaton Terrace Telephone 01323 866755
Eastbourne BN16 3RS Fax 01323 995655
VAT Reg No 544 2900 17 **Tax point** 16 May 20X0

Reason for credit Clerical error on invoice 38999

FAO Services Manager
Royal Hotel
Royal View
Eastbourne

Client code ROY 05

Name	Start	Finish	Hours	Grade	Rate £	Total excl VAT £
Clarke						12.90
				VAT at 17.5%		2.26
						15.16

CREDIT NOTE
ELLIOTT BROOK ASSOCIATES

12236

Address
25 Eaton Terrace Telephone 01323 866755
Eastbourne BN16 3RS Fax 01323 995655
VAT Reg No 544 2900 17 **Tax point** 16 May 20X0

Reason for credit Clerical error on invoice 39101

FAO Services Manager
Sandringham Hotel
101 The Promenade
Eastbourne

Client code SAN 10

Name	Start	Finish	Hours	Grade	Rate £	Total excl VAT £
						45.89
				VAT at 17.5%		8.03
						53.92

A Brook (signature)

SALES DAY BOOK

DATE	CLIENT	INVOICE	NET	VAT	GROSS

CREDIT NOTES DAY BOOK

DATE	CLIENT	INVOICE	NET	VAT	GROSS

ACTIVITY 47

Given below is a completed sales day book for the week ending 26 April 20X1.

Required

Post the totals of the sales day book to the main ledger accounts; and post each individual invoice to the subsidiary ledger (sales ledger) accounts.

Sales day book						
Date	Invoice No	Customer name	Code	Total	VAT	Net
				£	£	£
20X1						
22 April	4671	J T Howard	SL15	138.93	20.69	118.24
22 April	4672	F Parker	SL07	99.07	14.75	84.32
23 April	4673	Harlow Ltd	SL02	125.10	18.63	106.47
24 April	4674	Edmunds & Co	SL13	167.75	24.98	142.77
26 April	4675	Peters & Co	SL09	113.04	16.83	96.21
				643.89	95.88	548.01

UNIT 30 : WORKBOOK

▷ ACTIVITY 48

Given below is an analysed sales day book.

Required

Total the sales day book and check that the totals cross-cast; post the totals to the main ledger accounts; and post the individual entries to the subsidiary ledger accounts.

Sales day book

Date	Invoice No	Customer name	Code	Total £	VAT £	01 £	02 £	03 £
20X0								
6/9	04771	Harold Ellis	H03	93.77	13.96	15.68		64.13
7/9	04772	P Pilot	P01	134.67	20.05		114.62	
	04773	R Tracy	T02	83.30	12.40	23.22	30.80	16.88
8/9	C0612	Harold Ellis	H03	(15.51)	(2.31)			(13.20)
9/9	04774	Planet Inc	P04	165.34	24.62		64.82	75.90
10/9	04775	Harold Ellis	H03	47.23	7.03	23.80	16.40	
	C0613	C Calver	C01	(17.17)	(2.55)	(8.20)		(6.42)

▷ ACTIVITY 49

Today is 19 February 20X0. You are the cashier at Paperbox Ltd.

You are required to complete the following tasks.

Task 1 Using the remittance lists prepare the paying-in slip and credit card voucher summary for paying these amounts in to the bank.

Task 2 Write up the cash book for monies included on the paying-in slip. Mail order sales are recorded on the remittance list including VAT.

Task 3 Prepare a journal entry to post the totals from the cash receipts book to the accounts in the main ledger.

The last journal entry was number 105.

REMITTANCE LIST

Date: 19 - 2 - X0

Receipts from: TRADE DEBTORS

Customer name	Invoice No	Cheque £	Credit Card Express £	Credit Card Global £	Discount £
NJ Peal	5229, 5248	291.60			
Stationery Supplies	5392	245.30			5.01
Candle Company Ltd	5227, 5309	562.80			4.95
Pearce & Fellows	5308	659.18			13.45
Abraham Matthews Ltd	5291	117.93			
Total		1,876.81			23.41

REMITTANCE LIST

Date: 19 - 2 - X0

Receipts from: MAIL ORDER

Customer name	Invoice No	Cheque £	Credit Card Express £	Credit Card Global £	Discount £
KB Smith			22.60		
R Jones			5.83		
C Bastok			26.18		
J Rirolli			18.95		
Total			73.56		

KEY TECHNIQUES : QUESTIONS

		REMITTANCE LIST		Date	19 - 2 - X0
				Receipts from	Sundry

Customer name	Invoice No	Cheque £	Credit Card Express £	Credit Card Global £	Discount £
RF Wholesalers Ltd (Not trade debtor) (Exempt from VAT)	Rent	539.50			
Total		539.50			

UNIT 30 : WORKBOOK

Bank paying-in slip

To be retained by receiving bank

For the credit of <u>George Jones Scrapmerchants</u>
Cheques etc for collection to be included in total credit of £_____ paid in_____ 20____.

	£	Brought forward	£	Brought forward	£
Carried forward	£	Carried forward	£	Total cheques etc	£

Date _____

Cashier's stamp and initials

56 -28 - 48

FINANCIAL BANK PLC
GREENOCK

£50 Notes	
£20 Notes	
£10 Notes	
£5 Notes	
£2 Coins	
£1 Coins	
50p	
20p	
Silver	
Bronze	
Total Cash	
Cheques, POs etc	
TOTAL £	

Fee | No Chqs

Credit T-S DESIGNS
Paid in by _____

Address/Ref No. _____

Credit card voucher summary

Have you imprinted the summary with your Retailer's Card?
Bank processing copy of Summary with your Vouchers in correct order:
1 Summary
2 Sales Vouchers
3 Refund Vouchers
Keep Retailer's copy and
         Retailer's Duplicate copy
No more than 200 Vouchers to each Summary
Do not use Staples, Pins, Paper Clips

	Items	Amount
Sales vouchers		
Less Refund Vouchers		
		:

Retailer Summary

Retailer's Copy

Retailer Summary

_____
Retailer's Signature

Complete this summary for every Deposit of Sales Vouchers and enter the Total on your normal Current Account paying-in slip

KEY TECHNIQUES : **QUESTIONS**

		£ p
Please do not pin or staple this voucher as this will affect the machine processing.	1	_____
	2	_____
	3	_____
All sales vouchers must be deposited within three banking days of the dates shown on them.	4	_____
	5	_____
	6	_____
	7	_____
If you are submitting more than 26 vouchers please enclose a separate listing.	8	_____
	9	_____
	10	_____
If a voucher contravenes the terms of the retailer agreement then the amount shown on the voucher may be charged back to your bank account, either direct or via your paying in branch.	11	_____
	12	_____
	13	_____
	14	_____
	15	_____
	16	_____
Similarly, if the total amount shown on the Retail Voucher Summary does not balance with our total of vouchers, the difference will be credited (or debited) to your bank account.	17	_____
	18	_____
	19	_____
	20	_____
	21	_____
	22	_____
	23	_____
	24	_____
	25	_____
	26	_____
SALES VOUCHERS TOTAL		_____
		£ p
	1	_____
	2	_____
	3	_____
	4	_____
	5	_____
	6	_____
	7	_____
REFUND VOUCHERS TOTAL		_____

Cash Book Receipts

Date	Narrative	Paying-in slip no	Total	Debtors	Mail Order Sales	Other	VAT	Discount allowed

KEY TECHNIQUES : QUESTIONS

		Journal no.	106
		Date	
		Prepared by	

Code	Account	Debit	Credit
	Bank		
	Sales mail order		
	Trade debtors		
	VAT control account		
	Discounts allowed		
	Trade debtors		
Total			
Narrative			

Chapter 16
Credit purchases: documents

▷ **ACTIVITY 50**

Nethan Builders have just received the following credit note. You are required to check that the credit note is clerically accurate and note the details of any problems. Trade discount is 15%.

CREDIT NOTE

Credit note to:
Nethan Builders
Brecon House
Stamford Road
Manchester
M16 4PL

J M Bond & Co
North Park Industrial Estate
Manchester
M12 4TU
Tel: 0161 561 3214
Fax: 0161 561 3060

Credit note no: 06192
Tax point: 22 April 20X1
VAT reg no: 461 4367 91
Invoice no: 331624

Code	Description	Quantity	VAT rate %	Unit price £	Amount exclusive of VAT £
DGSS4163	Structural Softwood Untreated	6 m	17.5%	6.85	41.10

	41.10
Trade discount 15%	8.22
	32.88
VAT at 17.5%	5.75
Total amount of credit	38.63

ACTIVITY 51

You work in the accounts department of Nethan Builders and given below are three purchase invoices together with the related purchase orders and delivery note. You are to check each invoice carefully and note any problems or discrepancies that you find. You may assume that the **rates** of trade and settlement discounts are correct.

INVOICE

A J Broom & Company Limited
59 Parkway
Manchester
M2 6EG
Tel: 0161 560 3392
Fax: 0161 560 5322

Invoice to:
Nethan Builders
Brecon House
Stamford Road
Manchester
M16 4PL

Deliver to:
As above

Invoice no: 046123
Tax point: 22 April 20X1
VAT reg no: 661 2359 07
Purchase order no: 7164

Code	Description	Quantity	VAT rate %	Unit price £	Amount exclusive of VAT £
DGS472	SDG Softwood	9.6 m	17.5%	8.44	81.02
CIBF653	Joist hanger	7	17.5%	12.30	86.10

	167.12
Trade discount 10%	16.71
VAT at 17.5%	150.41
	26.32
Total amount payable	176.73

INVOICE

Jenson Ltd
30 Longfield Park
Kingsway
M45 2TP
Tel: 0161 511 4666
Fax: 0161 511 4777

Invoice to:
Nethan Builders
Brecon House
Stamford Road
Manchester
M16 4PL

Deliver to:
As above

Invoice no:	47792
Tax point:	22 April 20X1
VAT reg no:	641 3229 45
Purchase order no:	7162

Code	Description	Quantity	VAT rate %	Unit price £	Amount exclusive of VAT £
PL432115	Door lining set 32 X 115 mm	14	17.5%	30.25	423.50
PL432140	Door lining set 32 X 138 mm	8	17.5%	33.15	265.20
					688.70
Trade discount 15%					103.30
VAT at 17.5%					585.40
					102.44
Total amount payable					687.84

Deduct discount of 3% if paid within 14 days.

INVOICE

Haddow Bros
The White House
Standing Way
Manchester
M13 6FH
Tel: 0161 560 3140
Fax: 0161 560 6140

Invoice to:
Nethan Builders
Brecon House
Stamford Road
Manchester
M16 4PL

Deliver to:
As above

Invoice no: 033912
Tax point: 22 April 20X1
VAT reg no: 460 3559 71
Purchase order no: 7165

Code	Description	Quantity	VAT rate %	Unit price £	Amount exclusive of VAT £
PLY8FE1	Plywood Hardwood 2440 x 1220 mm	12 sheets	17.5%	17.80	213.60
					213.60
VAT at 17.5%					36.63
					250.23

Total amount payable

Deduct discount of 2% if paid within 10 days.

PURCHASE ORDER

Nethan Builders

Brecon House
Stamford Road
Manchester
M16 4PL
Tel: 0161 521 6411
Fax: 0161 521 6412
Date: 14 April 20X1
Purchase order no: 7162

To: Jenson Ltd
30 Longfield Park
Kingsway
M45 2TP

Delivery address
(If different from above)

Invoice address
(If different from above)

Code	Quantity	Description	Unit price (exclusive of VAT) £
PL432140	8	Door lining set 32 x 138 mm	33.15
PL432115	14	Door lining set 32 x 115 mm	30.25

PURCHASE ORDER

Nethan Builders

Brecon House
Stamford Road
Manchester
M16 4PL
Tel: 0161 521 6411
Fax: 0161 521 6412
Date: 14 April 20X1
Purchase order no: 7164

To: JA J Broom & Co Ltd
59 Parkway
Manchester
M2 6EG

Delivery address
(If different from above)

Invoice address
(If different from above)

Code	Quantity	Description	Unit price (exclusive of VAT) £
DGS472	9.6 m	SDG Softwood	8.44
CIBF653	5	Joist hanger	12.30

PURCHASE ORDER

Nethan Builders

Brecon House
Stamford Road
Manchester
M16 4PL
Tel: 0161 521 6411
Fax: 0161 521 6412
Date: 14 April 20X1
Purchase order no: 7165

To: Haddow Bros
        The White House
        Standing Way
        Manchester
        M13 6FH

Delivery address
(If different from above)

Invoice address
(If different from above)

Code	Quantity	Description	Unit price (exclusive of VAT) £
PLY8FE1	12 sheets	Plywood Hardwood 2440 x 1220 mm	17.80

UNIT 30 : WORKBOOK

DELIVERY NOTE

Deliver to:
Nethan Builders
Brecon House
Stamford Road
Manchester
M16 4PL

Jenson Ltd
30 Longfield Park
Kingsway
M45 2TP
Tel: 0161 511 4666
Fax: 0161 511 4777

Delivery note no: 771460
Date: 19 April 20X1
VAT reg no: 641 3229 45

Code	Description	Quantity	VAT rate %	Unit price £	Amount exclusive of VAT £
PL432115	Door lining set 32x115 mm	14			
PL432140	Door lining set 32x138 mm	8			

Goods received in good condition.

Print name .....C JULIAN..........

Signature .....C Julian..........

Date ....19/4/X1..........

DELIVERY NOTE

Deliver to:
Nethan Builders
Brecon House
Stamford Road
Manchester
M16 4PL

A J Broom & Company Limited
59 Parkway
Manchester
M2 6EG
Tel: 0161 560 3392
Fax: 0161 560 5322

Delivery note no: 076429
Date: 20 April 20X1
VAT reg no: 661 2359 07
Purchase order no: 7164

Code	Description	Quantity	VAT rate %	Unit price £	Amount exclusive of VAT £
CIBF653	Joist hanger	7			
DGS472	SDG Softwood	9.6 m			

Goods received in good condition.

Print name ....C JULIAN............

Signature ....C Julian............

Date ....19/4/X1............

UNIT 30 : WORKBOOK

DELIVERY NOTE

Deliver to:
Nethan Builders
Brecon House
Stamford Road
Manchester
M16 4PL

Haddow Bros
The White House
Standing Way
Manchester
M13 6FH
Tel: 0161 560 3140
Fax: 0161 560 6140

Delivery note no: 667713
Date: 17 April 20X1
VAT reg no: 460 3559 71

Code	Description	Quantity	VAT rate %	Unit price £	Amount exclusive of VAT £
PLY8FE1	Plywood Hardwood 2440x1220 mm	10			

Goods received in good condition.

Print name ....C JULIAN....

Signature ....C Julian....

Date ....17/4/X1....

Chapter 17
Making payments

▷ ACTIVITY 52

Given below are four invoices received by Nethan Builders that are to be paid today, 18 May 20X1. It is the business policy to take advantage of any settlement discounts possible. If the cheques are written out today then they will reach the supplier on 20 May.

You are required to complete a remittance advice and cheque, ready for signature by the owner, for each payment.

INVOICE

Invoice to:
Nethan Builders
Brecon House
Stamford Road
Manchester
M16 4PL

Building Contract Supplies
Unit 15
Royal Estate
Manchester
M13 2EF
Tel: 0161 562 3041
Fax: 0161 562 3042

Deliver to:
As above

Invoice no: 07742
Tax point: 8 May 20X1
VAT reg no: 776 4983 06

Code	Description	Quantity	VAT rate %	Unit price £	Amount exclusive of VAT £
SDGSL6	SDGS Softwood 47 x 225 mm	20.5 m	17.5%	8.30	170.15

	170.15
VAT at 17.5%	29.32
Total amount payable	199.47

Deduct discount of 1½% if paid within 14 days.

INVOICE

Invoice to:
Nethan Builders
Brecon House
Stamford Road
Manchester
M16 4PL

Deliver to:
As above

Jenson Ltd
30 Longfield Park
Kingsway
M45 2TP
Tel: 0161 511 4666
Fax: 0161 511 4777

Invoice no:	47811
Tax point:	5 May 20X1
VAT reg no:	641 3229 45
Purchase order no:	7174

Code	Description	Quantity	VAT rate %	Unit price £	Amount exclusive of VAT £
PL432115	Door Lining Set 32x115 mm	6	17.5%	30.25	181.50

Trade discount 15%

VAT at 17.5%
Total amount payable
Deduct discount of 3% if paid within 14 days

181.50
27.22
154.28
26.18
180.46

INVOICE

Invoice to:
Nethan Builders
Brecon House
Stamford Road
Manchester
M16 4PL

Magnum Supplies
140/150 Park Estate
Manchester
M20 6EG
Tel: 0161 501 3202
Fax: 0161 501 3200

Deliver to:
As above

Invoice no: 077422
Tax point: 11 May 20X1
VAT reg no: 611 4337 90

Code	Description	Quantity	VAT rate %	Unit price £	Amount exclusive of VAT £
BH47732	House Bricks – Red	600	17.5%	1.24	744.00

	744.00
Trade discount 15%	111.60
	632.40
VAT at 17.5%	108.45
Total amount payable	740.85
Deduct discount of 2% if paid within 10 days	

INVOICE

Invoice to:
Nethan Builders
Brecon House
Stamford Road
Manchester
M16 4PL

Deliver to:
As above

Haddow Bros
The White House
Standing Way
Manchester
M13 6FH
Tel: 0161 560 3140
Fax: 0161 560 6140

Invoice no: G33940
Tax point: 9 May 20X1
VAT reg no: 460 3559 71

Code	Description	Quantity	VAT rate %	Unit price £	Amount exclusive of VAT £
PLY8FE1	Plywood Hardwood 2440x1220 mm	24	17.5%	17.80	427.20

	427.20
VAT at 17.5%	73.26
Total amount payable	500.46

Deduct discount of 2% if paid within 10 days.

REMITTANCE ADVICE

To:

Nethan Builders
Brecon House
Stamford Road
Manchester
M16 4PL

Tel: 0161 521 6411
Fax: 0161 530 6412
VAT Reg no: 471 3860 42
Date:

Date	Invoice no	Amount £	Discount taken £	Paid £

Total paid £ _____

Cheque no _____

REMITTANCE ADVICE

To:

Nethan Builders
Brecon House
Stamford Road
Manchester
M16 4PL

Tel: 0161 521 6411
Fax: 0161 530 6412
VAT Reg no: 471 3860 42
Date:

Date	Invoice no	Amount £	Discount taken £	Paid £

Total paid £ _____

Cheque no _____

REMITTANCE ADVICE

To:

Nethan Builders
Brecon House
Stamford Road
Manchester
M16 4PL

Tel: 0161 521 6411
Fax: 0161 530 6412
VAT Reg no: 471 3860 42
Date:

Date	Invoice no	Amount £	Discount taken £	Paid £

Total paid £ _____

Cheque no _____

REMITTANCE ADVICE

To:

Nethan Builders
Brecon House
Stamford Road
Manchester
M16 4PL

Tel: 0161 521 6411
Fax: 0161 530 6412
VAT Reg no: 471 3860 42
Date:

Date	Invoice no	Amount £	Discount taken £	Paid £

Total paid £ _____

Cheque no _____

KEY TECHNIQUES : QUESTIONS

CENTRAL BANK PLC
18 Coventry Road
Birmingham
B13 2TU

19-14-60

_____ 20___

Pay _____ or order

Account payee

£

200550   19-14-60   50731247   **NETHAN BUILDERS**

CENTRAL BANK PLC
18 Coventry Road
Birmingham
B13 2TU

19-14-60

_____ 20___

Pay _____ or order

Account payee

£

200551   19-14-60   50731247   **NETHAN BUILDERS**

CENTRAL BANK PLC
18 Coventry Road
Birmingham
B13 2TU

19-14-60

_____ 20___

Pay _____ or order

Account payee

£

200552   19-14-60   50731247   **NETHAN BUILDERS**

UNIT 30 : WORKBOOK

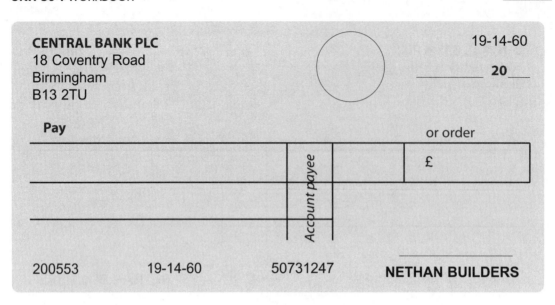

Chapter 18
Payroll procedures

▷ ACTIVITY 53

Given below are the totals of the wages book for the week ended 23 May 20X1.

Required

Enter these totals into the wages control account for the week.

Wages book totals

	Gross pay £	PAYE £	Employee's NIC £	Employer's NIC £	Net pay £
Total	167,384	35,129	14,043	20,086	118,212

▷ ACTIVITY 54

An employee has gross pay for a week of £368.70. The PAYE for the week is £46.45, the employer's NIC £30.97 and the employee's NIC £23.96.

What is the employee's net pay for the week?

▷ ACTIVITY 55

Given below is the wages book for the month of May 20X1 for a small business with four employees.

Wages book

Employee number	Gross pay £	PAYE £	Employee's NIC £	Employer's NIC £	Net pay £
001	1,200	151	78	101	971
002	1,400	176	91	118	1,133
003	900	113	58	76	729
004	1,550	195	101	130	1,254
	5,050	635	328	425	4,087

You are required to use the totals from the wages book for the month to write up the wages ledger accounts given below.

Gross wages control account

	£		£

Wages expense account

	£		£
30 April Balance b/d	23,446		

HM Revenue and Customs account

	£		£
19 May CPB	760	30 April Balance b/d	760

UNIT 30 : WORKBOOK

▷ ACTIVITY 56

Today is 4 May 20X1. You are the cashier at Park Foods Group plc, a manufacturer of confectionery products. You are responsible for all cash records.

TASK 1 Write up the analysed cash book for the week ended 30 April 20X1, from the:
- Cheques paid listing
- Standing order schedule
- Direct debit schedule
- BACS listing

Note that VAT is only payable on the English Telecom invoice.

TASK 2 Complete the journal entry for the posting of the totals of the cash payments book.

TASK 3 Post the totals of the cash payments book to the main ledger accounts (excluding the salaries).

TASK 4 Post the individual payments to the four subsidiary ledger, (purchases) accounts given.

TASK 5 Using the wages book totals given, write up the main ledger accounts for wages for the month – the salaries expense account (the net salary paid should already have been entered), the gross salaries control account and the HMRC account.

CHEQUES PAID LISTING
Milton Keynes
Cheque run 24/4/X1

Creditors

2374	Fowler & Kenworthy Ltd	17,678.67
75	Vinegar Supply Company Ltd	1,657.99
76	Western Farmers Ltd	34,766.45
77	Fish Supply Group plc	14,365.00
78	General Grain Supply Co Ltd	2,334.45
79	Tamar Flour Millers Ltd	1,766.38
80	Angus Meat Suppliers plc	5,443.12
81	Hobbs and Davies Ltd	773.56
82	Jersey Foods Ltd	3,716.33
83	Flour Products Ltd	12,674.99
84	DI Ltd	543.92
85	Finer Products Ltd	23,894.34
86	Greengates Ltd	9,333.25
87	Catering Supplies Ltd	112.32
88	Plastic Products Ltd	6,833.28
89	Simpson Foods Ltd	346.60
90	Paper Bag Company Ltd	10,004.43
91	United Food Producers Ltd	9,567.76
92	TY Foods Ltd	17,334.78
93	Bell Distribution International Ltd	3,885.38
94	Winter & White Ltd	267.56
95	Dairy Produce Company Ltd	245.87
96	Ghanwani Foods Ltd	844.20
97	Cross & Fordingham Ltd	18,794.95
98	T & P Importers Ltd	10,339.27
2399	Golden Grains Ltd	5,680.11
2400	Imperial Foods plc	605.02

Salaries

2401	L Freeborough	76.83

UNIT 30 : WORKBOOK

STANDING ORDER SCHEDULE

DATE	PAYEE	AMOUNT £	SPECIAL INSTRUCTIONS
19th Monthly	Feed producers Assoc	60.00	Last payment 19/4/XI
28th Quarterly	Kennedy Property	6,547.45	Rent of warehouse April, July, Oct & January
15th Quarterly	Northern Gas	60.65	March, June, Sept, Dec

DIRECT DEBIT SCHEDULE

DATE	PAYEE	AMOUNT £	SPECIAL INSTRUCTIONS
24th Quarterly	Security Insurance	546.90	April, July, Oct, Dec
27th Quarterly	English Telecomm	Variable	April, July, Oct, Dec

The April bill from English Telecomm totalled £378.65 inclusive of £56.39 VAT.

KEY TECHNIQUES : **QUESTIONS**

BACS Listing

Milton Keynes
25/4/X1

		£
Salaries	01	23,564.22
	02	12,453.64
	03	35,555.25
	04	3,630.66

Cash Book Payments

Date	Narrative	Cheque no	Total	Creditors	Salaries	Other	VAT

UNIT 30 : WORKBOOK

JOURNAL

	Journal no	78
	Date	
	Authorised	Patricia Konig
	Dr	Cr

Reason

MAIN LEDGER ACCOUNTS

Purchases ledger control account

	£		£
		23/4/X1 Balance b/f	346,589.45

Rent account

	£		£
23/4/X1 Balance b/f	7,235.46		

Insurance account

	£		£
23/4/X1 Balance b/f	478.69		

Telephone account

	£		£
23/4/X1 Balance b/f	412.56		

VAT account

	£		£
		23/4/X1	20,376.43

KEY TECHNIQUES : QUESTIONS

Gross salaries control account

	£		£

Salaries expense account

	£		£
23/4/X1 Balance b/f	250,437.36		

HMRC account

	£		£
		12/4/X1 Balance b/f	18,584.34

SUBSIDIARY LEDGER – PURCHASES LEDGER ACCOUNTS

Fowler & Kenworthy Ltd   2374

	£		£
		23/4/X1 Balance b/f	23,475.68

Hobbs and Davies Ltd   2381

	£		£
		23/4/X1 Balance b/f	1,043.50

Paper Bag Company Ltd   2390

	£		£
		23/4/X1 Balance b/f	10,004.43

T & P Importers Ltd   2398

	£		£
		23/4/X1 Balance b/f	15,364.89

WAGES BOOK SUMMARY

Department	Gross pay	PAYE	Employee's NIC	Employer's NIC	Net pay
	£	£	£	£	£
01	29,222.55	3,682.04	1,899.46	2,454.70	23,641.05
02	15,393.87	1,939.63	1,000.60	1,293.08	12,453.64
03	43,949.63	5,537.65	2,856.73	3,691.77	35,555.25
04	4,487.84	565.47	291.71	376.98	3,630.66
	93,053.89	11,724.79	6,048.50	7,816.53	75,280.60

Chapter 19
Accounting for purchases – summary

▶ ACTIVITY 57

Julian Hargreaves is a self-employed painter and decorator. He uses an analysed purchases day book and analyses his purchases into paints, wallpaper and other purchases.

Given below are three purchase invoices that he has received. The purchase ledger codes for the three suppliers are:

Mortimer & Co	PL03
F L Decor Supplies	PL06
Specialist Paint Ltd	PL08

Today's date is 22 March 20X1 and you are to enter these invoices into the analysed purchases day book given and total each of the columns.

INVOICE

Invoice to:
Julian Hargreaves
28 Flynn Avenue
Corton
TN16 4SJ

Mortimer & Co
Pearl Park Estate
Tonbridge
TN14 6LM
Tel: 01883 461207
Fax: 01883 461208

Deliver to:
As above

IInvoice no:	047992
Tax point:	20 March 20X1
VAT reg no:	641 3299 07

Code	Description	Quantity	VAT rate %	Unit price £	Amount exclusive of VAT £
LP4882	Lining Paper Grade 2	40 rolls	17.5%	2.80	112.00
GL117	Wallpaper Glue	4 tins (2 litres)	17.5%	10.65	42.60
					154.60
VAT at 17.5%					26.37
Total amount payable					180.97

Deduct discount of 2½% if paid within 14 days.

INVOICE

Invoice to:
Julian Hargreaves
28 Flynn Avenue
Corton
TN16 4SJ

F L Decor Supplies
64/66 Main Road
Flimfield
TN22 4HT
Tel: 01883 714206
Fax: 01883 714321

Deliver to:
As above

Invoice no: 61624
Tax point: 18 March 20X1
VAT reg no: 743 2116 05

Code	Description	Quantity	VAT rate %	Unit price £	Amount exclusive of VAT £
AG461	Anaglypta Wallpaper – White	16 rolls	17.5%	3.80	60.80

	60.80
Trade discount 10%	6.08
	54.72
VAT at 17.5%	9.57
Total amount payable	64.29

UNIT 30 : WORKBOOK

INVOICE

Invoice to:
Julian Hargreaves
28 Flynn Avenue
Corton
TN16 4SJ

Specialist Paint Ltd
Cedar House
Otford Way
Tonbridge
TN3 6AS
Tel: 01883 445511
Fax: 01883 445512

Deliver to:
As above

Invoice no: 05531
Tax point: 20 March 20X1
VAT reg no: 666 4557 28

Code	Description	Quantity	VAT rate %	Unit price £	Amount exclusive of VAT £
PT4168	Eggshell Paint – Fuchsia	6 tins (2 litres)	17.5%	16.40	98.40
BS118	Horse Hair Paint Brush 50 mm	10	17.5%	8.85	88.50
					186.90
VAT at 17.5%					32.21
Total amount payable					219.11

Deduct discount of 1½% if paid within 14 days

Purchases day book

Date	Invoice no	Code	Supplier	Total	VAT	Paint	Wallpaper	Other

ACTIVITY 58

Given below is the purchases day book for a business for the week ending 12 March 20X1.

You are required to:
- prepare the journal entry for the posting of the totals to the main ledger - the last journal number was 0253;
- post the individual entries to the subsidiary ledger accounts given.

Purchases day book

Date	Invoice no	Code	Supplier	Total £	VAT £	01 £	02 £	03 £	04 £
08/3/X1	06121	PL12	Homer Ltd	223.87	33.34	68.90			121.63
	11675	PL07	Forker & Co	207.24	30.86		70.20	106.18	
09/3/X1	46251	PL08	Print Associates	230.04	34.26			64.88	130.90
10/3/X1	016127	PL02	ABG Ltd	292.58	43.57	118.60	130.41		
	C4366	PL07	Forker & Co	(23.73)	(3.53)		(20.20)		
11/3/X1	77918	PL19	G Greg	169.69	25.27	69.82		74.60	
	06132	PL12	Homer Ltd	189.33	28.19	70.24			90.90
12/3/X1	CN477	PL02	ABG Ltd	(48.31)	(7.19)	(16.80)	(24.32)		
				1,240.71	184.77	310.76	156.09	245.66	343.43

JOURNAL ENTRY		No:	
Prepared by:			
Authorised by:			
Date:			
Narrative:			

Account	Debit	Credit
TOTALS		

Subsidiary ledger

ABG Ltd   PL02

	£			£
		5/3	Balance b/d	486.90

Forker & Co — PL07

£			£
	5/3	Balance b/d	503.78

Print Associates — PL08

£			£
	5/3	Balance b/d	229.56

Homer Ltd — PL12

£			£
	5/3	Balance b/d	734.90

G Greg — PL19

£			£
	5/3	Balance b/d	67.89

▷ ACTIVITY 59

Below you are given the purchases day book for a business for the week ending 24 February 20X1. You are required to:
- post the totals to the main ledger accounts given;
- post the individual entries to the subsidiary ledger accounts given.

Purchases day book

Date	Invoice no	Code	Supplier	Total £	VAT £	01 £	02 £	03 £	04 £
20/2/X1	46118	PL11	Fred Janitor	218.70	32.57	84.93		101.20	
	46119	PL07	S Doorman	189.53	28.22		86.51	74.80	
21/2/X1	46120	PL03	P & F Davis & Co	166.54	24.80	68.92	23.30		49.52
22/2/X1	CN462	PL11	Fred Janitor	(30.99)	(4.61)	(10.20)		(16.18)	
	46121	PL06	Clooney & Partner	230.58	34.34		87.54	60.08	48.62
23/2/X1	CN463	PL07	S Doorman	(21.51)	(3.20)		(18.31)		
24/2/X1	46122	PL03	P & F Davis & Co	189.23	28.18	78.40		82.65	
				942.08	140.30	222.05	179.04	302.55	98.14

Main ledger

Purchases ledger control account

£			£
	17/2	Balance b/d	2,357.57

VAT account

			£				£
				17/2	Balance b/d		662.47

Purchases – 01 account

		£			£
17/2	Balance b/d	14,275.09			

Purchases – 02 account

		£			£
17/2	Balance b/d	12,574.26			

Purchases – 03 account

		£			£
17/2	Balance b/d	29,384.74			

Purchases – 04 account

		£			£
17/2	Balance b/d	9,274.36			

Subsidiary ledger

P & F Davis & Co   PL03

			£				£
				17/2	Balance b/d		368.36

Clooney & Partner   PL06

			£				£
				17/2	Balance b/d		226.48

S Doorman   PL06

			£				£
				17/2	Balance b/d		218.47

Fred Janitor   PL06

			£				£
				17/2	Balance b/d		111.45

UNIT 30 : WORKBOOK

▷ ACTIVITY 60

Given below is the cheque payment listing for a business for the week ending 8 May 20X1.

Cheque payment listing

Supplier	Code	Cheque number	Cheque amount £	Discount taken £
G Rails	PL04	001221	177.56	4.43
L Jameson	PL03	001222	257.68	7.73
Cash purchases		001223	216.43	
K Davison	PL07	001224	167.89	
T Ives	PL01	001225	289.06	5.79
Cash purchases		001226	263.78	
H Samuels	PL02	001227	124.36	

The cash purchases include VAT at the standard rate.

You are required to:
- enter the payments into the cash payments book given and total all of the columns;
- complete the journal for the posting of the totals to the main ledger - the last journal entry was number 1467;
- post the individual entries to the subsidiary ledger accounts given.

Cash payments book

Date	Details	Cheque no	Code	Total £	VAT £	Purchases ledger £	Cash purchases £	Other £	Discounts received £

KEY TECHNIQUES : QUESTIONS

JOURNAL ENTRY	No:	
Prepared by:		
Authorised by:		
Date:		
Narrative:		
Account	Debit	Credit
TOTALS		

Subsidiary ledger

T Ives — PL01

	£			£
		1 May	Balance b/d	332.56

H Samuels — PL02

	£			£
		1 May	Balance b/d	286.90

L Jameson — PL03

	£			£
		1 May	Balance b/d	623.89

G Rails — PL04

	£			£
		1 May	Balance b/d	181.99

K Davison — PL07

	£			£
		1 May	Balance b/d	167.89

Chapter 20
Petty cash systems

▷ ACTIVITY 61

Given below are the petty cash vouchers that have been paid during the week ending 12 January 20X1 out of a petty cash box run on an imprest system of £150 per week. At the end of each week a cheque requisition is drawn up for a cheque for cash to bring the petty cash box back to the imprest amount.

Voucher no	Amount £	Reason
03526	13.68	Postage
03527	25.00	Staff welfare
03528	14.80	Stationery (including £2.20 VAT)
03529	12.00	Taxi fare (including £1.79 VAT)
03530	6.40	Staff welfare
03531	12.57	Postage
03532	6.80	Rail fare
03533	7.99	Stationery (including £1.19 VAT)
03534	18.80	Taxi fare (including £2.80 VAT)

You are required to:
- write up the petty cash book given;
- prepare the cheque requisition for the cash required to restore the petty cash box to the imprest amount;
- post the petty cash book totals to the main ledger accounts given.

Petty cash book										
Receipts			Payments							
Date	Narrative	Total £	Date	Narrative	Voucher no	Total £	Postage £	Staff welfare £	Stationery £	Travel expenses £	VAT £

KEY TECHNIQUES : QUESTIONS

CHEQUE REQUISITION FORM
CHEQUE DETAILS
Date ....
Payee ....
Amount £ ....
Reason ....
Invoice no. (attached/to follow) ....
Receipt (attached/to follow) ....
Required by   (Print) ....
                      (Signature ....
Authorised by: ....

Main ledger accounts

Postage account

	£		£
5 Jan Balance b/d	248.68		

Staff welfare account

	£		£
5 Jan Balance b/d	225.47		

Stationery account

	£		£
5 Jan Balance b/d	176.57		

Travel expenses account

	£		£
5 Jan Balance b/d	160.90		

VAT account

	£		£
		5 Jan Balance b/d	2,385.78

UNIT 30 : WORKBOOK

▷ ACTIVITY 62

A business runs its petty cash on an imprest system with an imprest amount of £100 per week.

At the end of the week ending 22 May 20X1 the vouchers in the petty cash box were:

Voucher no	£
02634	13.73
02635	8.91
02636	10.57
02637	3.21
02638	11.30
02639	14.66

The cash remaining in the petty cash box was made up as follows:

£10 note	1
£5 note	2
£2 coin	3
£1 coin	7
50p coin	5
20p coin	4
10p coin	1
5p coin	2
2p coin	3
1p coin	6

You are required to reconcile the petty cash in the box to the vouchers in the box at 22 May 20X1 and if it does not reconcile to suggest reasons for the difference.

KEY TECHNIQUES : QUESTIONS

▷ ACTIVITY 63

A business runs an imprest system with an imprest amount of £120. The rules of the petty cash system are as follows:
- only amounts of less than £30 can be paid out of petty cash, any larger claims must be dealt with by filling out a cheque requisition form;
- all petty cash claims over £5 must be supported by a receipt or invoice;
- the exception to this is that rail fares can be reimbursed without a receipt provided that the petty cash voucher is authorised by the department head;
- all other valid petty cash vouchers can be authorised by you, the petty cashier;
- all petty cash vouchers that are authorised are given a sequential number.

You have on your desk ten petty cash vouchers which have been completed and you must decide which can be paid and which cannot.

PETTY CASH VOUCHER			
Authorised by	Claimed by J Athersych	No	
Date	Description	Amount	
15/3/X1	Coffee	4	83
	Milk	1	42
	Biscuits	0	79
	Total	7	04

Receipt is attached.

PETTY CASH VOUCHER			
Authorised by	Claimed by J Athersych	No	
Date	Description	Amount	
15/3/X1	Envelopes	4	85
	Total	4	85

No receipt.

UNIT 30 : WORKBOOK

PETTY CASH VOUCHER				
Authorised by Department head	Claimed by F Rivers		No	
Date	Description		Amount	
16/3/X1	Rail fare		12	80
		Total	12	80

No receipt.

PETTY CASH VOUCHER				
Authorised by	Claimed by M Patterson		No	
Date	Description		Amount	
16/3/X1	Computer discs		4	20
	Printer paper		2	40
		Total	6	60

No receipt.

PETTY CASH VOUCHER				
Authorised by	Claimed by D R Ray		No	
Date	Description		Amount	
17/3/X1	Lunch – entertaining clients		42	80
		Total	42	80

Bill attached

KEY TECHNIQUES : QUESTIONS

PETTY CASH VOUCHER			
Authorised by	Claimed by J Athersych	No	
Date	Description	Amount	
17/3/X1	Milk	1	42
	Tea bags	2	28
	Total	3	70

No receipt

PETTY CASH VOUCHER			
Authorised by	Claimed by D R Ray	No	
Date	Description	Amount	
18/3/X1	Rail fare	12	50
	Total	12	50

No receipt

PETTY CASH VOUCHER			
Authorised by	Claimed by M Patterson	No	
Date	Description	Amount	
18/3/X1	Special delivery postage	19	50
	Total	19	50

Receipt attached

UNIT 30 : WORKBOOK

PETTY CASH VOUCHER

Authorised by	Claimed by M T Noble	No	
Date	Description	Amount	
18/3/X1	Ink for printer	17	46
	Total	17	46

Receipt attached

PETTY CASH VOUCHER

Authorised by	Claimed by J Norman	No	
Date	Description	Amount	
18/3/X1	Rail fare	7	60
	Total	7	60

No receipt

▷ ACTIVITY 64

A business runs its petty cash system on an imprest system with an imprest amount of £100 per week. During the week ended 30 April 20X1 the following, petty cash vouchers were paid:

Voucher no	Amount £	Reason
002534	4.68	Coffee/milk
002535	13.26	Postage
002536	10.27	Stationery (including £1.53 VAT)
002537	15.00	Taxi fare (including £2.23 VAT)
002538	6.75	Postage
002539	7.40	Train fare
002540	3.86	Stationery (including £0.57 VAT)

KEY TECHNIQUES : QUESTIONS

You are required to:

- write up these vouchers in petty cash book given;
- post the totals of the petty cash book to the main ledger accounts given.

Petty cash book											
Receipts			Payments								
Date	Narrative	Total £	Date	Narrative	Voucher no	Total £	Postage £	Tea and coffee £	Stationery £	Travel expenses £	VAT £

Main ledger accounts

Postage account

		£			£
23 Apr	Balance b/d	231.67			

Staff welfare account

		£			£
23 Apr	Balance b/d	334.78			

Stationery account

		£			£
23 Apr	Balance b/d	55.36			

Travel expenses account

		£			£
23 Apr	Balance b/d	579.03			

VAT account

	£			£
		23 April	Balance b/d	967.44

▷ ACTIVITY 65

SCENARIO
You are the cashier at Toybox Games Ltd, a manufacturer of children's board games. Part of your duties is the management of petty cash.

Personnel
Managing director   Andrew Pritchard

Department heads
Production director   Ian Grahamson
Buying director   Eric Connelly
Sales director   Derek Gibb
Management accountant   Sarah Chesterton

Accounts function
Accounts assistant   Andrew Donnelly
Credit controller   Stanley Green
Cashier   You

Account codes are as follows:
Sales   01
Production   02
Buying   03
Finance   04
Entertainment   20
Education   21
Travelling   22
Welfare   23
Stationery/post   24

Procedures
Here is an extract from the group's procedures manual.

Petty cash

1   The main source of petty cash is cheques drawn on the main bank account. An imprest system is maintained. (Levels of cash held are set locally.)

2   Petty cash can only be paid out on the production of a petty cash voucher authorised by a department head.

In addition there are authorisation limits for each department head of £100.00. Any amount over £100.00 must be authorised by the managing director.

All petty cash vouchers over £5.00 must be supported by receipts/invoices (even if these are not proper VAT receipts/invoices).

Petty cash will not be paid out if the above rules are not followed.

3   Correctly completed petty cash vouchers must be numbered and correctly filed. If a voucher cannot be coded it must not be numbered or written up and the cash will not be paid.

4   Expenditure must be correctly coded and analysed in the petty cash book. The analysis must be performed at the same time as the petty cash book is written up.
    VAT may only be reclaimed where the company holds a proper VAT invoice/receipt.

5   The petty cash book must be written up weekly. The balance of cash in hand must be reconciled to the records.
    A cheque requisition must be completed for the balance needed to restore the level of cash held.

6   A journal must be prepared to post the totals of expenditure to the correct main ledger accounts.

Terms of trade

The company is registered for VAT. All sales of board games are standard-rated.

THE TASKS TO BE COMPLETED

Today is 4 December 20X1.

TASK 1 Produce a schedule of vouchers that cannot be paid, giving reasons for non-payment.

TASK 2 Write up the petty cash book to 30 November 20X1 from the acceptable vouchers provided. The last voucher before this batch was number 334.

TASK 3 Prepare a journal entry to post totals of expenditure to the correct ledger accounts. The last journal was number 3345.

UNIT 30 : WORKBOOK

PETTY CASH VOUCHER				
Authorised by DG	Received by	Code		No
Date	Description			Amount
25/11	flowers for D Gibbs			16	99
	Secretary				
			Total	16	99

No receipt is available.

PETTY CASH VOUCHER				
Authorised by SAC	Received by	Code		No
Date	Description			Amount
30/11	Coffee / tea			6	51
	Finance dept				
			Total	6	51

A receipt is available but it is not a proper VAT receipt.

PETTY CASH VOUCHER				
Authorised by DG	Received by	Code		No
Date	Description			Amount
30/11	Biscuits / coffee / sugar			6	78
	Sales & Marketing				
	Kitchen				
			Total	6	78

A proper VAT receipt is available. VAT of 30 pence is recoverable.

PETTY CASH VOUCHER

Authorised by DG	Received by	Code	No
Date	Description		Amount
28/11	Coffee / milk		3	51
	Production			
		Total	3	51

PETTY CASH VOUCHER

Authorised by SAC	Received by	Code	No
Date	Description		Amount
28/11	Stamps -		3	68
	Finance dept (franking			
	machine empty)			
		Total	3	68

PETTY CASH VOUCHER

Authorised by DG	Received by	Code	No
Date	Description		Amount
27/11	Sales conference		12	99
	- Taxi home to station			
		Total	12	99

A receipt is available.

UNIT 30 : WORKBOOK

PETTY CASH VOUCHER			
Authorised by EJC	Received by	Code	No
Date	Description		Amount
28/11	Food for staff party		13 | 71
	– Buying Department		
	Total		13 | 71

A proper VAT receipt is available – VAT of £1.50 reclaimable.

PETTY CASH VOUCHER			
Authorised by DG	Received by	Code	No
Date	Description		Amount
27/11	Sales conference		179 | 00
	– Rail tickets		
	Total		179 | 00

A receipt is available.

PETTY CASH VOUCHER			
Authorised by IG	Received by	Code	No
Date	Description		Amount
30/11	Window cleaner		7 | 00
	Total		7 | 00

A receipt is available. The window-cleaner is not registered for VAT. There is no code for this expense.

PETTY CASH VOUCHER

Authorised by	Received by	Code	No
Date	*Description*		*Amount*
26/11	VAT Book – Finance Dept		15	78
	Total		15	78

A receipt is available.

PETTY CASH BOOK

Date	Voucher number	£	£ 01 Sales	£ 02 Production	£ 03 Buying	£ 04 Finance	£ VAT	Code

JOURNAL PETTY CASH EXPENDITURE			No	

Prepared by _____ **Week ending** _____

Authorised by _____

Department	Expense	Account code	Debit	Credit
Sales / marketing	Entertainment	01 20		
	Education	21		
	Travelling	22		
	Welfare	23		
	Stationery/Post	24		
Production	Entertainment	02 20		
	Education	21		
	Travelling	22		
	Welfare	23		
	Stationery/Post	24		
Buying	Entertainment	03 20		
	Education	21		
	Travelling	22		
	Welfare	23		
	Stationery/Post	24		
Finance	Entertainment	04 20		
	Education	21		
	Travelling	22		
	Welfare	23		
	Stationery/Post	24		
VAT				
Petty cash				
TOTALS				

Chapter 21
Bank reconciliations

▷ ACTIVITY 66

Given below are the cash receipts book, cash payments book and bank statement for a business for the week ending 11 March 20X1.

Required

- Compare the bank statement to the cash book.
- Correct the cash receipts and payments books for any items which are unmatched on the bank statement.
- Total the cash receipts book and cash payments book.
- Find the balance on the cash book if the opening balance on 7 March was £860.40 cash in hand.
- Explain why the amended cash book balance and the bank statement balance at 11 March are different.

Cash receipts book

Date	Narrative	Total £	VAT £	Debtors £	Other £	Discount £
20X1						
7/3	Paying in slip 0062	1,112.60	78.80	583.52	450.28	23.60
8/3	Paying in slip 0063	1,047.80	60.24	643.34	344.22	30.01
9/3	Paying in slip 0064	1,287.64	71.20	809.59	406.85	34.20
10/3	Paying in slip 0065	987.80	49.90	652.76	285.14	18.03
11/3	Paying in slip 0066	1,127.94	51.84	779.88	296.22	23.12

Cash payments book

Date	Details	Cheque No	Code	Total £	VAT £	Creditors £	Cash purchases £	Other £	Discounts received £
20X1									
7/3	P Barn	012379	PL06	383.21		383.21			
	Purchases	012380	ML	268.33	39.96		228.37		
	R Trevor	012381	PL12	496.80		496.80			6.30
8/3	F Nunn	012382	PL07	218.32		218.32			
	F Taylor	012383	PL09	467.28		467.28			9.34
	C Cook	012384	PL10	301.40		301.40			
9/3	L White	012385	PL17	222.61		222.61			
	Purchases	012386	ML	269.40	40.12		229.28		
	T Finn	012387	PL02	148.60		148.60			
10/3	S Penn	012388	PL16	489.23		489.23			7.41
11/3	P Price	012389	PL20	299.99		299.99			
	Purchases	012390	ML	264.49	39.39		225.10		

KEY TECHNIQUES : **QUESTIONS**

FINANCIAL BANK plc CONFIDENTIAL

You can bank on us!

10 Yorkshire Street   Account   CURRENT   Sheet 00614
Headingley
Leeds LS1 1QT   Account name   T R FABER LTD
Telephone: 0113 633061
           Statement date   11 March 20X1   Account Number   27943316

Date	Details	Withdrawals (£)	Deposits (£)	Balance (£)
7/3	Balance from sheet 00613			860.40
	Bank giro credit L Fernley		406.90	1,267.30
9/3	Cheque 012380	268.33		
	Cheque 012381	496.80		
	Credit 0062		1,112.60	1,614.77
10/3	Cheque 012383	467.28		
	Cheque 012384	301.40		
	Credit 0063		1,047.80	
	SO – Loan Finance	200.00		1,693.89
11/3	Cheque 012379	383.21		
	Cheque 012386	269.40		
	Cheque 012387	148.60		
	Credit 0064		1,287.64	
	Bank interest		6.83	2,187.15

SO Standing order   DD Direct debit   CP Card purchase
AC Automated cash   OD Overdrawn   TR Transfer

UNIT 30 : WORKBOOK

▷ ACTIVITY 67

Given below is the cash book of a business and the bank statement for the week ending 20 April 20X1.

Required

Compare the cash book to the bank statement and note any differences that you find.

T Ives

Receipts		£	Payments		£
16/4	Donald & Co	225.47	16/4	Balance b/d	310.45
17/4	Harper Ltd	305.68	17/4	Cheque 03621	204.56
	Fisler Partners	104.67	18/4	Cheque 03622	150.46
18/4	Denver Ltd	279.57	19/4	Cheque 03623	100.80
19/4	Gerald Bros	310.45		Cheque 03624	158.67
20/4	Johnson & Co	97.68	20/4	Cheque 03625	224.67
			20/4	Balance c/d	173.91
		1,323.52			1,323.52

EXPRESS BANK   CONFIDENTIAL

High Street	Account	CURRENT	Sheet 0213
Fenbury			
TL4 6JY	Account name	P L DERBY LTD	
Telephone: 0169 422130			

Statement date 20 April 20X1   Account Number 40429107

Date	Details	Withdrawals (£)	Deposits (£)	Balance (£)
16/4	Balance from sheet 0212			310.45 OD
17/4	DD – District Council	183.60		494.05 OD
18/4	Credit		225.47	268.58 OD
19/4	Credit		104.67	
	Cheque 03621	240.56		
	Bank interest	3.64		408.11 OD
20/4	Credit		305.68	
	Credit		279.57	
	Cheque 03622	150.46		
	Cheque 03624	158.67		131.99 OD

SO Standing order	DD Direct debit	CP Card purchase
AC Automated cash	OD Overdrawn	TR Transfer

KEY TECHNIQUES : QUESTIONS

▷ ACTIVITY 68

Graham

The cash account of Graham showed a debit balance of £204 on 31 March 20X3. A comparison with the bank statements revealed the following:

		£
1	Cheques drawn but not presented	3,168
2	Amounts paid into the bank but not credited	723
3	Entries in the bank statements not recorded in the cash account	
	(i) Standing orders	35
	(ii) Interest on bank deposit account	18
	(iii) Bank charges	14
4	Balance on the bank statement at 31 March	2,618

Tasks

(a) Show the appropriate adjustments required in the cash account of Graham bringing down the correct balance at 31 March 20X3.

(b) Prepare a bank reconciliation statement at that date.

▷ ACTIVITY 69

Data

The following are the cash book and bank statements of Kiveton Cleaning.

Receipts June 20X1

CASH BOOK – JUNE 20X1				CB 117
Date	Details	Total	Sales ledger control	Other
1 June	Balance b/d	7,100.45		
8 June	Cash and cheques	3,200.25	3,200.25	–
15 June	Cash and cheques	4,100.75	4,100.75	–
23 June	Cash and cheques	2,900.30	2,900.30	–
30 June	Cash and cheques	6,910.25	6,910.25	–
		£24,212.00	£17,111.55	

UNIT 30 : WORKBOOK

Payments June 20X1

Date	Payee	Cheque no	Total	Purchase ledger control	Operating overhead	Admin overhead	Other
1 June	Hawsker Chemical	116	6,212.00	6,212.00			
7 June	Wales Supplies	117	3,100.00	3,100.00			
15 June	Wages and salaries	118	2,500.00		1,250.00	1,250.00	
16 June	Drawings	119	1,500.00				1,500.00
18 June	Blyth Chemical	120	5,150.00	5,150.00			
25 June	Whitby Cleaning Machines	121	538.00	538.00			
28 June	York Chemicals	122	212.00	212.00			
			£19,212.00	£15,212.00	£1,250.00	£1,250.00	£1,500.00

Crescent Bank plc Statement no: 721
High Street
Sheffield Page 1
Account: Alison Robb t/a Kiveton Cleaning
Account no: 57246661

Date	Details	Payments £	Receipts £	Balance £
20X1				
1 June	Balance b/fwd			8,456.45
1 June	113	115.00		8,341.45
1 June	114	591.00		7,750.45
1 June	115	650.00		7,100.45
4 June	116	6,212.00		888.45
8 June	CC		3,200.25	4,088.70
11 June	117	3,100.00		988.70
15 June	CC		4,100.75	5,089.45
15 June	118	2,500.00		2,589.45
16 June	119	1,500.00		1,089.45
23 June	120	5,150.00		4,060.55 O/D
23 June	CC		2,900.30	1,160.25 O/D

Key:	S/O	Standing Order	DD	Direct Debit
	CC	Cash and cheques	CHGS	Charges
	BACS	Bankers automated clearing	O/D	Overdrawn

Task

Examine the business cash book and the business bank statement shown in the data provided above. Prepare a bank reconciliation statement as at 30 June 20X1. Set out your reconciliation in the proforma below.

Proforma

BANK RECONCILIATION STATEMENT AS AT 30 JUNE 20X1

£

Balance per bank statement
Outstanding lodgements:

Unpresented cheques:

Balance per cash book   £
                                    ─────

▷ ACTIVITY 70 ▷▷▷▷

Task

Refer to the business cash book and the business bank statement reproduced below. You are required to perform a bank reconciliation as at 31 December 20X8. Set out your reconciliation in the proforma below.

CASH BOOK: RECEIPTS – DECEMBER 20X8

Date	Details	Total £	VAT £	Sales £	Other £
20X8					
01 Dec	Balance b/d	7,809.98			
01 Dec	Cash and cheques banked	5,146.02	710.58	4,060.44	375.00
08 Dec	Cash and cheques banked	4,631.42	689.79	3,941.63	
15 Dec	Cash and cheques banked	5,094.56	758.76	4,335.80	
23 Dec	Cash and cheques banked	6,488.47	966.37	5,522.10	
31 Dec	Cash and cheques banked	4,744.66	706.65	4,038.01	
		33,915.11	3,832.15	21,897.98	375.00

CASHBOOK: PAYMENTS – DECEMBER 20X8

Date	Payee	Cheque no	Total £	VAT £	Purchases ledger control £	Admin expenses £	CBP221 Other £
20X8							
01 Dec	Morland Estates	17330	2,500.00			2,500.00	
01 Dec	Vitesse Cars	17331	5,000.00				5,000.00
03 Dec	Robin Toys Limited	17332	2,596.50		2,596.50		
07 Dec	Bonchester Land Ltd	17333	3,000.00			3,000.00	
09 Dec	Warner & Co	17334	1,500.00		1,500.00		
15 Dec	Brewer & Partners	17335	423.00	63.00		360.00	
15 Dec	Creative Play	17336	1,915.09		1,915.09		
16 Dec	Louise Montgomery	17337	800.00				800.00
22 Dec	Grain Studios	17338	2,393.86		2,393.86		
24 Dec	Carved Angels	17339	1,436.32		1,436.32		
29 Dec	Wages and salaries	17340	9,968.35			9,968.35	
31 Dec	Balance c/d		2,381.99				
			33,915.11	63.00	9,841.77	15,828.35	5,800.00

Royal Westminster Bank plc
28 High Street, Bonchester, BN3 7OT
Account: Cloudberry Crafts
Account no: 61324288

STATEMENT
50 - 66 - 11

Statement no: 93

Date	Details	Payments £	Receipts £	Balance £
20X8				
01 Dec	Balance forward			7,069.75
01 Dec	CC		5,095.66	
01 Dec	17328	869.35		11,296.06
03 Dec	17325	1,619.42		9,676.64
07 Dec	CC		5,146.02	
07 Dec	17330	2,500.00		12,322.66
08 Dec	17329	1,866.66		10,456.00
09 Dec	CC		4,631.42	15,087.42
14 Dec	17331	5,000.00		
14 Dec	17333	3,000.00		7,087.42
16 Dec	CC		5,094.56	
16 Dec	17334	1,500.00		10,681.98
17 Dec	17332	2,596.50		8,085.48
20 Dec	17335	423.00		7,662.48
27 Dec	CC		6,488.47	14,150.95
29 Dec	17338	2,393.86		
29 Dec	17336	1,915.09		9,842.00

Key	S/O	Standing order
	DD	Direct debit
	CC	Cash and/or cheques
	CHGS	Charges
	BACS	Bankers automated clearing services
	O/D	Overdrawn

BANK RECONCILIATION STATEMENT – 31 DECEMBER 20X8

£

Balance per the cash book
Less items not yet credited

Add items not yet debited

Balance per bank statement

UNIT 30 : WORKBOOK

▷ ACTIVITY 71

You are the cashier at Natural Products Ltd, a manufacturer of cosmetics. Your duties include writing up the cash book.

Today is 6 July 20X1.

TASK 1 Total the receipts and payments side of the cash book and determine the balance on the cash account if the balance at the start of the week was £84,579.77 in hand.

TASK 2 Post the totals of the cash receipts book and cash payments book to the main ledger accounts given.

TASK 3 Compare the cash book to the bank statement.

Take each item on the bank statement and then tick it when it is agreed to a cash book entry – also tick the cash book entry. Any cheques earlier than 389 will remain unticked on the bank statement in this example as the cash payments book does not go far enough back. (In practice these would be agreed to earlier pages in the cash payments book and therefore ticked.)

TASK 4 Send the cash book to your supervisor Caroline Everley with a memo documenting any errors found.

TASK 5 Calculate the revised balance on the cash book once the errors noted have been dealt with.

Note: You should keep a note of any errors you find to include in the memo in Task 4.

Cash book receipts

Date	Narrative	Paying-in slip	Total	Debtors	Mail order	VAT control	Discount allowed
26/6	Trade debtors	598	15,685.23	15,685.23			
	Mail order (Chq/PO)	599	386.29		328.76	57.53	
	Mail order (CC)	600	189.80		76.43	13.37	
27/6	Trade debtors	601	6,650.28	6,650.28			
	Mail order	602	115.98		98.71	17.27	
	Megastores plc	CHAPS	11,755.25	11,755.25			204.17
28/6	Trade debtors	603	12,223.81	12,223.81			
	Mail order	604	609.22		518.49	90.73	
29/6	Trade debtors	605	5,395.40	5,395.40			
	Mail order	606	98.60		83.91	14.69	
30/6	Trade debtors	607	2,641.68	2,641.68			
	Mail Order/shop	608	249.59		212.43	37.16	
29/6	Freeman Foods Group	CHAPS	14,776.04	14,776.04			256.64
30/6	Totals						

156

Cash book payments

Date	Narrative	Cheque	Total	Creditors	Salaries	Other	VAT control	Discount received
26/6	Blackwood Foodstuffs	389	325.99	325.99				
	Bruning & Soler	390	683.85	683.85				
	Dehlavi Kosmetatos	391	2,112.16	2,112.16				
	Environmentally Friendly Co Ltd	392	705.77	705.77				
	Greig Handling (Import)	393	1,253.98	1,253.98				
	Halpern Freedman	394	338.11	338.11				
	Kobo Design Studio	395	500.00	500.00				
	Rayner Food Co	396	375.22	375.22				
	Year 2000 Produce Co	397	1,100.68	1,100.68				
27/6	HM Revenue & Customs	398	23,599.28				23,599.28	
28/6	Salaries - Bank Giro	400	48,995.63		48,995.63			
30/6	Arthur Chong Ltd	401	235.55	235.55				
	Dwyer & Co (Import)	402	469.55	469.55				23.48
	Earthworld Ltd	403	449.28	449.28				22.46
	English Electricity	DD	159.78			135.98	23.80	
	English Telecom	DD	224.47			191.04	33.43	
	Totals							

Main ledger accounts

Sales ledger control account

	£			£
24/6	Balance b/d	312,465.99		

Mail order sales account

	£			£
		24/6	Balance b/d	26,578.46

VAT control account

	£			£
		24/6	Balance b/d	29,375.32

Discount allowed account

	£			£
24/6	Balance b/d	4,627.56		

Purchases ledger control account

	£			£
		24/6	Balance b/d	25,476.34

Salaries account

			£			£
24/6	Balance b/d		105,374.36			

Electricity account

			£			£
24/6	Balance b/d		1,496.57			

Telephone account

			£			£
24/6	Balance b/d		967.47			

Discount received account

			£			£
				24/6	Balance b/d	336.58

KEY TECHNIQUES : **QUESTIONS**

FINANCIAL BANK plc CONFIDENTIAL

You can bank on us!

467 HIGH STREET	Account	CURRENT	Sheet 455
TAUNTON			
TA1 9WE	Account name	NATURAL PRODUCTS LIMITED	
Telephone: 01832 722098			
20X1 Statement date	30 JUNE 20X1	Account Number	34786695

Date	Details		Withdrawals (£)	Deposits (£)	Balance (£)
27 JUN	Balance from sheet 454				11,305.11
27 JUN	MEGASTORES PLC	CHAPS		11,755.25	
	COUNTER CREDIT 591			13,604.01	
	COUNTER CREDIT 592			112.13	
	374		127.09		
	376		5,955.80		
	ENGLISH ELECTRIC	DD	159.78		30,533.83
28 JUN	COUNTER CREDIT 593			11,655.24	
	COUNTER CREDIT 594			683.11	
	COUNTER CREDIT 595			112.19	
	372		87.93		
	389		325.99		
	ENGLISH TELECOM	DD	224.47		42,345.98
29 JUN	COUNTER CREDIT 596			325.11	
	COUNTER CREDIT 597			60,331.90	
	391		2,112.16		
	382		331.80		
	FREEMAN FOODS GRP CHAPS			14,776.04	
	COUNTER CREDIT 598			15,685.23	
	COUNTER CREDIT 599			386.29	
	COUNTER CREDIT 600			89.80	
	394		338.11		
	395		500.00		
	386		441.09		
	388		111.94		130,105.25
30 JUN	COUNTER CREDIT 601			6,650.28	
	COUNTER CREDIT 602			115.98	
	381		117.54		
	384		3,785.60		
	387		785.11		
	390		683.85		
	393		1,253.98		
	399		175.10		
	COUNTER CREDIT 603			12,223.81	
	COUNTER CREDIT 604			609.22	142,903.36

key SO Standing order   DD Direct debit   CP Card purchase
     AC Automated cash   OD Overdrawn
     CHAPS Clearing House Automated Payments System
     BACS Bankers Automated Clearing Service

UNIT 30 : WORKBOOK

MEMORANDUM

To:

From:

Subject:

Date:

Chapter 22
Ledger balances and control accounts

▷ ACTIVITY 72

Basil Spence is a dealer in fancy goods. At 1 January 20X9 his ledger included the following balances.

	£
Debtors	17,349
Creditors	16,593

The debtors at 1 January 20X9 were as follows:

	£
N Pevsner	5,700
R Hackney	5,823
The Prince of Wales Hotel	5,826

The creditors at 1 January 20X9 were as follows:

	£
E Lutyens	5,481
M Hutchinson	5,553
H Falkner	5,559

During January 20X9 Basil's books of prime entry showed the following:

Purchases day book

	£
Lutyens	2,850
Hutchinson	2,055
Falkner	3,360
	8,265

Sales day book

	£
Pevsner	150
Hackney	5,280
Prince of Wales Hotel	4,995
	10,425

Cash payments book

	£
Lutyens	2,700
Hutchinson	150
Falkner	2,469
	5,319

Cash receipts book

	£
Hackney	5,700
Prince of Wales Hotel	5,826
	11,526

Hackney argued about £123 of his outstanding balance, saying that the goods concerned were of the wrong design. Basil decided to write off this amount.

UNIT 30 : WORKBOOK

Required

For the month of January 20X9, write up the:
(a) individual debtors' and creditors' accounts;
(b) sales ledger and purchases ledger control accounts;
(c) bad debt expense account;

▷ ACTIVITY 73

The following totals are taken from the books of a business:

		£
1 January 20X1	Credit balance on purchases ledger control account	5,926
	Debit balance on sales ledger control account	10,268
31 January 20X1	Credit sales	71,504
	Credit purchases	47,713
	Cash received from credit customers	69,872
	Cash paid to creditors	47,028
	Sales ledger balances written off as bad	96
	Sales returns	358
	Purchases returns	202
	Discounts allowed	1,435
	Discounts received	867
	Contra entry	75

Required

(a) Prepare the purchases ledger control account and balance at the end of the month.
(b) Prepare the sales ledger control account and balance at the end of the month.

▷ ACTIVITY 74

The purchases ledger control account of Birkett is as follows:

Purchases ledger control account

	£		£
Purchase returns	13,418	Balance b/f	84,346
Cash book	525,938	Purchases (purchases day book)	552,196
Balance c/f	97,186		
	636,542		636,542
		Balance b/f	97,186

Balances extracted from the purchases ledger totalled £96,238.

The following errors have been discovered.

1   The purchases day book was undercast by £6,000.
2   A cash account total of £10,858 was posted to the control account as £9,058.
3   A credit balance of £1,386 on the purchases ledger had been set off against a sales ledger debit balance but no entry had been made in the control accounts (a contra entry).
4   A debit balance of £40 in the list of purchases ledger balances had been extracted as a credit balance.
5   A credit balance of £3,842 had been omitted from the list of balances.

Required

(a) Correct the control account.
(b) Reconcile the adjusted account with the sum of the balances extracted.

▷ ACTIVITY 75

The balance on the sales ledger control account of Robin & Co on 30 September 20X0 amounted to £3,825 which did not agree with the net total of the list of sales ledger balances at that date of £3,362.

The errors discovered were as follows:
1   Debit balances in the sales ledger, amounting to £103, had been omitted from the list of balances.

2   A bad debt amounting to £400 had been written off in the sales ledger but had not been posted to the bad debts expense account or entered in the control accounts.

3   An item of goods sold to Sparrow, £250, had been entered once in the sales day book but posted to his account twice.

4   No entry had been made in the control account in respect of the transfer of a debit of £70 from Quail's account in the sales ledger to his account in the purchases ledger (a contra entry).

5   The discount allowed column in the cash account had been undercast by £140.

Required

(a) Make the necessary adjustments in the sales ledger control account and bring down the balance.
(b) Show the adjustments to the net total of the original list of balances to reconcile with the amended balance on the sales ledger control account.

UNIT 30 : WORKBOOK

▷ ACTIVITY 76

When carrying out the sales ledger control account reconciliation the following errors were discovered:
(a) a bad debt of £800 had been written off in the subsidiary ledger but not in the main ledger;
(b) a contra entry of £240 had been made in the subsidiary ledger but not in the main ledger;
(c) the discount allowed column in the cash receipts book had been undercast by £100.

Required

Produce journal entries to correct each of these errors.

▷ ACTIVITY 77

When carrying out the purchases ledger control account reconciliation the following errors were discovered:
(a) the purchases day book was overcast by £1,000;
(b) the total of the discount received column in the cash payments book was posted to the main ledger as £89 instead of £98;
(c) a contra entry of £300 had been entered in the subsidiary ledger but not in the main ledger.

Required

Produce journal entries to correct each of these errors.

Chapter 23
Drafting an initial trial balance

▷ ACTIVITY 78

Given below are the balances of a business at 31 May 20X1.

	£
Purchases	385,800
Creditors	32,000
Computer	8,000
Motor car	19,200
Discount received	3,850
Telephone	4,320
Sales returns	6,720
Wages	141,440
VAT (credit balance)	7,200
Drawings	60,000
Discount allowed	6,400
Rent and rates	26,200
Debtors	53,500
Motor expenses	7,700
Sales	642,080
Stock	38,880
Inland Revenue	3,800
Purchases returns	2,560
Electricity	6,080
Bank (debit balance)	1,920
Capital	74,670

Required

Prepare the trial balance as at 31 May 20X1.

▷ ACTIVITY 79

Given below are the ledger accounts for the first month of trading for a small business.

Capital account

	£			£
		1 Mar	Bank	12,000

Bank account

		£			£
1 Mar	Capital	12,000	2 Mar	Motor car	4,500
7 Mar	Sales	3,000	2 Mar	Purchases	2,400
20 Mar	Sales	2,100	14 Mar	Rent	600
26 Mar	Debtors	3,800	18 Mar	Stationery	200
			25 Mar	Creditors	3,100
			28 Mar	Drawings	1,600

Motor car account

		£		£
2 Mar	Bank	4,500		

Purchases account

		£		£
2 Mar	Bank	2,400		
4 Mar	Creditors	2,500		
12 Mar	Creditors	4,100		

Creditors' account

		£			£
25 Mar	Bank	3,100	4 Mar	Purchases	2,500
			12 Mar	Purchases	4,100

Sales account

	£			£
		7 Mar	Bank	3,000
		10 Mar	Debtors	4,600
		15 Mar	Debtors	3,500
		20 Mar	Bank	2,100

Debtors' account

		£			£
10 Mar	Sales	4,600	26 Mar	Bank	3,800
15 Mar	Sales	3,500			

Rent account

		£		£
14 Mar	Bank	600		

Stationery account

	£		£
18 Mar Bank	200		

Drawings account

	£		£
28 Mar Bank	1,600		

Required

Balance off the ledger accounts and produce a trial balance at the end of the first month of trading.

▷ ACTIVITY 80

Given below is a list of the balances for a business at the end of June 20X1.

	£
Debtors	33,440
Bank (debit balance)	1,200
Sales	401,300
Stock	24,300
Wages	88,400
Telephone	2,700
Motor car	12,000
VAT (credit balance)	7,000
Electricity	3,800
Rent	16,400
Purchases	241,180
Purchases returns	1,600
Sales returns	4,200
Office equipment	5,000
Capital	49,160
Motor expenses	4,840
Discounts allowed	4,010
Discounts received	2,410
Creditors	20,000
Drawings	40,000

Required

Draw up the trial balance at 30 June 20X1.

ACTIVITY 81

Introduction

Music World Ltd operates as a wholesaler supplying cassette tapes and compact discs throughout the UK.

The managing director is Jane Alder whilst Tony Bryant is the accountant and company secretary. You are employed as an accounting technician to assist Tony Bryant.

Data

The following transactions all occurred on 1 December 20X1 and have been entered for you into summarised books of original entry. VAT has been calculated to the nearest pound at a rate of 17.5% and you should continue to use this rate for any subsequent calculations.

Treat 'other customers' and 'other suppliers' as individual accounts.

Sales day book

	Total £	VAT £	Net £
Hit Records Ltd	4,279	637	3,642
Smiths & Co	6,023	897	5,126
Classic Music	1,978	295	1,683
Other customers	12,307	1,833	10,474
	24,587	3,662	20,925

Purchases day book

	Total £	VAT £	Net £	Goods for resale £	Heating & lighting £
HMI Ltd	10,524	1,567	8,957	8,957	
Atlantic Imports Ltd	12,528	1,866	10,662	10,662	
Southern Electric	606	90	516		516
Other suppliers	5,652	842	4,810	4,810	
	29,310	4,365	24,945	24,429	516

Sales returns day book

	Total £	VAT £	Net £
Classic Music	167	25	142

Purchases returns day book

	Total £	VAT £	Net £
Atlantic Imports Ltd	32	5	27

Cash book

				£
Opening balance at start of day				14,492 (debit)
Receipts		Discount £		Amount received £
Classic Music		45		1,755
				1,755
				16,247
Payments	Discount £	VAT £	Total amount paid £	
Atlantic Imports Ltd	112		4,388	
Equipment purchased		144	970	
Equipment repairs		15	102	
Unpaid cheque – Classic Music			1,000	
Bank charges			67	
Cash purchases		34	230	
Other suppliers			10,565	
				17,322
Closing balance at end of day				1,075 (credit)

UNIT 30 : WORKBOOK

The following balances are available to you at the start of the day on 1 December 20X1:

	£
Customers:	
Hit Records Ltd	10,841
Smiths & Co	18,198
Classic Music	16,742
Other customers	491,702
Suppliers:	
HMI Ltd	82,719
Atlantic Imports Ltd	43,607
Southern Electric	Nil
Other suppliers	278,220
Other:	
Purchases	2,432,679
Sales	3,284,782
Sales returns	10,973
Purchases returns	9,817
Heating and lighting	1,728
Equipment	4,182
Equipment repairs	166
Bank charges	82
VAT (credit balance)	63,217
Discount allowed	11,420
Discount received	8,516
Sales ledger control account	537,483
Purchases ledger control account	404,546
Various other debit balances – total	1,368,815
Various other credit balances – total	611,142

THE TASKS TO BE COMPLETED

Complete all the following tasks.

TASK 1 Enter the opening balances into the following accounts on the ledger sheets provided.

    Sales ledger control account
    Purchases ledger control account
    Equipment
    Heating and lighting
    Purchases
    VAT
    Classic Music
    Atlantic Imports Ltd

TASK 2 Enter all relevant entries into the accounts shown in Task 1.

TASK 3 Balance off all the accounts in which you have made entries in Task 2.

TASK 4 Calculate the closing balances of the remaining accounts. Complete the list of balances given by inserting the updated figure for each account in either the debit balances column or the credit balances column as appropriate. Total the two columns. The two totals should be the same. If they do not agree try to trace and correct any errors you have made within the time you have available. If you are still unable to make the totals balance, leave the work incomplete.

Note: It is not a requirement to draw up all the individual accounts in order to calculate the closing balances for Task 4. Candidates may, however, adopt that approach if they wish.

Main ledger

Sales ledger control account

Date	Details	Amount £	Date	Details	Amount £

Purchase ledger control account

Date	Details	Amount £	Date	Details	Amount £

Equipment

Date	Details	Amount £	Date	Details	Amount £

Heating and lighting

Date	Details	Amount £	Date	Details	Amount £

Purchases

Date	Details	Amount £	Date	Details	Amount £

VAT

Date	Details	Amount £	Date	Details	Amount £

Subsidiary (sales) ledger

Classic Music

Date	Details	Amount £	Date	Details	Amount £

KEY TECHNIQUES : QUESTIONS

Subsidiary (purchases) ledger
Atlantic Imports Ltd

Date	Details	Amount £	Date	Details	Amount £

List of updated balances at the end of the day:

	Debit balances £	Credit balances £
Customers:		
Hit Records Ltd	....	....
Smiths & Co	....	....
Classic Music	....	....
Other customers	....	....
Suppliers:		
HMI Ltd	....	....
Atlantic Imports Ltd	....	....
Southern Electric	....	....
Other suppliers	....	....
Other:		
Purchases	....	....
Sales	....	....
Sales returns	....	....
Purchases returns	....	....
Heating and lighting	....	....
Equipment	....	....
Equipment repairs	....	....
Bank charges	....	....
VAT	....	....
Bank	....	....
Discount allowed	....	....
Discount received	....	....
Other debit balances	1,368,815	....
Other credit balances	....	611,142
Totals		

MOCK SIMULATION 1
QUESTIONS

UNIT 30 : WORKBOOK

BRAMALL TOYS LTD

DATA AND TASKS

Instructions

This simulation is designed to test your ability to record and account for income and receipts.

The situation is provided on the next page.

The simulation is divided into three parts, each containing tasks. You are advised to look through the whole simulation first to gain a general appreciation of your tasks.

Part one: Credit sales
Task 1 Prepare sales invoices
Task 2 Prepare credit notes
Task 3 Enter sales invoices and credit notes in the day books

Part two: Receipts
Task 4 Validate cheque and credit card receipts
Task 5 Prepare paying-in documentation
Task 6 Write up the cash receipts book

Part three: Main ledger and subsidiary (sales) ledger posting
Task 7 Post invoices and credit notes to the subsidiary (sales) ledger
Task 8 Post cheque receipts to the subsidiary (sales) ledger
Task 9 Post the day book and cash receipts book totals to the main ledger

The simulation also contains a large volume of data which you will need in order to complete the tasks.

You are advised to read the whole of the simulation before commencing as all of the information may be of value and is not necessarily supplied in the sequence in which you might wish to deal with it.

Your answers should be set out in the answer booklet, using the forms provided.

You are allowed **three hours** to complete your work.

A high level of accuracy is required. Check your work carefully before handing it in.

The situation

Your name is A Student and you are the bookkeeper for Bramall Toys Limited, a wholesaler of children's toys. The address of Bramall Toys is Blades Parade, Burslem Road, Sheffield S2 4SV. Today is Friday 21 November 20X1. Bramall Toys also has a small retail outlet for seconds and slightly damaged toys.

Your duties as bookkeeper include:
- preparing sales invoices and credit notes by reference to despatch notes, goods returned notes and the company's price list. Note that it is the company's policy (a) to round VAT amounts down to the nearest whole penny (in line with HM Revenue & Customs requirements) and (b) to round trade discounts up to the nearest whole penny;
- posting sales and purchases invoices and credit notes, as well as any necessary adjustments, to ledger accounts. Note that any adjustments to the ledger accounts, other than those which derive from routine postings from the books of prime entry, must be authorised in writing by the Accountant;
- to act as duty cash supervisor in the retail outlet and to prepare paying-in slips for cash sales receipts;
- to periodically post receipts to the cash receipts book.

Sales and purchases
Sales are analysed into two categories:
(a) pre-school toys (product codes beginning with P);
(b) school age toys (product codes beginning with S).

All sales are subject to VAT at 17.5%.

Purchases of goods for resale are analysed into the same two categories as sales.

Ledgers
The company maintains a main ledger together with subsidiary (sales and purchase) ledgers.

The main ledger contains control accounts for the subsidiary (sales) ledger and subsidiary (purchase) ledger. These control accounts are part of the double entry system. The accounts for individual debtors and creditors in the subsidiary ledgers are not part of the double entry system, but are for memorandum only.

The tasks to be completed

PART 1

TASK 1
Refer to the despatch notes given and prepare sales invoices using the forms in the answer booklet. The invoices should be numbered consecutively, beginning with number 1325.

You will need to refer to the customer details given and the extract from the Bramall price list.

TASK 2
Refer to the goods returned notes given and provided that you are satisfied with them prepare credit notes using the forms provided in the answer booklet. You should number the credit notes consecutively, beginning with number 513.

UNIT 30 : WORKBOOK

If you are not satisfied with the goods returned documentation, explain what action you would take using the blank page in the answer booklet.

TASK 3
Refer to the sales day book and the sales returns day book in the answer booklet which have already been written up to 20 November 20X1.

You are required to enter all invoices and credit notes for 21 November 20X1 in the day books, including full analysis into the appropriate columns and then to total the two books for the week ended 21 November 20X1.

PART TWO

TASK 4
It is Friday 21 November 20X1 and you are acting as duty cash supervisor in the retail outlet during the normal supervisor's lunch break. While you are on duty shop staff bring you the cheques and credit card vouchers that have been received so far during the day.

You are required to scrutinise the cheques, cheque card details and credit card vouchers to ensure they are in order. Any discrepancies should be explained to the member of staff concerned so that they can be rectified. On the page given in the answer booklet set out what you would do in respect of each payment, either approving the sale or explaining the discrepancy that needs to be rectified.

TASK 5
At the end of the day you are given the cash, cheque and credit card takings for the day. These are made up as follows:

Notes and coins

Denomination	Number
£50	2
£20	19
£10	15
£5	11
£1	22
50p	15
20p	14
10p	23
5p	10
2p	16
1p	12

MOCK SIMULATION 1 : QUESTIONS

Cheques

Name of payer	Amount £
D Page	31.76
L Thew	19.05
C Boardman	33.75
K Martin	48.09
G Kelly	72.11
S Hicks	18.82
I Ironside	28.30
J Rockett	22.65
L Harper	10.67
N Trebble	15.55
O Heald	54.44

Credit card vouchers

Name of payer	Amount £
E Smith	33.14
P Laine	19.75
P Easton	35.90
N Wanchope	24.23
R Sykes	18.99
E James	75.28
P Somers	14.58
J Singh	12.66

You are required to complete the bank paying slip and the credit card summary, both given in the answer booklet, in preparation for depositing the day's takings in the night safe of your bank branch. Assume that any problems with the cheques and credit cards from Task 4 have been correctly dealt with and are now all valid payments.

TASK 6

The cash takings banked earlier in the week are detailed below. You are required to enter all cash takings for the week, including those for Friday 21 November 20X1, in the cash book (receipts side) given in the answer booklet. Your entries should include extension of totals into analysis columns. You are reminded that all of Bramall's sales are subject to VAT at 17.5%. Note that cheque receipts from credit customers have already been entered into the cash receipts book (total column only) and these will need to be entered in the analysis column(s).

Takings banked

Date	Amount £
17 November	1,146.73
18 November	1,225.78
19 November	1,234.05
20 November	900.14

UNIT 30 : WORKBOOK

On completion total all of the columns in the cash receipts book.

All of these cash sales are for pre-school toys.

PART THREE

TASK 7
You are required to post the invoices and credit notes for the week ending 21 November 20X1 to the subsidiary (sales) ledger accounts given in the answer booklet.

TASK 8
Using the cash receipts book you are required to post the cheque receipts from individual credit customers to their accounts in the subsidiary (sales) ledger.

TASK 9
You are required to post the totals of the sales day book, sales returns day book and the cash receipts book for the week ended 21 November 20X1 to the main ledger accounts given in the answer booklet.

PART 1, TASKS 1 AND 2

DATA

Extracts from the Bramall Toys price list

Item description	Item code	Price (excl VAT) £
Pre-school toys		
Chime bear	P094	4.25
Activity centre	P121	10.50
Activity arch	P145	14.50
Musical teether	P172	2.80
Cot mobile	P182	6.70
Bubble ball	P189	3.10
Trike	P309	8.75
Pop-up farm	P322	6.50
Toddler truck	P335	12.60
Plastic garage	P370	7.25
Musical phone	P381	5.50
School age toys		
Water ball	S151	3.75
Trolley	S375	10.40
Painting easel	S513	15.00
Magnetic easel	S520	28.30
Painting overall	S522	2.50
Stencil set	S529	5.80
Compact keyboard	S546	15.20
Trampoline	S558	31.50
Tree house	S571	85.60

MOCK SIMULATION 1 : **QUESTIONS**

PART 1, TASKS 1 AND 2, CONTINUED

DATA

Customer details

Name	Address	Discount
Angell Flo Ltd	75 Britholme Street Slough Berks SL3 3MN	35%
Blake Ltd	34 Exley Road Triverton TN2 6WY	30%
Hodges & Co	108 Wyndale Road Brooking Herts BK12 1ER	30%
Hutchison Ltd	Nicholson Centre Ramley Northants RY3 4AY	25%
Walker plc	Walker House Ardrees Avenue Twycroft BN3 7PS	25%
White & Veart	216 Breech Street Holyfield M32 5FG	35%
Whitehouse Stores Ltd	Unit 8 Hockley Trading Estate Hammerfold LR2 8DT	30%

PART ONE, TASK 1

DESPATCH NOTE

Bramall Toys Ltd, Blades Parade, Burslem Road SHEFFIELD S2 4SV
Telephone: 0114 273 5895

To: Hutchison Ltd
Nicholson Centre
Ramley Northants RY3 4AY

Despatch Note No 397
Date 21 November 20X1
Customer Order No 4260

We would like to advise you that the following goods have now been despatched.

Quantity	Description	Item Code
10	Cot mobile	P182
5	Compact keyboard	S546

On behalf of Bramall Toys   *Amir Guha*

DESPATCH NOTE

Bramall Toys Ltd, Blades Parade, Burslem Road SHEFFIELD S2 4SV Telephone: 0114 273 5895

To: Walker plc
Walker House Ardrees Avenue
Twycroft BN3 7PS

Despatch Note No 398
Date 21 November 20X1
Customer Order No 3178

We would like to advise you that the following goods have now been despatched.

Quantity	Description	Item Code
12	Activity Centre	P121
20	Stencil set	S529

On behalf of Bramall Toys   *Amir Guha*

DESPATCH NOTE

Bramall Toys Ltd, Blades Parade, Burslem Road SHEFFIELD S2 4SV Telephone: 0114 273 5895

To: Hodges & Co
108 Wyndale Road
Brooking Herts BK12 1ER

Despatch Note No 399
Date 21 November 20X1
Customer Order No 909

We would like to advise you that the following goods have now been despatched.

Quantity	Description	Item Code
15	Pop-up farm	P322

On behalf of Bramall Toys   *Amir Guha*

DESPATCH NOTE

Bramall Toys Ltd, Blades Parade, Burslem Road SHEFFIELD S2 4SV Telephone: 0114 273 5895

To: Whitehouse Stores Ltd Unit 8
Hockley Trading Estate
Hammerfold LR2 8DT

Despatch Note No 400
Date 21 November 20X1
Customer Order No 463

We would like to advise you that the following goods have now been despatched.

Quantity	Description	Item Code
2	Tree house	S571
30	Bubble ball	P189

On behalf of Bramall Toys   *Amir Guha*

DESPATCH NOTE

Bramall Toys Ltd, Blades Parade, Burslem Road SHEFFIELD S2 4SV Telephone: 0114 273 5895

To: Walker plc
Walker House Ardrees Avenue
Twycroft BN3 7PS

Despatch Note No 401
Date 21 November 20X1
Customer Order No 3192

We would like to advise you that the following goods have now been despatched.

Quantity	Description	Item Code
10	Toddler truck	P335
5	Magnetic easel	S520

On behalf of Bramall Toys   *Amir Guha*

DESPATCH NOTE

Bramall Toys Ltd, Blades Parade, Burslem Road SHEFFIELD S2 4SV Telephone: 0114 273 5895

To: White & Veart
216 Breech Street
Holyfield M32 5FG

Despatch Note No 402
Date 21 November 20X1
Customer Order No 284

We would like to advise you that the following goods have now been despatched.

Quantity	Description	Item Code
20	Plastic garage	P370
4	Trampoline	S558

On behalf of Bramall Toys   *Amir Guha*

DESPATCH NOTE

Bramall Toys Ltd, Blades Parade, Burslem Road SHEFFIELD S2 4SV Telephone: 0114 273 5895

To: Blake Ltd
34 Exley Road
Triverton TN2 6WY

Despatch Note No 403
Date 21 November 20X1
Customer Order No 392

We would like to advise you that the following goods have now been despatched.

Quantity	Description	Item Code
50	Painting overall	S522
20	Chime bear	P094

On behalf of Bramall Toys   *Amir Guha*

UNIT 30 : WORKBOOK

DESPATCH NOTE

Bramall Toys Ltd, Blades Parade, Burslem Road SHEFFIELD S2 4SV Telephone: 0114 273 5895

To: Angell Flo Ltd
75 Britholme Street
Slough Berks SL3 3MN

Despatch Note No 404
Date 21 November 20X1
Customer Order No 1603

We would like to advise you that the following goods have now been despatched..

Quantity	Description	Item Code
10	Trike	P309
10	Activity centre	P121

On behalf of Bramall Toys   *Amir Guha*

GOODS RETURNED NOTE

Date: 21 November 20X1   **Returned by: Hodges & Co**

Quantity	Item Code	Item Description
2	P121	Activity Centre

On behalf of Bramall Toys   *Adam Barton*

GOODS RETURNED NOTE

Date: 21 November 20X1   **Returned by: Blake Ltd**

Quantity	Item Code	Item Description
1	S520	Magnetic easel

On behalf of Bramall Toys   *Adam Barton*

GOODS RETURNED NOTE

Date: 21 November 20X1 Returned by: White & Veart

Quantity	Item Code	Item Description
2	S558	Magnetic easel

On behalf of Bramall Toys   Adam Barton

GOODS RETURNED NOTE

Date: 21 November 20X1 Returned by: Angell Flo Ltd

Quantity	Item Code	Item Description
3	P335	Toddler truck

On behalf of Bramall Toys   Adam Barton

PART TWO, TASK 4

1

WADSWORTH BANK PLC
Plumtree Street
Wimbledon, SW19 4AE

25-34-78

21 November 20 X1

Pay   Bramall Toys Limited   or order

Thirty-three pounds and 75p

£ 33.75

Account payee

C BOARDMAN

C Boardman

342206   25 - 34 - 78   54329816

Card details: Name of holder   Account No   Limit   Date
C Boardman   54329816   £50   2/X0 – 1/X2

UNIT 30 : WORKBOOK

2

NORTH BANK PLC   20–35–65
Hillhead Branch 4 Langley Road
Hillhead HD2 5JC   21 November 20 X1

Pay   Bramall Toys Limited   or order

Forty-eight pounds and 9p   £ 48.09

                                                      K Martin

                                                           K Martin

01247   20 - 35 - 65   10024566

Card details:	Name of holder	Account No	Limit	Date
	K Martin	10024566	£100	11/W9 –10/X1

3

SOUTHERN BANK PLC   40–20–36
Market Street
Hambourn HN1 8AQ   21 November 20 X1

Pay   Bramall Toys Limited   or order

Seventy-two pounds and 11p   £ 72.11

                                                      G Kelly

                                                           G Kelly

103297   40 - 20 - 36   60412570

Card details:	Name of holder	Account No	Limit	Date
	G Kelly	60412570	£100	5/X0 – 4/X2

4

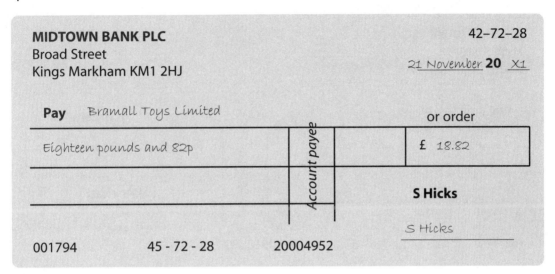

Card details:	Name of holder	Account No	Limit	Date
	S Hicks	20004952	£100	12/X0 – 11/X2

5

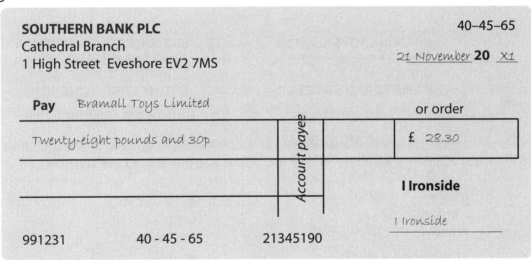

Card details:	Name of holder	Account No	Limit	Date
	I Ironside	21345180	£50	6/X0 – 5/X2

UNIT 30 : WORKBOOK

6

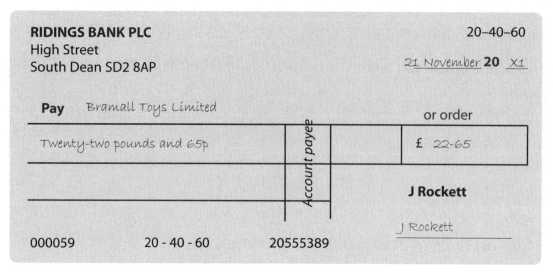

Card details:	Name of holder	Account No	Limit	Date
	J Rockett	20555389	£100	3/X0 – 2/X2

7

BRAMALL TOYS LIMITED
Blades Parade, Burslem Road,
Sheffield, S2 4SV

CREDIT CARD VOUCHER

This is not a VAT receipt

VISA   4556 4701 2389 6214
Expires   6/X2 Ref 10010097
Date   21/11/X1
Time   13.07
Amount   £24.23
Holder   N WANCHOPE

Cardholder's signature
N Wanchope

Please debit my credit card account with the total amount shown.

8

BRAMALL TOYS LIMITED
Blades Parade, Burslem Road,
Sheffield, S2 4SV

CREDIT CARD VOUCHER

This is not a VAT receipt

VISA   4556 4701 4265 8312
Expires   2/X2 Ref 10010102
Date   21/11/X1
Time   13.36
Amount   £18.99
Holder   R SYKES

Cardholder's signature
R Sykes

Please debit my credit card account with the total amount shown.

9

BRAMALL TOYS LIMITED
Blades Parade, Burslem Road,
Sheffield, S2 4SV

CREDIT CARD VOUCHER

This is not a VAT receipt

ACCESS   5224 0067 4832 3157
Expires   6/X2 Ref 10010175
Date   21/11/X1
Time   13.41
Amount   £75.28
Holder   E JAMES

Cardholder's signature

Please debit my credit card account with the total amount shown.

10

BRAMALL TOYS LIMITED
Blades Parade, Burslem Road,
Sheffield, S2 4SV

CREDIT CARD VOUCHER

This is not a VAT receipt

ACCESS   5224 0067 3942 1106
Expires   5/X3 Ref 10010234
Date   21/11/X1
Time   13.52
Amount   £14.58
Holder   P SOMERS

Cardholder's signature
P Somers

Please debit my credit card account with the total amount shown.

UNIT 30 : WORKBOOK

MOCK SIMULATION 2
QUESTIONS

UNIT 30 : WORKBOOK

DATA AND TASKS

Instructions
This simulation is designed to test your ability to make and record payments.

The situation is provided on the next page.

The simulation is divided into three parts as follows:

PART ONE: PETTY CASH
Task 1 Authorisation of petty cash claims
Task 2 Entries in petty cash book
Task 3 Reconciliation of cash box contents with petty cash book balance

PART TWO: CASH PAYMENTS
Task 4 Preparing cheques and remittance advices
Task 5 Entering cheques in cash book

PART THREE: WRITING UP LEDGER
Task 6 Posting from cash book and petty cash book to ledger accounts
Task 7 Drafting memo

Note that the final task referred to above will require you to explain any discrepancies you have encountered in the course of the simulation; you are advised to make a brief note of such discrepancies as you come across them by way of reminder.

This booklet also contains a large amount of data which you will need to complete the tasks and you are advised to read the whole of the simulation before commencing as all of the information may be of value and is not necessarily supplied in the sequence in which you might wish to deal with it.

Your answers should be set out in the answer booklet using the specimen forms provided.

You are allowed **three hours** to complete your work.

A high level of accuracy is required. Check your work carefully before handing it in.

Correcting fluid should not be used. Errors should be crossed out neatly and clearly. You should write in black ink, not pencil.

MOCK SIMULATION 2 : **QUESTIONS**

The situation

Your name is A Student and you work for Seamer Retail Limited, 37 Cain Road, Scarborough YO12 4HF. Seamer is a retailer of gardening and DIY (do-it-yourself) supplies. Your duties involve both bookkeeping and, occasionally, acting as a cash supervisor in the retail area of the company's premises. The transactions you are required to deal with take place in the week ending Friday 7 November 20X1.

Petty cash
Petty cash is maintained on an imprest system, with a float of £100 replenished at the end of each accounting week. When staff incur petty cash expenditure they complete a voucher (which must be supported by a receipt) and then submit it to you. Provided the amount is not above £10, you authorise the expenditure yourself by signing and dating the petty cash voucher and then pay the cash. For amounts above £10, authorisation is required by the Accountant.

Expenditure
Another of your duties is to make out cheques to pay suppliers. You are not an authorised signatory of the company bank account: once you have prepared the cheques, they are passed for signing to Gillian Russell, the company accountant.

It is Gillian Russell who decides when invoices should be paid. She prepares a list each week, which is passed to you for the preparation of appropriate remittance advices and cheques. When preparing cheques to suppliers who offer settlement discounts, it is your responsibility to ensure that advantage is taken of any discounts available.

The tasks to be completed

PART ONE

TASK 1
Refer to the petty cash receipts given. The related petty cash vouchers are given in the answer booklet. For each claim that you are satisfied with you are required to complete the relevant voucher ready for entering in the petty cash book. The vouchers are to be numbered in sequence, beginning with number 175.

In the case of any claim you do not feel able to process, explain what action you would take. Use the form given in the answer booklet.

(**Note:** In the final task of this simulation you will be required to write a memo to the Accountant setting out any discrepancies of which she should be aware, including any you discover in this task.)

TASK 2
The petty cash book for Seamer Retail is given in the answer booklet. You are required to enter in it the petty cash vouchers that you have processed in task

KAPLAN PUBLISHING

UNIT 30 : WORKBOOK

1 above, and then to total and balance off the petty cash book for the week ended 7 November 20X1, including the entries necessary to restore the imprest.

TASK 3
The contents of the petty cash box at close of business on 7 November 20X1 are listed below. You are required to reconcile the total of cash on hand with the balance shown in the petty cash book. Use the blank in the answer booklet to set out your reconciliation.

Contents of petty cash box

£10 notes x 4
£5 notes   x 3
£1 coins   x 6
50p coins x 3
20p coins x 4
10p coins x 9
2p coins   x 8
1p coins   x 11

PART TWO

TASK 4
The Accountant has informed you that the following invoices can now be paid.

Supplier	Invoice number	Invoice date	Amount Goods (ex VAT) £	VAT £	Terms
Baxley Limited Station Road Horsford TV12 3EW	4132	26/10/X1	1,788.56	309.86	1% cash discount for settlement within 10 days
Harborne Limited 12 Barton Street Apton AN3 4RT	2541	7/10/X1	2,076.22	363.33	Net 30 days
Hurley Limited 241 Steels Avenue Picton SR5 9TY	1008	1/10/X1	300.17	52.52	Net 30 days
Allen and Banks 49 Exley Road Traxham TM5 1UJ	1673	27/10/X1	654.08	112.74	1.5% cash discount for settlement within 14 days
Wallace Limited 101-105 Knighton Rd Brixley BY2 3FR	4321	10/10/X1	102.66	17.96	Net 30 days

MOCK SIMULATION 2 : **QUESTIONS**

You are required to complete cheques ready for signature by Gillian Russell in respect of each of these invoices. You should ensure in each case that any discount to which the company is entitled is accounted for in calculating the amount of the cheques (the cheques will be posted on 7 November 20X1). You are also required to complete remittance advices.

Blank cheques and remittance advices are provided in the answer booklet.

TASK 5
An extract from the company's cash book (payments side) appears in the answer booklet. You are required to enter in the book all of the cheques prepared in task 4, and also the petty cash imprest cheque (cheque no 305081) calculated earlier in task 2. Total all of the cash book columns.

PART THREE

TASK 6
In the answer booklet certain main ledger and subsidiary (purchases) ledger accounts have been extracted from the books of Seamer Retail Limited.
You are required to make the following postings to these ledger accounts.

(a) Post from the cash book (payments side) for the week ended 7 November 20X1 to the appropriate main ledger accounts.
(b) Post from the cash book (payments side) for the week ended 7 November 20X1 to the appropriate subsidiary (purchases) ledger accounts.
(c) Post from the petty cash book for the week ended 7 November 20X1 to the appropriate main ledger accounts.

TASK 7
You are required to write a memo to Gillian Russell, the Accountant, explaining any discrepancies you encountered in the course of the tasks above. Use the blank memo form in the answer booklet.

Stationery Supplies	
Hill Street, Scarborough	
Telephone 01723 23478	
5 November 20X1	
Goods	13.07
VAT	2.28
Total	15.35
Amount tendered	20.00
Change	4.65
Vat registration no: 245 9162 47	

Stationery Supplies	
Hill Street, Scarborough	
Telephone 01723 23478	
7 November 20X1	
Goods	9.45
VAT	1.65
Total	11.10
Amount tendered	15.00
Change	3.90
Vat registration no: 245 9162 47	

UNIT 30 : WORKBOOK

Stationery Supplies	
Hill Street, Scarborough	
Telephone 01723 23478	
4 November 20X1	
Goods	6.24
VAT	1.09
Total	7.33
Amount tendered	10.00
Change	2.67
Vat registration no: 245 9162 47	

Stationery Supplies	
Hill Street, Scarborough	
Telephone 01723 23478	
5 November 20X1	
Goods	5.92
VAT	1.03
Total	6.95
Amount tendered	10.00
Change	3.05
Vat registration no: 245 9162 47	

Ace Taxis	
Telephone 01723 29865	
Date 4 November 20X1	
Received with thanks £5 - 20	
Vat registration no: 337 8714 29	

Ace Taxis	
Telephone 01723 29865	
Date 7 November 20X1	
Received with thanks £6 - 10	
Vat registration no: 337 8714 29	

POST OFFICE P325
Order for stamps, etc
*This is **not** a certificate of posting*

Postage stamps		Miscellaneous	
	£		£
Stamps	5-25		
		B/F FROM COLUMN 1	
		GRAND TOTAL	5-25
TOTAL COLUMN 1		**4 November 20X1**	

POST OFFICE P325
Order for stamps, etc
*This is **not** a certificate of posting*

Postage stamps		Miscellaneous	
	£		£
Stamps	0-76		
		B/F FROM COLUMN 1	
		GRAND TOTAL	0-76
TOTAL COLUMN 1		**4 November 20X1**	

MOCK SIMULATION 2 : QUESTIONS

POST OFFICE		P325	
Order for stamps, etc			
*This is **not** a certificate of posting*			
Postage stamps		Miscellaneous	
	£		£
Stamps	3-94		
		B/F FROM COLUMN 1	
		GRAND TOTAL	3-94
TOTAL COLUMN 1		**6 November 20X1**	

POST OFFICE		P325	
Order for stamps, etc			
*This is **not** a certificate of posting*			
Postage stamps		Miscellaneous	
	£		£
Stamps	12-35		
		B/F FROM COLUMN 1	
		GRAND TOTAL	12-35
TOTAL COLUMN 1		**7 November 20X1**	

MOCK SIMULATION 3
QUESTIONS

UNIT 30 : WORKBOOK

This mock simulation is in two parts. In each part the double entry takes place in the main ledger and the individual accounts of debtors and creditors in the subsidiary ledgers are therefore regarded as memorandum only.

You are advised to spend approximately 1 hour on each part of the test.

DATA AND TASKS
Instructions
The situation and the tasks to be completed are set out on the following pages.

The test is divided into **two** parts:

Part 1 – **five** tasks
Part 2 – **four** tasks

This test also contains a large amount of data which you may need to complete the tasks. You are advised to read the whole of the test before commencing as all of the information may be of value and is not necessarily supplied in the sequence in which you might wish to deal with it.

PART ONE

DATA
Balances
The following balances are relevant to you at the start of the day on 1 June 20X1:

	£
Credit suppliers	
Hadley Turf Supplies	12,500
Blackwood Nurseries	8,260
Lawnmower Repair Shop	970
Western Electricity	40
Other suppliers	10,000
Purchases	88,039
Purchases returns	1,000
Purchases (Creditors) ledger control	32,109
Sales	180,770
Sales (Debtors) ledger control	66,468
Heat and light	566
VAT (credit balance)	8,078

The following transactions all occurred on 1 June 20X1 and have been entered into the relevant books of prime entry (given below). However, no entries have yet been made into the ledger system. VAT has been calculated at a rate of $17\frac{1}{2}$%.

Day books

PURCHASES DAY BOOK (PDB)

Date 20X1	Details	Invoice	Total £	VAT £	Purchases £	Heat &Light £
1 June	Hadley Turf Supplies	5461	2,538	378	2,160	
1 June	Blackwood Nurseries	76105	1,598	238	1,360	
1 June	Lawnmower Repair Shop	124	4,700	700	4,000	
1 June	Western Electricity	8066	470	70		400
	Totals		9,306	1,386	7,520	400

PURCHASES RETURNS DAY BOOK (PRDB)

Date 20X1	Details	Credit Note	Total £	VAT £	Net £
1 June	Blackwood Nurseries	CR12	705	105	600
1 June	Hadley Turf Supplies	CR13	517	77	440
	Totals		1,222	182	1,040

SALES DAY BOOK (SDB)

Date 20X1	Details	Invoice	Total £	VAT £	Net £
1 June	G Brown	G104	1,175	175	1,000
1 June	S Cox	G105	940	140	800
1 June	Swinford Council	G106	3,525	525	3,000
	Totals		5,640	840	4,800

Journal

The following correction has been entered into the journal. (This journal does not refer to double entry in the main ledger.)

Date	Details	Debit £	Credit £
1 June	Lawnmower Repair Shop	235	
1 June	Blackwood Nurseries To correct purchase invoice 165 being posted to the account of Lawnmower Repair Shop in error.		235

UNIT 30 : WORKBOOK

Bank statement

The following bank statement was also received on 1 June 20X1.

Western Bank plc
Bradbury Way
Swinford LE1 8OU

Gregson Garden Services Limited
Account 86759485

STATEMENT OF ACCOUNT

Date 20X1	Details	Debit £	Credit £	Balance £
26 May	Balance b/f			8,070C
27 May	Cheque 111987	4,760		3,310C
28 May	Bank Giro Credit: Carter & Son		7,000	10,310C
28 May	Cheque 111988	2,198		8,112C
31 May	Bank charges	55		8,057C
31 May	Direct Debit: Contract Cleaning	235		7,822C
31 May	Credit		1,880	9,702C

D = Debit C = Credit

The Cash Book is also given, written up until the end of May 20X1.

Cash Book (bank columns only)

20X1		£	20X1		£
20 May	Balance b/d	8,070	21 May	Patio Pavers	4,760
26 May	B Bradley	1,880	22 May	L Briggs	2,198
31 May	Park Maintenance	2,170	31 May	T Brown	1,500

THE TASKS TO BE COMPLETED

Complete all five tasks

TASK 1

Enter the opening balances at the start of 1 June 20X1 into the following accounts, which are given in the answer booklet provided:
- Hadley Turf Supplies
- Blackwood Nurseries
- Lawnmower Repair Shop

Western Electricity
Other suppliers
Purchases
Purchases returns
Purchases (Creditors) ledger control
Sales
Sales (Debtors) ledger control
Heat and light
VAT

TASK 2

Using the data given in the day books and journal enter all the relevant transactions into the accounts in the Subsidiary (Purchases) Ledger and Main Ledger.

TASK 3

Balance off all of the accounts *showing clearly the balances carried down*.

TASK 4

Reconcile the Purchases (Creditors) ledger control account with the list of the Subsidiary (Purchases) ledger balances. The following notes are relevant:

(a) The total column of the Purchases Day Book in May was overcast by £200.
(b) An invoice for £163 from Hadley Turf Supplies was correctly entered in the PDB but not posted to Hadley's account in the Subsidiary (Purchases) ledger.
(c) A credit note for £24 (inc VAT) from Blackwood Nurseries was correctly entered in their account in the Subsidiary (Purchases) ledger but entered twice in the Purchases Returns Day Book. (You do not have to make any other adjustments to the ledger accounts other than the one needed to correct the PLCA.)

TASK 5

Compare the bank statement and the cash book and then update the cash book given using appropriate information taken from the bank statement. Balance off the cash book *showing clearly the balance carried down*. You should tick the amounts which are shown finally in the cash book and bank statement to identify the differences between them.

UNIT 30 : WORKBOOK

PART TWO

Various transactions have taken place in a business today and they are as follows:

	Total £	VAT £	Net £
Invoices issued			
Barnes Department Stores	562	84	478
Sportsworld Ltd	2,191	326	1,865
Birmingham Sports	889	132	757
Hi-sport	1,738	259	1,479
	5,380	801	4,579
Invoices received			
Royal Sports Ltd	15,910	2,370	13,540
Leisurewear UK Ltd	8,204	1,222	6,982
	24,114	3,592	20,522
Credit notes issued			
Sportsworld Ltd	126	19	107
Credit notes received			
Leisurewear UK Ltd	28	4	24
Receipts from debtors			
Sportsworld Ltd	1,485		
Hi-sport	527		
	2,012		
Payments			
Royal Sports Ltd	7,991		
Bad debt written off			
Keysports	3,678		

The various accounts where the balance changed during the day were as follows:

Balances at the start of the day	£
Customers	
Barnes Department Stores	10,629
Sportsworld Ltd	3,523
Birmingham Sports	4,890
Hi-sport	5,917
Keysports	3,678
Suppliers	
Royal Sports Ltd	24,236
Leisurewear UK Ltd	40,802
Sales	352,871
Purchases	188,295
Sales returns	2,166
Purchases returns	1,843
Bank overdraft	10,068
VAT (credit balance)	4,110
Other balances which did not change during the day:	
Debit balances	486,775
Credit balances	271,943

The tasks to be completed

Complete all the following tasks.

Your work should be neat, legible and accurate. Use the answer booklet provided.

TASK 6
Draw up the VAT account as it would appear in the ledger, balancing off the account at the end of the day.

TASK 7
At the beginning of the day the balance of the sales ledger control account amounted to £78,852. Produce an updated sales ledger control account which shows clearly the individual debits and credits and the closing balance for the day.

TASK 8
Enter the appropriate transactions into the accounts for Sportsworld Ltd and Royal Sports Ltd showing clearly the opening and closing balances for the day.

TASK 9
Update the opening balances to take account of the day's transactions. Complete the list of balances provided by inserting the updated figure for each individual account shown in either the debit balances column or the credit balances column as appropriate. Total the two columns. The two totals

should be the same. If they do not agree, try to trace and correct any errors you have made within the time you have available. If you are still unable to make the totals balance, leave the work incomplete.

Note: It is not a requirement to draw up all the individual accounts in order to update the opening balances although candidates may, if they wish, adopt this approach. Workings should, however, be shown wherever possible.

SPECIMEN EXAM PAPER QUESTIONS

UNIT 30 : WORKBOOK

This examination paper is in TWO sections.

You must show competence in BOTH sections.

You should therefore attempt and aim to complete EVERY task in EACH section.

You should spend about 75 minutes on Section 1 and 105 minutes on Section 2.

Both sections are based on the business described below.

Introduction

- Marian Walker is the owner of The Garden Warehouse, a business which supplies gardening equipment.
- You are employed by the business as a bookkeeper.
- The business uses a manual accounting system.
- Double entry takes place in the Main (General) ledger. Individual accounts of debtors and creditors are kept in subsidiary ledgers as memorandum accounts.
- Bank payments and receipts are recorded in the cash book, which is part of the double entry system.
- Assume today's date is 30 June 2005 unless you are told otherwise.

SPECIMEN EXAMINATION : **QUESTIONS**

Section 1 – Double entry bookkeeping and trial balance

You should spend 75 minutes on this section.

Note: Please show your answer by inserting a tick, text or figures, as appropriate.

Task 1.1

On 1 June there were opening balances on all the accounts in the Subsidiary (sales) ledger which represent money owing to The Garden Warehouse.

Would the opening balances in the Subsidiary (sales) ledger be shown as debit or credit entries? Tick the correct answer.

	✓
Debit	
Credit	

Task 1.2

On 1 June the following opening balances were in the Main ledger.

Would the opening balances in the Main ledger be shown as a debit or credit entry?

Account name	Amount £	Debit/Credit
Office equipment	3,500	
Sales	321,650	
Sales returns	15,800	
Sales ledger control	112,636	
Discount allowed	750	
Motor expenses	1,225	
Rent and rates	3,600	

Task 1.3

The following transactions all took place on 30 June 2005 and have been entered into the Sales day book as shown below. No entries have yet been made into the ledger system

Sales day book

Date 2005	Details	Invoice number	Total £	VAT at 17.5% £	Net £
30 June	Creations Ltd	849	2,115	315	1,800
30 June	Jackson and Company	850	9,870	1,470	8,400
30 June	Loxley Ltd	851	3,055	455	2,600
30 June	PTT Ltd	852	7,050	1,050	6,000
	Totals		22,090	3,290	18,800

(a) What will be the entries in the Subsidiary (sales) ledger?

Account name	Amount £	Debit/Credit

(b) What will be the entries in the Main ledger?

Account name	Amount £	Debit/Credit

Task 1.4

The following transactions all took place on 30 June 2005 and have been entered into the Sales returns day book as shown below. No entries have yet been made into the ledger system.

Sales returns day book

Date 2005	Details	Credit note number	Total £	VAT £	Net £
30 June	Creations Ltd	131	4,700	700	4,000
30 June	Loxley Ltd	132	423	63	360
	Totals		5,123	763	4,360

(a) What will be the entries in the Subsidiary (sales) ledger?

Account name	Amount £	Debit/Credit

(b) What will be the entries in the main ledger?

Account name	Amount £	Debit/Credit

Task 1.5

The following transactions all took place on 30 June 2005 and have been entered into the Purchases day book as shown below. No entries have yet been made into the ledger system.

Purchases day book

Date 2005	Details	Invoice number	Total £	VAT £	Net £
30 June	Lee Ltd	39872	3,525	525	3,000
30 June	Ball and McGee	128949	1,410	210	1,200
30 June	Horner and Company	Z694	12,690	1,890	10,800
30 June	H & H Ltd	H302	4,700	700	4,000
	Totals		22,325	3,325	19,000

(a) What will be the entries in the Subsidiary (purchases) ledger?

Account name	Amount £	Debit/Credit

(b) What will be the entries in the Main ledger?

Account name	Amount £	Debit/Credit

Task 1.6

The following transactions all took place on 30 June 2005 and have been entered into the Cash book as shown below. No entries have yet been made into the ledger system.

Cash book

Date 2005	Receipt type	Details	Discount allowed £	Bank £	Date 2005	Cheque details	Bank £
30 June		Balance b/f		8,190	30 June	Motor expenses	350
30 June	BACS	Jackson and Company	100	3,650	30 June	Rent and rates	1,200
					30 June	Office equipment	3,250
					30 June	Croxford Ltd	2,000
					30 June	Balance c/d	5,040
			100	11,840			11,840
1 July		Balance b/d		5,040			

UNIT 30 : WORKBOOK

(a) What will be the entries to record this receipt and these payments in the Subsidiary (sales) ledger, Subsidiary (purchases) ledger and Main ledger?

Subsidiary (sales) ledger

Account name	Amount £	Debit/Credit

Subsidiary (purchases) ledger

Account name	Amount £	Debit/Credit

Main ledger

Account name	Amount £	Debit/Credit

Task 1.7

The following two accounts are in the main ledger at the close of day on 30 June.

(a) Insert the balance carried down together with date and details.
(b) Insert the totals.
(c) Insert the balance brought down together with date and details.

Hotel expenses

Date 2005	Details	Amount £	Date 2005	Details	Amount £
01 June	Balance b/f	3,000			
26 June	Bank	595			
	Total			Total	

SPECIMEN EXAMINATION : QUESTIONS

Loan from bank

Date 2005	Details	Amount £	Date 2005	Details	Amount £
18 June	Bank	700	1 June	Balance b/f	15,000
	Total			Total	

Task 1.8

Record the journal entries needed in the Main ledger to deal with the following. Note: You do not need to give narratives. You may not need to use all the lines.

(a) An amount of £70 has been debited to the miscellaneous account instead of the motor expenses account.

Account name	Amount £	Debit/Credit

(b) Credit purchases of £500 have been entered as £5,000 in the relevant Main ledger accounts (ignore VAT).

Account name	Amount £	Debit/Credit

(c) A credit customer, L G Whitburn, has ceased trading. It owes The Garden Warehouse £200 plus VAT. The net amount and VAT must be written off in the Main ledger.

Account name	Amount £	Debit/Credit

KAPLAN PUBLISHING

UNIT 30 : WORKBOOK

Task 1.9

During the month a trial balance was extracted which did not balance and an amount of £75 was credited to the suspense account. The following two errors have now been discovered.

(i) Rent paid has been understated by £10.

(ii) A figure in the heat and light account has been overstated by £85.

What entries are needed in the Main ledger to correct these errors?

Account name	Amount £	Debit/Credit

Task 1.10

Below is a list of balances to be transferred to the trial balance as at 30 June.

Place the figures in the debit or credit column, as appropriate, and total each column.

Account name	Amount £	Debit £	Credit £
Motor vehicles	5,200		
Office equipment	8,750		
Stock	17,000		
Cash at bank	5,040		
Petty cash control	60		
Sales ledger control	125,853		
Purchases ledger control	56,713		
VAT owing to H M Revenue & Customs	13,990		
Loan from bank	14,300		
Capital	32,373		
Sales	340,450		
Sales returns	20,160		
Purchases	206,511		
Purchases returns	862		
Discount received	248		
Discount allowed	850		
Wages	50,425		

Account name	Amount £	Debit £	Credit £
Heat and light	963		
Motor expenses	1,645		
Rent and rates	4,810		
Travel expenses	1,650		
Hotel expenses	3,595		
Telephone	1,006		
Accountancy fees	2,530		
Bad debts written off	200		
Miscellaneous expenses	2,688		
Totals			

UNIT 30 : WORKBOOK

Section 2 – Accounting processes

You should spend about 105 minutes on this section.

Note 1: You do not need to adjust any accounts in Section 1 as part of any of the following tasks.

Note 2: Please show your answer by inserting a tick, text or figures, as appropriate.

Task 2.1

The Garden Warehouse has received the following purchase invoice.

Wentworth Supplies
18 High Street, Droitwich, Worcestershire, WR15 01W
Tel: 01943 567392

VAT Registration Number: 374 8219 00

To: The Garden Warehouse   29 June 2005
     2a Lower Parade
     Droitwich
     Worcestershire WR16 81S

I N V O I C E N O: P/1674

		£
20 …….. Garden spades		200.00
Less 10% trade discounts		20.00
		180.00
VAT at 17.5%		30.87
Total		210.87

Terms: 2% settlement discount for payment within 7 days

Marian Walker has asked you to pay this invoice immediately.

(a) What is the amount to be paid to Wentworth Supplies?

		✓
(i)	£206.65	
(ii)	£210.87	
(iii)	£207.27	
(iv)	£207.90	

(b) What is the purpose of a TRADE discount?

		✓
(i)	To reward customers who pay in cash	
(ii)	To offer a lower price to an organisation within the same trade	
(iii)	To reduce the price of goods that are damaged	

(c) To which customers might The Garden Warehouse offer a BULK discount?

		✓
(i)	Those placing large orders	
(ii)	Those with many branches	
(iii)	Those who have been customers for many years	

Task 2.2

If the VAT account in the main ledger of The Garden Warehouse showed a debit balance, what would this indicate?

		✓
(i)	There had been an accounting error	
(ii)	The Garden Warehouse is entitled to a refund from H M Revenue & Customs	
(iii)	The Garden Warehouse does not have to charge VAT	

Task 2.3

On 1 June a manufacturer telephoned The Garden Warehouse and offered to supply some gardening equipment at a greatly reduced price. Marian Walker said she would think about it and reply by post. On 2 June Marian posted an acceptance of the offer to the supplier, who received it on 5 June.

What is the date on which the contract was formed?

		✓
(i)	1 June	
(ii)	2 June	
(iii)	5 June	

Task 2.4

The Garden Warehouse has just opened a credit account for a new supplier, Wright Brothers, which brings the total number of suppliers to 50.

(a) Suggest an appropriate four-character alphanumeric ledger code for this account.

(b) In which ledger would you expect to see this account?

	✓
(i) Main ledger	
(ii) Subsidiary (sales) ledger	
(iii) Subsidiary (purchases) ledger	

Task 2.5

The following errors have been made in the accounting records of The Garden Warehouse.

Show whether the errors cause an imbalance in the trial balance.

(a) A purchase invoice is lost in the post and not received at The Garden Warehouse.

	✓
(i) The trial balance will balance	
(ii) The trial balance will not balance	

(b) Discount allowed has not been taken by a customer.

	✓
(i) The trial balance will balance	
(ii) The trial balance will not balance	

(c) A purchase invoice has been correctly entered in the Main ledger but omitted from the Subsidiary (purchases) ledger.

	✓
(i) The trial balance will balance	
(ii) The trial balance will not balance	

(d) An entry has been made to the Purchases and VAT accounts but omitted from the Purchases ledger control account.

	✓
(i) The trial balance will balance	
(ii) The trial balance will not balance	

Task 2.6

A cheque has been received at The Garden Warehouse which has been dated 30 June 2004 and the bank will not accept it.

After what amount of time does a cheque become out of date?

	✓
3 months	
6 months	
12 months	
24 months	

Task 2.7

The Garden Warehouse buys goods from and sells goods to Pascoe Plants. It has been agreed to set off the amounts owing between them by a contra entry.

What accounts in the main ledger of The Garden Warehouse would be adjusted to record this set-off?

Account name	Debit/Credit

Task 2.8

Which TWO items listed below would you expect to see in a Wages and salaries control account?

	✓
Total of net wages paid to employees	
Payment to Jackson Brothers for cleaning windows	
Total of trade union fee deductions	
Payment to creditors	

Task 2.9

The Garden Warehouse's transactions in June included the items listed below.

State whether each is a capital transaction or a revenue transaction.

Transaction	Capital or Revenue
Purchase of office stationery	
Annual decoration of offices	
Purchase of a delivery van	
Purchase of fuel for the delivery van	

Task 2.10

The petty cash control account shown below is in the Main ledger of The Garden Warehouse.

Petty cash control

Date 2005	Details	Amount £	Date 2005	Details	Amount £
1 July	Balance b/f	60.00	5 July	Window cleaning	10.00
			10 July	Tea and coffee	5.00
			15 July	Stamps	30.00

What will be the amount required to restore the imprest level to £60?

£

Task 2.11

The Sale of Goods Act sets out what a customer is entitled to expect when buying goods from a shop.

Which one of the following statements is NOT included in this Act?

	✓
Goods must be of a satisfactory quality	
Goods must be worth the price asked	
Goods must be fit for purpose	
Goods must be as described	

Task 2.12

During the last VAT quarter sales amounted to £122,000 plus VAT. Purchases totalled £9,870 including VAT.

(a) What was the amount of VAT payable on sales made?

(b) What was the amount of VAT included in the purchases figure?

(c) What would have been the balance on the VAT account at the end of the quarter?

[   ]

(d) Is the amount you calculated in (c) above payable to H M Revenue & Customs or receivable from them?

	✓
Payable to H M Revenue & Customs	
Receivable from H M Revenue & Customs	

Task 2.13

Marian Walker has given you a list of new customers and has asked you to apply credit limits to each account.

What is a credit limit?

	✓
The maximum amount allowed on any one invoice	
The term for a customer with no credit account	
The amount of time a debt may be outstanding	
The maximum amount allowed to be outstanding at any one time	

Task 2.14

The Garden Warehouse has received a cheque for £800 plus VAT for goods sold. The customer does not have a credit account.

(a) What will be the accounting entries required to record this receipt?

Account name	Amount £	Debit/Credit

(b) Prepare the paying-in slip to pay this cheque into the bank on 1 July 2005, together with cash amounting to £120 and made up of two £20 notes, four £10 notes and eight £5 notes.

Date	MBC Bank plc Worcester	£50 notes	
		£20 notes	
	Account The Garden Warehouse	£10 notes	
		£5 notes	
No. of items	Paid in by Marian Walker	£2 coin	
		£1 coin	
		Other coin	
		Total cash	
		Cheques, POs	
	49-20-40 39287594 78	£	

Task 2.15

Which one of the following documents is used to accompany goods and, when provided in duplicate, acts as proof of delivery?

✓

Sales order acknowledgement	
Advice note	
Delivery note	
Despatch note	

Task 2.16

What documents would The Garden Warehouse send out in each of the following circumstances?

✓

(a) To accompany a cheque in payment of an account	Statement of account	
	Remittance advice	
	Credit note	
	Invoice	
	Confirmation order	
(b) To list unpaid invoices and ask for payment each month	Statement of account	
	Remittance advice	
	Credit note	
	Invoice	
	Confirmation order	

(c)	To correct an overcharge on	Statement of account	
	an invoice issued	Remittance advice	
		Credit note	
		Invoice	
		Confirmation order	

Task 2.17

(a) This is a summary of transactions with suppliers during the month of June.

Show whether each entry will be a debit or credit in the Purchases ledger control account.

Debit/Credit

Balance of creditors at 1 June 2005	£53,386	
Goods bought on credit	£20,500	
Money paid to credit suppliers	£16,193	
Discounts received	£380	
Goods returned to credit suppliers	£600	

(b) What will be the balance brought down on 1 July on the above account?

Dr	£89,099	
Cr	£89,099	
Dr	£56,713	
Cr	£56,713	✓
Dr	£57,473	
Cr	£57,473	

(c) The following closing credit balances were in the Subsidiary (purchases) ledger on 30 June.

Reconcile the balances shown below with the Purchases ledger control account balance you have calculated in part (b).

	£
Gardens Unlimited	15,620
P Lower	1,695
L Brown	23,000
White Brothers	16,200
Hoe and Dig	578

	£
Purchase ledger control account balance as at 30 June 2005	
Total of Subsidiary (purchases) ledger accounts as at 30 June 2005	
Difference	

UNIT 30 : WORKBOOK

(d) What may have caused the difference you calculated in part (c)?

	✓
Goods returned have been omitted from Subsidiary (purchases) ledger	
Discounts received have been omitted from the Subsidiary (purchases) ledger	
Goods returned have been entered twice in the Subsidiary (purchases) ledger	
Discounts received have been entered twice in the Subsidiary (purchases) ledger	

Task 2.18

On 28 June The Garden Warehouse received the following bank statement as at 24 June.

MIDDLE BANK plc
12 High Street, Droitwich, WR15 7LW

To: The Garden Warehouse   Account No: 867287234   24 June 2005

STATEMENT OF ACCOUNT

Date 2005	Details	Paid out £	Paid in £	Balance £	Tick
1 June	Balance b/f			15,619 C	
6 June	Cheque 008301	2,650		12,969 C	
8 June	Cheque 008302	1,986		10,983 C	
10 June	Bank Giro Credit A Parker		550	11,533 C	
10 June	Bank Giro Credit L Westwood		6,140	17,673 C	
13 June	Cheque 008303	8,432		9,241 C	
15 June	Direct Debit Droitwich CC	100		9,141 C	
20 June	Direct Debit Cranston Insurance	250		8,891 C	
22 June	Overdraft facility fee	50		8,841 C	
22 June	Bank charges	16		8,825 C	
22 June	Bank interest		26	8,851 C	

D = Debit C = Credit

The Cash book as at 28 June 2005 is shown below.

Cash book

Date 2005	Details	Tick	Bank £	Date 2005	Cheque Number	Details	Tick	Bank £
1 June	Balance b/f		15,619	1 June	008301	Portman Brothers		2,650
10 June	A Parker		550	1 June	008302	Tether & Tie		1,986
10 June	L Westwood		6,140	6 June	008303	D Price		8,432
15 June	CCC Ltd		1,260	6 June	008304	Mundon Ltd		1,407
22 June	B Williams		142	22 June	008305	Hackett Ltd		350
				28 June		Balance c/d		
29 June	Balance b/d							

(a) Check the items on the bank statement against the items in the cash book, highlighting each item that matches.

(b) Enter any items in the cash book as needed.

(c) Total the cash book and clearly show the balance carried down at 28 June (closing balance) and brought down at 29 June (opening balance).

Note: You do not need to adjust the accounts in Section 1.

(d) Now complete the bank reconciliation statement as at 28 June.

Do not make any entries in the shaded boxes.

Bank reconciliation statement as at 28 June 2005		
Balance per bank statement		£
Add:		
	Name:	£
	Name:	£
Total to add		
Less:		
	Name:	£
	Name:	£
Total to subtract		£
Balance as per cash book		£

Task 2.19

This is an order from a customer of The Garden Warehouse. The goods were delivered on 1 July and all documentation is in order. The discount policy is to offer a 2% settlement discount on all orders over £1,000 excluding VAT.

TGL Limited
The Avenue, Broadway, West Midlands, B84 3LD

Order No: 290

To: The Garden Warehouse

Date: 17 June 2005

Please supply 500 heavy duty gardening forks code F60
at £12 each plus VAT as per your quotation.

Prepare the sales invoice below.

The Garden Warehouse
2a Lower Parade
Droitwich
Worcestershire, WR16 8IS
VAT Registration No. 387 2987 00

Invoice No: 853

Your Order No:

Date:

Quantity	Description	Product code	Net £	VAT £	Total £

2% settlement discount for payment within 7 days

UNIT 30 : WORKBOOK

Task 2.20

On 1 July Swindon Spades, a customer of The Garden Warehouse, has an amount outstanding in the subsidiary ledger of £3,525. This relates to invoice number 110 dated 16 January 2005.

Draft a letter from Marian Walker requesting payment of the overdue account by return.

**The Garden Warehouse
2a Lower Parade
Droitwich
Worcestershire, WR16 81S**

Swindon Spades
18 High Street
Swindon
FR3 1JH

MOCK SIMULATION 1
ANSWER BOOKLET

UNIT 30 : WORKBOOK

PART ONE

TASK 1

INVOICE　　　　　　　　　　　　　　　　　　NO:

BRAMALL TOYS LTD
BLADES PARADE, BURSLEM ROAD, SHEFFIELD S2 4SV
Telephone: 0114 273 5895

To:

Date / tax point :
Customer Order No :

Quantity	Description	Item Code	Unit Price £	Trade discount £	Total amount £

Total goods	
VAT @ 17½%	
Total Due	

Terms: net, 30 days　　　　　　　VAT registration number 643 782 692

INVOICE　　　　　　　　　　　　　　　　　　NO:

BRAMALL TOYS LTD
BLADES PARADE, BURSLEM ROAD, SHEFFIELD S2 4SV
Telephone: 0114 273 5895

To:

Date / tax point :
Customer Order No :

Quantity	Description	Item Code	Unit Price £	Trade discount £	Total amount £

Total goods	
VAT @ 17½%	
Total Due	

Terms: net, 30 days　　　　　　　VAT registration number 643 782 692

INVOICE

BRAMALL TOYS LTD
BLADES PARADE, BURSLEM ROAD, SHEFFIELD S2 4SV
Telephone: 0114 273 5895

NO:

To:

Date / tax point :
Customer Order No :

Quantity	Description	Item Code	Unit Price £	Trade discount £	Total amount £

Total goods	
VAT @ 17½%	
Total Due	

Terms: net, 30 days

VAT registration number 643 782 692

INVOICE

BRAMALL TOYS LTD
BLADES PARADE, BURSLEM ROAD, SHEFFIELD S2 4SV
Telephone: 0114 273 5895

NO:

To:

Date / tax point :
Customer Order No :

Quantity	Description	Item Code	Unit Price £	Trade discount £	Total amount £

Total goods	
VAT @ 17½%	
Total Due	

Terms: net, 30 days

VAT registration number 643 782 692

UNIT 30 : WORKBOOK

INVOICE NO:

BRAMALL TOYS LTD
BLADES PARADE, BURSLEM ROAD, SHEFFIELD S2 4SV
Telephone: 0114 273 5895

To:

Date / tax point :
Customer Order No :

Quantity	Description	Item Code	Unit Price £	Trade discount £	Total amount £

Total goods	
VAT @ 17½%	
Total Due	

Terms: net, 30 days

VAT registration number 643 782 692

INVOICE NO:

BRAMALL TOYS LTD
BLADES PARADE, BURSLEM ROAD, SHEFFIELD S2 4SV
Telephone: 0114 273 5895

To:

Date / tax point :
Customer Order No :

Quantity	Description	Item Code	Unit Price £	Trade discount £	Total amount £

Total goods	
VAT @ 17½%	
Total Due	

Terms: net, 30 days

VAT registration number 643 782 692

MOCK SIMULATION 1 : **ANSWER BOOKLET**

INVOICE					NO:

BRAMALL TOYS LTD
BLADES PARADE, BURSLEM ROAD, SHEFFIELD S2 4SV
Telephone: 0114 273 5895

To:

Date / tax point :
Customer Order No :

Quantity	Description	Item Code	Unit Price £	Trade discount £	Total amount £

Total goods	
VAT @ 17½%	
Total Due	

Terms: net, 30 days

VAT registration number 643 782 692

INVOICE					NO:

BRAMALL TOYS LTD
BLADES PARADE, BURSLEM ROAD, SHEFFIELD S2 4SV
Telephone: 0114 273 5895

To:

Date / tax point :
Customer Order No :

Quantity	Description	Item Code	Unit Price £	Trade discount £	Total amount £

Total goods	
VAT @ 17½%	
Total Due	

Terms: net, 30 days

VAT registration number 643 782 692

UNIT 30 : WORKBOOK

TASK 2

CREDIT NOTE					**NO:**
BRAMALL TOYS LTD					
BLADES PARADE, BURSLEM ROAD, SHEFFIELD S2 4SV					
Telephone: 0114 273 5895					

To:

Date / tax point :

Quantity	Description	Item Code	Unit Price £	Trade discount £	Total amount £

REASON FOR CREDIT

Total goods	
VAT @ 17½%	
Total Credit Due	

VAT registration number 643 782 692

CREDIT NOTE					**NO:**
BRAMALL TOYS LTD					
BLADES PARADE, BURSLEM ROAD, SHEFFIELD S2 4SV					
Telephone: 0114 273 5895					

To:

Date / tax point :

Quantity	Description	Item Code	Unit Price £	Trade discount £	Total amount £

REASON FOR CREDIT

Total goods	
VAT @ 17½%	
Total Credit Due	

VAT registration number 643 782 692

MOCK SIMULATION 1 : **ANSWER BOOKLET**

CREDIT NOTE NO:

BRAMALL TOYS LTD
BLADES PARADE, BURSLEM ROAD, SHEFFIELD S2 4SV
Telephone: 0114 273 5895

To:

Date / tax point :

Quantity	Description	Item Code	Unit Price £	Trade discount £	Total amount £

REASON FOR CREDIT

Total goods	
VAT @ 17½%	
Total Credit Due	

VAT registration number 643 782 692

CREDIT NOTE NO:

BRAMALL TOYS LTD
BLADES PARADE, BURSLEM ROAD, SHEFFIELD S2 4SV
Telephone: 0114 273 5895

To:

Date / tax point :

Quantity	Description	Item Code	Unit Price £	Trade discount £	Total amount £

REASON FOR CREDIT

Total goods	
VAT @ 17½%	
Total Credit Due	

VAT registration number 643 782 692

UNIT 30 : WORKBOOK

TASK 2, CONTINUED

Details of goods returned note	Action

MOCK SIMULATION 1 : **ANSWER BOOKLET**

TASK 3

SALES DAY BOOK

SDB 73

Date	Invoice	Customer	Total	VAT	Pre-school toys	School-age toys
20X1			£	£	£	£
17 Nov	1318	Bigston Ltd	243.75	36.30	114.70	92.75
17 Nov	1319	Dalglish Ltd	490.62	73.07	204.65	212.90
18 Nov	1320	Hodges & Co	411.60	61.30	28.90	321.40
19 Nov	1321	Whitehouse Stores Ltd	631.38	94.03	346.75	190.60
19 Nov	1322	Blake Ltd	340.69	50.74	187.50	102.45
19 Nov	1323	Walker plc	519.87	77.42	301.55	140.90
20 Nov	1324	Angell Flo Ltd	182.88	27.23	55.60	100.05

SALES RETURNS DAY BOOK

SRDB 17

Date	Credit Note	Customer	Total	VAT	Pre-school toys	School-age toys
20X1			£	£	£	£
17 Nov	510	Whitehouse Stores Ltd	54.40	8.10	46.30	
19 Nov	511	Walker plc	67.91	10.11		57.80
20 Nov	512	Hutchison Ltd	71.85	10.70	42.20	18.95

KAPLAN PUBLISHING

UNIT 30 : WORKBOOK

PART TWO

TASK 4

Document number	Action
1	
2	
3	
4	
5	
6	
7	
8	
9	
10	

MOCK SIMULATION 1 : **ANSWER BOOKLET**

TASK 5

Bank Giro Credit

Date _____

Credit _____

£50 Notes		
£20 Notes		
£10 Notes		
£5 Notes		
£2, £1		
50p		
20p		
10p, 5p		
2p, 1p		
Total cash		
Cheques, etc *see over*		
£		

Date _____
Cashier's stamp and initials

Code no 25 - 46 - 70

Bank   Wadworth Bank Ltd

Branch _____

Credit   Bramall Toys Ltd

Account no   21758391

No of cheques

Paid in by _____

£50 Notes		
£20 Notes		
£10 Notes		
£5 Notes		
£2, £1		
50p		
20p		
10p, 5p		
2p, 1p		
Total cash		
Cheques, etc *see over*		
£		

Cheques, etc

	£	Brought forward £		
Carried forward £		Carried over £		

Counterfoil

Carried over £

UNIT 30 : WORKBOOK

TASK 5, CONTINUED

HAVE YOU IMPRINTED THE SUMMARY WITH YOUR RETAILER'S CARD?

BANK Processing (White) copy of Summary with your vouchers in correct order:
1. SUMMARY
2. SALES VOUCHERS
3. REFUND VOUCHERS

KEEP Retailer's copies (Blue & Yellow)
NO MORE THAN 200 Vouchers to each Summary.
DO NOT USE Staples, Pins, Paper Clips

WADSWORTH BANK

BANKING SUMMARY

	ITEMS	AMOUNT
SALES VOUCHERS (LISTED OVERLEAF)		
LESS REFUND VOUCHERS		
DATE	TOTAL £	

SUMMARY – RETAILER'S COPY

RETAILER'S SIGNATURE

Complete this summary for every deposit of sales vouchers and enter the total on your normal current account paying-in slip

	£	p
1		
2		
3		
4		
5		
6		
7		
8		
9		
10		
11		
12		
13		
14		
15		
16		
17		
18		
19		
20		
Total		

Carried overleaf

DO NOT TICK OR MAKE ANY MARKS OUTSIDE THE LISTING AREA

MOCK SIMULATION 1 : **ANSWER BOOKLET**

TASK 6

	Cash Book Receipts					41
Date	Narrative	Total	Debtors	Cash Sales	VAT	Discount allowed
18 Nov	Hutchison Ltd	152.81				
18 Nov	White & Veart	526.74				
19 Nov	Bigston Ltd	82.53				
19 Nov	Walker plc	272.19				

PART THREE
TASKS 7 AND 8

SUBSIDIARY (SALES) LEDGER ACCOUNTS

Account: Angell Flo Ltd

Debit   Credit

Date 20X1	Details	Amount £	Date 20X1	Details	Amount £
14 Nov	Balance b/f	691.29			

Account: Bigston Ltd

Debit			Credit		
Date 20X1	Details	Amount £	Date 20X1	Details	Amount £
14 Nov	Balance b/f	274.04		

Account: Blake Ltd

Debit			Credit		
Date 20X1	Details	Amount £	Date 20X1	Details	Amount £
14 Nov	Balance b/f	577.03		

Account: Dalglish Ltd

Debit			Credit		
Date 20X1	Details	Amount £	Date 20X1	Details	Amount £
14 Nov	Balance b/f	1,521.11		

Account: Hodges & Co

Debit			Credit		
Date 20X1	Details	Amount £	Date 20X1	Details	Amount £
14 Nov	Balance b/f	546.62		

MOCK SIMULATION 1 : **ANSWER BOOKLET**

Account: Hutchison Ltd

Debit			Credit		
Date 20X1	Details	Amount £	Date 20X1	Details	Amount £
14 Nov	Balance b/f	426.89			

Account: Walker plc

Debit			Credit		
Date 20X1	Details	Amount £	Date 20X1	Details	Amount £
14 Nov	Balance b/f	522.74			

Account: White & Veart

Debit			Credit		
Date 20X1	Details	Amount £	Date 20X1	Details	Amount £
14 Nov	Balance b/f	926.38			

Account: Whitehouse Stores Ltd

Debit			Credit		
Date 20X1	Details	Amount £	Date 20X1	Details	Amount £
14 Nov	Balance b/f	641.56			

UNIT 30 : WORKBOOK

TASK 9

MAIN LEDGER ACCOUNTS

Account: Sales ledger control

Debit			Credit		
Date 20X1	Details	Amount £	Date 20X1	Details	Amount £
14 Nov	Balance b/f	14,890.75			

Account: VAT

Debit			Credit		
Date 20X1	Details	Amount £	Date 20X1	Details	Amount £
			14 Nov	Balance b/f	2,533.40

Account: Sales: pre-school toys

Debit			Credit		
Date 20X1	Details	Amount £	Date 20X1	Details	Amount £
			14 Nov	Balance b/f	52,147.60

Account: Sales returns: pre-school toys

Debit			Credit		
Date 20X1	Details	Amount £	Date 20X1	Details	Amount £
14 Nov	Balance b/f Sales	2,430.91			

MOCK SIMULATION 1 : **ANSWER BOOKLET**

Account: Sales: school-age toys

Debit | | | Credit | | |

Date 20X1	Details	Amount £	Date 20X1	Details	Amount £
			14 Nov	Balance b/f Sales	37,182.58

Account: Sales returns: school-age toys

Debit | | | Credit | | |

Date 20X1	Details	Amount £	Date 20X1	Details	Amount £
14 Nov	Balance b/f Sales	1,724.49			

MOCK SIMULATION 2
ANSWER BOOKLET

UNIT 30 : WORKBOOK

PART ONE

TASK 1

Petty Cash Voucher		
Folio _____		
Date _____		
	AMOUNT	
For what required	£	p
Stationery	11	10
	11	10
Signature Adam Haynes		
Passed by		

Petty Cash Voucher		
Folio _____		
Date _____		
	AMOUNT	
For what required	£	p
Stationery	6	95
	6	95
Signature Adam Haynes		
Passed by		

Petty Cash Voucher		
Folio _____		
Date _____		
	AMOUNT	
For what required	£	p
Stationery	4	94
	4	94
Signature Adam Haynes		
Passed by		

Petty Cash Voucher		
Folio _____		
Date _____		
	AMOUNT	
For what required	£	p
Stationery	7	33
	7	33
Signature Adam Haynes		
Passed by		

MOCK SIMULATION 2 : **ANSWER BOOKLET**

Petty Cash Voucher		
Folio _____		
Date _____		
	AMOUNT	
For what required	£	p
Stationery	15	35
	15	35
Signature Adam Haynes		
Passed by		

Petty Cash Voucher		
Folio _____		
Date _____		
	AMOUNT	
For what required	£	p
Stationery	12	35
	12	35
Signature Jane Hawkins		
Passed by		

Petty Cash Voucher		
Folio _____		
Date _____		
	AMOUNT	
For what required	£	p
Stamps	5	25
	5	25
Signature Jane Hawkins		
Passed by		

Petty Cash Voucher		
Folio _____		
Date _____		
	AMOUNT	
For what required	£	p
Stamps	3	94
	3	94
Signature Jane Hawkins		
Passed by		

Petty Cash Voucher		
Folio _____		
Date _____		
	AMOUNT	
For what required	£	p
Stamps	0	76
	0	76
Signature Jane Hawkins		
Passed by		

Petty Cash Voucher		
Folio _____		
Date _____		
	AMOUNT	
For what required	£	p
Taxi fare (meeting with auditors)	5	20
	5	20
Signature Gillian Russell		
Passed by		

KAPLAN PUBLISHING

UNIT 30 : WORKBOOK

Petty Cash Voucher

Folio _____

Date _____

For what required	AMOUNT	
	£	p
Taxi fare (meeting with supplier)	6	10
	6	10

Signature   *Ben Thornley*

Passed by

TASK 1, CONTINUED

MEMORANDUM OF DISCREPANCIES
FOR LETTER TO GILLIAN RUSSELL

Details of claim	Action

MOCK SIMULATION 2 : **ANSWER BOOKLET**

TASK 2

PETTY CASH BOOK								PCB22
Receipts £	Date 20X1	Details	Voucher	Total £	VAT £	Travel £	Stationery £	Postage £
100.00	31-Oct	Balance b/d						

RECONCILIATION OF PETTY CASH

Petty Cash Book

£

Opening balance of imprest
Payments

Closing balance

Cash counted

UNIT 30 : WORKBOOK

PART TWO

TASK 4

REMITTANCE ADVICE

From: Seamer Retail Limited
        37 Cain Road
        Scarborough
        YO12 4HF

To:

Date:

Details	Amount	
	£	p
Cheque no enclosed		

In case of query, please contact

Date

Payee

£

305082

WADSWORTH BANK PLC
Chambers Street, Scarborough, YO12 3NZ

25–46–70

_____ 20 ___

Pay   or order

£

For Seamer Retail Ltd

305082   25 - 46 - 70   21758391

MOCK SIMULATION 2 : **ANSWER BOOKLET**

REMITTANCE ADVICE	
From: **Seamer Retail Limited** **37 Cain Road** **Scarborough** **YO12 4HF**	
To:	
Date:	

Details	Amount	
	£	p
Cheque no enclosed		

In case of query, please contact

Date
_____

Payee
_____
_____
_____

£ _____

305083

WADSWORTH BANK PLC
Chambers Street, Scarborough, YO12 3NZ

25–46–70

_____ 20____

Pay   or order

                                                                      £

                                                              For Seamer Retail Ltd

305083   25 - 46 - 70   21758391   _____

KAPLAN PUBLISHING

UNIT 30 : WORKBOOK

REMITTANCE ADVICE

From: **Seamer Retail Limited**
37 Cain Road
Scarborough
YO12 4HF

To:

Date:

Details	Amount £	p
Cheque no enclosed		

In case of query, please contact

Date

Payee

£

305084

WADSWORTH BANK PLC
Chambers Street, Scarborough, YO12 3NZ

25–46–70

20

Pay   or order

£

For Seamer Retail Ltd

305084   25 - 46 - 70   21758391

MOCK SIMULATION 2 : **ANSWER BOOKLET**

REMITTANCE ADVICE

From: **Seamer Retail Limited**
37 Cain Road
Scarborough
YO12 4HF

To:

Date:

Details	Amount	
	£	p
Cheque no enclosed		

In case of query, please contact

Date

Payee

£

305085

WADSWORTH BANK PLC
Chambers Street, Scarborough, YO12 3NZ

25–46–70

_____ 20 ___

Pay   or order

£

For Seamer Retail Ltd

305085   25 - 46 - 70   21758391

UNIT 30 : WORKBOOK

REMITTANCE ADVICE

From: Seamer Retail Limited
       37 Cain Road
       Scarborough
       YO12 4HF

To:

Date:

Details	Amount £	p
Cheque no enclosed		

In case of query, please contact

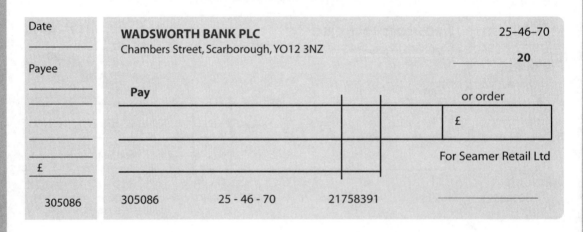

MOCK SIMULATION 2 : **ANSWER BOOKLET**

TASK 5

CASH BOOK PAYMENTS

CPB 53

Date 20X1	Payee/details	Cheque no	Total £	VAT £	Creditors £	Discount Received £	Sundry £

TASK 6

MAIN LEDGER

Account: Postage

Debit / Credit

Date 20X1	Details	Amount £	Date 20X1	Details	Amount £
31-Oct	Bal b/f	213.76			

Account: Stationery

Debit / Credit

Date 20X1	Details	Amount £	Date 20X1	Details	Amount £
31-Oct	Bal b/f	543.09			

Account: Travel

Debit			Credit		
Date 20X1	Details	Amount £	Date 20X1	Details	Amount £
31-Oct	Bal b/f	513.88			

Account: Purchase ledger control

Debit			Credit		
Date 20X1	Details	Amount £	Date 20X1	Details	Amount £
			31-Oct	Bal b/f	28,996.21

Account: VAT

Debit			Credit		
Date 20X1	Details	Amount £	Date 20X1	Details	Amount £
			31-Oct	Bal b/f	2,499.04

Account: Cash sales

Debit			Credit		
Date 20X1	Details	Amount £	Date 20X1	Details	Amount £
			31-Oct	Bal b/f	51,235.99

MOCK SIMULATION 2 : ANSWER BOOKLET

Account: Discount received

Debit			Credit		
Date 20X1	Details	Amount £	Date 20X1	Details	Amount £
			31-Oct	Bal b/f	147.39

SUBSIDIARY (PURCHASES) LEDGER

Account: Allen and Banks

Debit			Credit		
Date 20X1	Details	Amount £	Date 20X1	Details	Amount £
			31-Oct	Bal b/f	1,152.90

Account: Baxley Limited

Debit			Credit		
Date 20X1	Details	Amount £	Date 20X1	Details	Amount £
			31-Oct	Bal b/f	3,012.75

Account: Harborne Limited

Debit			Credit		
Date 20X1	Details	Amount £	Date 20X1	Details	Amount £
			31-Oct	Bal b/f	3,225.67

UNIT 30 : WORKBOOK

Account: **Hurley Limited**

Debit			Credit		
Date 20X1	Details	Amount £	Date 20X1	Details	Amount £
			31-Oct	Bal b/f	961.44

Account: **Wallace Limited**

Debit			Credit		
Date 20X1	Details	Amount £	Date 20X1	Details	Amount £
			31-Oct	Bal b/f	546.08

PART THREE

TASK 7

MEMO

To:
From:
Subject:
Date:

MOCK SIMULATION 2 : **ANSWER BOOKLET**

MOCK SIMULATION 3
ANSWER BOOKLET

UNIT 30 : WORKBOOK

PART ONE

TASKS 1, 2 and 3

SUBSIDIARY (PURCHASES) LEDGER

Hadley Turf Supplies

Date	Details	Amount £	Date	Details	Amount £

Blackwood Nurseries

Date	Details	Amount £	Date	Details	Amount £

Lawnmower Repair Shop

Date	Details	Amount £	Date	Details	Amount £

Western Electricity

Date	Details	Amount £	Date	Details	Amount £

Other suppliers

Date	Details	Amount £	Date	Details	Amount £

MAIN LEDGER

Purchases

Date	Details	Amount £	Date	Details	Amount £

Purchases returns

Date	Details	Amount £	Date	Details	Amount £

Purchases (Creditors) ledger control

Date	Details	Amount £	Date	Details	Amount £

UNIT 30 : WORKBOOK

Sales

Date	Details	Amount £	Date	Details	Amount £

Sales (Debtors) ledger control

Date	Details	Amount £	Date	Details	Amount £

Heat and light

Date	Details	Amount £	Date	Details	Amount £

VAT

Date	Details	Amount £	Date	Details	Amount £

MOCK SIMULATION 3 : **ANSWER BOOKLET**

TASK 4

Reconciliation of Purchases ledger control account at 1 June 20X1.

List of creditors

Name	Amount £

Total

Adjustments

Revised total

Balance per control account

Adjustments

Revised total

UNIT 30 : WORKBOOK

TASK 5

Western Bank plc
Bradbury Way
Swinford LE1 8OU

Gregson Garden Services Limited
Account 86759485

STATEMENT OF ACCOUNT

Date 20X1	Details	Debit £	Credit £	Balance £
26 May	Balance b/f			8,070C
27 May	Cheque 111987	4,760		3,310C
28 May	Bank Giro Credit: Carter & Son		7,000	10,310C
28 May	Cheque 111988	2,198		8,112C
31 May	Bank charges	55		8,057C
31 May	Direct Debit: Contract Cleaning	235		7,822C
31 May	Credit		1,880	9,702C

D = Debit C = Credit

Cash Book

20X1		£	20X1		£
20 May	Balance b/d	8,070	21 May	Patio Pavers	4,760
26 May	B Bradley	1,880	22 May	L Briggs	2,198
31 May	Park Maintenance	2,170	31 May	T Brown	1,500

MOCK SIMULATION 3 : **ANSWER BOOKLET**

PART 2

TASK 6

VAT

£	£

TASK 7

Sales ledger control account

£	£

TASK 8

Sportsworld Ltd

£	£

Royal Sports Ltd

£	£

UNIT 30 : WORKBOOK

TASK 9

List of updated balances at the end of the day

	Debit balances £	Credit balances £
Customers:		
Barnes Department Stores		
Sportsworld Ltd		
Birmingham Sports		
Hi-sport		
Keysports		
Suppliers:		
Royal Sports Ltd		
Leisurewear UK Ltd		
Sales		
Purchases		
Sales returns		
Purchases returns		
Bank		
VAT		
Bad debts		
Other debit balances	486,775	
Other credit balances		271,943
Totals		

KEY TECHNIQUES ANSWERS

Chapter 1
Double entry bookkeeping – introduction

▲ ACTIVITY 1

(a) Opening capital

		£		£
Assets	Cash	5,000	Capital	5,000

(b) Cash purchase

		£		£
Assets	Stock	500	Capital	5,000
	Cash (5,000 – 500)	4,500		
		5,000		5,000

(c) Credit purchase

		£		£
Assets	Stock (500 + (5 x 200))	1,500	Capital	5,000
	Cash	4,500		
		6,000		
Liabilities	Creditors	(1,000)		
		5,000		5,000

(d) Cash sale

		£		£
Assets	Stock (1,500 – 500)	1,000	Capital	5,000
	Cash (4,500 + 750)	5,250	Profit (750 – 500)	250
		6,250		
	Liabilities Creditors	(1,000)		
		5,250		5,250

(e) Cash sale

		£		£
Assets	Stock (1,000 – 800)	200	Capital	5,000
	Debtors	1,200	Profit (250 + 1,200 – 800)	650
	Cash	5,250		
		6,650		
Liabilities	Creditors	(1,000)		
		5,650		5,650

KEY TECHNIQUES : **ANSWERS**

(f) **Rent payment**

		£		£
Assets	Stock	200	Capital	5,000
	Debtors	1,200	Profit (650 – 250)	400
	Cash (5,250 – 250)	5,000		
		6,400		
Liabilities	Creditors	(1,000)		
		5,400		5,400

(g) **Drawings**

		£		£
Assets	Stock	200	Capital	5,000
	Debtors	1,200	Profit	400
	Cash (5,000 – 100)	4,900		
		6,300	Drawings	(100)
Liabilities	Creditors	(1,000)		
		5,300		5,300

(h) **Sundry income**

		£		£
Assets	Stock	200	Capital	5,000
	Debtors (1,200 + 50)	1,250	Profit (400 + 50)	450
	Cash	4,900		
		6,350	Drawings	(100)
Liabilities	Creditors	(1,000)		
		5,350		5,350

(i) **Payment to creditor**

		£		£
Assets	Stock	200	Capital	5,000
	Debtors	1,250	Profit	450
	Cash (4,900 – 500)	4,400		
		5,850	Drawings	(100)
Liabilities	Creditors (1,000 – 500)	(500)		
		5,350		5,350

(j) **Receipt from debtor**

		£		£
Assets	Stock	200	Capital	5,000
	Debtors (1,250 – 1,200)	50	Profit	450
	Cash (4,400 + 1,200)	5,600		
		5,850	Drawings	(100)
Liabilities	Creditors	(500)		
		5,350		5,350

UNIT 30 : WORKBOOK

(k) Purchase of van

		£		£
Assets	Van	4,000	Capital	5,000
	Stock	200	Profit	450
	Debtors	50		
	Cash (5,600 – 4,000)	1,600		5,450
		5,850	Drawings	(100)
Liabilities	Creditors	(500)		
		5,350		5,350

(l) Telephone bill

		£		£
Assets	Van	4,000	Capital	5,000
	Stock	200	Profit (450 – 150)	300
	Debtors	50		
	Cash	1,600		5,300
		5,850	Drawings	(100)
Liabilities	Creditors (500 + 150)	(650)		
		5,200		5,200

△ ACTIVITY 2

Accounting equation at 31 January 20X6

		£		£
Assets	Display equipment	50	Capital	3,000
	Stocks of sports equipment (W1)	2,000	Profit (balancing figure)	230
	Debtors	30		3,230
	Cash (W2)	2,500		
		4,580		
Liabilities	Creditors	1,500	Drawings	150
		3,080		3,080

WORKINGS

(1) Stock

	£
Purchased 10 January (½ x £1,000)	500
Purchased 31 January	1,500
	2,000

KEY TECHNIQUES : ANSWERS

(2) Cash

		£	£
Receipts	Capital paid in		3,000
	From customers		800
			3,800
Payments	Rent	100	
	Suppliers of stock	1,000	
	Suppliers of display equipment	50	
	Drawings	150	
			(1,300)
Balance at 31 January			2,500

Chapter 2
Ledger accounting

△ ACTIVITY 3

Bank

		£			£
(a)	Capital	4,000	(b)	Computer	1,000
(d)	Sales	800	(c)	Rent	400

Capital

		£			£
			(a)	Bank	4,000

Rent

		£		£
(c)	Bank	400		

Sales

		£			£
			(d)	Bank	800

Computers

		£		£
(b) Bank		1,000		

UNIT 30 : WORKBOOK

△ ACTIVITY 4

Transaction	Debit		Credit	
	Account	Reason	Account	Reason
(a) £4,000 capital	Bank	Cash paid into the bank - an asset	Capital	Cash paid in by owner – a liability
(b) Computer £1,000	Computer	Increase in assets	Bank	Cash paid out of the bank – a reduction in the value of the asset
(c) Rent £400	Rent	An expense	Bank	Cash paid out of the bank – a reduction in the value of the asset
(d) Consultancy £800	Bank	Cash paid into the bank – an asset	Sales	Increase in income

△ ACTIVITY 5

Bank

		£			£
(a)	Capital	5,000	(b)	Purchases	800
(e)	Sales	600	(c)	Rent	500
(f)	Sales	700	(d)	Van	2,000
			(g)	Purchases	1,000
			(h)	Stationery	200
			(i)	Drawings	500

Purchases

		£			£
(b)	Bank	800			
(g)	Bank	1,000			

Capital

		£			£
			(a)	Bank	5,000

Rent

		£			£
(c)	Bank	500			

KEY TECHNIQUES : **ANSWERS**

Van

	£			£
(d) Bank	2,000			

Sales

	£			£
		(e)	Bank	600
		(f)	Bank	700

Stationery

	£		£
(h) Bank	200		

Drawings

	£		£
(i) Bank	500		

△ ACTIVITY 6

Capital

	£			£
		(a)	Bank	4,000

Purchases

	£		£
(b) Bank	700		
(g) Bank	1,200		

Entertainment

	£		£
(c) Bank	300		

Computers

	£		£
(d) Bank	3,000		

Sales

	£			£
		(e)	Bank	1,500

Drawings

	£		£
(f) Bank	500		

Telephone

		£			£
(h)	Bank	600	(i)	Bank	200

Stationery

		£			£
(j)	Bank	157			

Bank

		£			£
(a)	Capital	4,000	(b)	Purchases	700
(e)	Sales	1,500	(c)	Entertainment	300
(i)	Telephone	200	(d)	Computers	3,000
			(f)	Drawings	500
			(g)	Purchases	1,200
			(h)	Telephone	600
			(j)	Stationery	157

ACTIVITY 7

Capital

		£			£
			(a)	Bank	2,000

Purchases

		£			£
(b)	Bank	1,000			
(f)	Bank	1,000			

Van

		£			£
(c)	Bank	900			

Sales

		£			£
			(d)	Bank	2,500

Consultancy services

		£			£
			(e)	Bank	3,000

Stationery

		£			£
(g)	Bank	260	(j)	Bank	100

KEY TECHNIQUES : ANSWERS

Rent

		£		£
(h)	Bank	750		

Wages

		£		£
(i)	Bank	600		

Bank

		£			£
(a)	Capital	2,000	(b)	Purchases	1,000
(d)	Sales	2,500	(c)	Van	900
(e)	Consultancy	3,000	(f)	Purchases	1,000
(j)	Stationery	100	(g)	Stationery	260
			(h)	Rent	750
			(i)	Wages	600

△ ACTIVITY 8

Sales

	£		£
		B	1,000
		C	90

B

	£		£
Sales	1,000	Bank	500

C

	£		£
Sales	90	Bank	90

Bank

	£		£
B	500		
C	90		

UNIT 30 : WORKBOOK

▲ ACTIVITY 9

Purchases

	£		£
Y	600		
Z	750		

Y

	£		£
Bank	300	Purchases	600

Z

	£		£
Bank	500	Purchases	750

Bank

	£		£
		Y	300
		Z	500

Chapter 3
Balancing the ledger accounts

▲ ACTIVITY 10

Bank

	£		£
Capital	10,000	Computer	1,000
Sales	2,000	Telephone	567
Sales	3,000	Rent	1,500
Sales	2,000	Rates	125
		Stationery	247
		Petrol	49
		Purchases	2,500
		Drawings	500
		Petrol	42
Sub-total	17,000	Sub-total	6,530
		Balance c/d	10,470
	17,000		17,000
Balance b/d	10,470		

KEY TECHNIQUES : **ANSWERS**

△ ACTIVITY 11

Bank

	£		£
Capital	5,000	Purchases	850
Sales	1,000	Fixtures	560
Sales	876	Van	1,500
Rent rebate	560	Rent	1,300
Sales	1,370	Rates	360
		Telephone	220
		Stationery	120
		Petrol	48
		Car repairs	167
Sub-total	8,806	Sub-total	5,125
		Balance c/d	3,681
	8,806		8,806
Balance b/d	3,681		

△ ACTIVITY 12

Bank

	£		£
Balance b/f	23,700	Drawings	4,000
Sales	2,300	Rent	570
Sales	1,700	Purchases	6,000
Debtors	4,700	Rates	500
		Salaries	3,600
		Car expenses	460
		Petrol	49
		Petrol	38
		Electricity	210
		Stationery	89
Sub-total	32,400	Sub-total	15,516
		Balance c/d	16,884
	32,400		32,400
Balance b/d	16,884		

△ ACTIVITY 13

	North	South	East	West	Total
Garden plants	253,865	27,598	315,634	109,521	706,618
Garden equipment	2,734,384	274,393	382,726	3,726,125	7,117,628
Consultancy	2,438,549	374,385	3,728,398	37,261	6,578,593
TOTAL	5,426,798	676,376	4,426,758	3,872,907	14,402,839

KAPLAN PUBLISHING

UNIT 30 : WORKBOOK

ACTIVITY 14

Date	Narrative	Folio	Total	Creditors	Stationery	Rent	Telephone	Postage	Fixed assets	Sundry
			35,800	23,894	678	4,563	5,675	456	456	78
			62,643	6,743					55,433	467
			58,547	56,432	654	675				786
			8,421	5,643	564		786	78	564	786
			11,147	675	89			675	765	8,943
			9,287	6,754	675		785	78	897	98
TOTAL			185,845	100,141	2,660	5,238	7,246	1,287	58,115	11,158

Chapter 4
Credit sales – discounts and VAT

ACTIVITY 15

(a) VAT = £140.00 x 17.5% = £24.50
(b) VAT = £560.00 x 17.5% = £98.00
(c) VAT = £780.00 x $\frac{17.5}{117.5}$ = £116.17
(d) VAT = £970.00 x $\frac{17.5}{117.5}$ = £144.46

ACTIVITY 16

(a) VAT = £(280 – (2% x 280)) x 17.5% = £48.02
(b) VAT = £(480 – (3% x 480)) x 17.5% = £81.48
(c) VAT = £(800 – (5% x 800)) x 17.5% = £133.00
(d) VAT = £(650 – (4% x 650)) x 17.5% = £109.20

KEY TECHNIQUES : **ANSWERS**

△ ACTIVITY 17

(a) B takes the settlement discount:

	£
Net price	600.00
VAT £(600 – (3% x 600)) x 17.5%	101.85
Invoice value	701.85

Amount paid by B:

	£
Invoice value	701.85
Less: 3% x 600	(18.00)
Amount paid	683.85

(b) B does not take the settlement discount:

	£
Net price	600.00
VAT £(600 – (3% x 600)) x 17.5%	101.85
Invoice value	701.85

If B does not take the settlement discount, B will pay the full £701.85.

△ ACTIVITY 18

(a) C takes the settlement discount:

	£
Net price	700.00
VAT £(700 – (5% x 700)) x 17.5%	116.37
Invoice value	816.37
Less: 5% discount = 700 x 5%	(35.00)
Amount paid by C	781.37

Sales

	£		£
		SLCA	700.00

SLCA

	£		£
Sales + VAT	816.37	Bank	781.37
		Discount allowed	35.00
	816.37		816.37

Bank

	£		£
SLCA	781.37		

KAPLAN PUBLISHING

VAT

	£		£
		SLCA	116.37

Discount allowed

	£		£
SLCA	35.00		

(b) C does not take the settlement discount:

	£
Invoice value (per (a))	816.37

As C does not take the settlement discount, he pays the full amount (£816.37).

Sales

	£		£
		SLCA	700.00

SLCA

	£		£
Sales + VAT	816.37	Bank	816.37

Bank

	£		£
SLCA	816.37		

VAT

	£		£
		SLCA	116.37

KEY TECHNIQUES : ANSWERS

Chapter 5
The sales day book – main and subsidiary ledgers

▲ ACTIVITY 19

Sales day book

Date	Invoice No	Customer name	Code	Total £	VAT £	Net £
20X1						
1/5	03466	Fraser & Co	SL14	151.19	22.51	128.68
	03467	Letterhead Ltd	SL03	303.03	45.13	257.90
2/5	03468	Jeliteen Traders	SL15	113.48	16.90	96.58
	CN0746	Garner & Co	SL12	(80.72)	(12.02)	(68.70)
3/5	03469	Harper Bros	SL22	315.07	46.92	268.15
	03470	Juniper Ltd	SL17	123.82	18.44	105.38
4/5	03471	H G Frank	SL30	346.23	51.56	294.67
	CN0747	Hill Traders	SL26	(138.27)	(20.59)	(117.68)
5/5	03472	Keller Assocs	SL07	129.93	19.35	110.58
				1,263.76	188.20	1,075.56

▲ ACTIVITY 20

Sales day book

Date	Invoice No	Customer name	Code	Total £	VAT £	01 £	02 £	03 £	04 £
18/4/X1	06116	B Z S Music	SL01	1,426.15	206.95		432.00		787.20
18/4/X1	06117	M T Retail	SL29	628.62	93.62	210.00			325.00
18/4/X1	06118	Harmer & Co	SL17	1,016.51	147.51		575.00	294.00	
				3,071.28	448.08	210.00	1,007.00	294.00	1,112.20

Note that when a trade discount has been deducted on the invoice in total it must be deducted from each type of sale when entering the figures in the analysed sales day book.

KAPLAN PUBLISHING

UNIT 30 : WORKBOOK

ACTIVITY 21

Sales day book

Date	Invoice No	Customer name	Code	Total £	VAT £	Maintenance £	Decorating £
01/5/X1	07891	Portman & Co	P2	162.83	23.83	139.00	
03/5/X1	07892	Stanton Assocs	S3	1,288.65	188.65		1,100.00
05/5/X1	07893	Boreham Bros	B7	277.30	41.30	106.00	130.00
				1,728.78	253.78	245.00	1,230.00

ACTIVITY 22

Sales day book

Date	Invoice No	Customer name	Code	Total £	VAT £	Group 01 £	Group 02 £
20X0							
1 Feb	61612	Worker Ltd	SL11	217.37	32.37	68.90	116.10
4 Feb	61613	P T Associates	SL04	122.38	18.22		104.16
5 Feb	61614	Paul Bros	SL13	289.27	43.08	106.19	140.00
8 Feb	61615	S D Partners	SL07	109.54	16.31	72.40	20.83
9 Feb	61616	Harper Ltd	SL08	399.97	59.57	160.18	180.22
11 Feb	C241	P T Associates	SL04	(23.68)	(3.52)		(20.16)
15 Feb	61617	Worker Ltd	SL11	144.26	21.48	50.60	72.18
17 Feb	61618	P T Associates	SL04	201.67	30.03	60.41	111.23
18 Feb	61619	Harper Ltd	SL08	345.15	51.40	110.15	183.60
22 Feb	C242	Paul Bros	SL13	(35.72)	(5.32)	(10.18)	(20.22)
25 Feb	61620	P T Associates	SL04	129.01	19.21	62.17	47.63
26 Feb	61621	S D Partners	SL07	56.58	8.42	48.16	
				1,955.80	291.25	728.98	935.57

KEY TECHNIQUES : ANSWERS

Main ledger accounts

Sales ledger control account

	£		£
28/2 SDB	1,955.80		

Sales account – 01

	£		£
		28/2 SDB	728.98

Sales account – 02

	£		£
		28/2 SDB	935.57

VAT account

	£		£
		28/2 SDB	291.25

Subsidiary ledger accounts

Worker Ltd — SL11

		£		£
1/2	SDB 61612	217.37		
15/2	SDB 61617	144.26		

P T Assocs — SL04

		£			£
4/2	SDB 61613	122.38	11/2	SDB C241	23.68
17/2	SDB 61618	201.67			
25/2	SDB 61620	129.01			

Paul Bros — SL13

		£			£
5/2	SDB 61614	289.27	22/2	SDB C242	35.72

S D Partners — SL07

		£		£
8/2	SDB 61615	109.54		
26/2	SDB 61621	56.58		

Harper Ltd — SL08

		£		£
9/2	SDB 61616	399.97		
18/2	SDB 61619	345.15		

UNIT 30 : WORKBOOK

▲ ACTIVITY 23

Main ledger accounts

Sales ledger control account

		£			£
			30/4	SRDB	140.19

Sales returns – 01

		£			£
30/4	SRDB	54.01			

Sales returns – 02

		£			£
30/4	SRDB	32.06			

Sales returns – 03

		£			£
30/4	SRDB	33.25			

VAT account

		£			£
30/4	SRDB	20.87			

Subsidiary ledger accounts

Gerard & Co   G01

		£			£
			7/4	SRDB 2114	34.36

Filmer Ltd   F02

		£			£
			15/4	SRDB 2115	44.92

T Harrison   H04

		£			£
			20/4	SRDB 2116	24.44

Rolls Ltd   R01

		£			£
			28/4	SRDB 2117	36.47

KEY TECHNIQUES : **ANSWERS**

Chapter 6
The analysed cash receipts book

△ ACTIVITY 24

(a) **Cash receipts book**

			Cash receipts book				
Date	Narrative	SL Code	Total £	VAT £	Debtors £	Cash sales £	Discount £
20X1							
28/4	G Heilbron	SL04	108.45		108.45		
	L Tessa	SL15	110.57		110.57		3.31
	J Dent	SL17	210.98		210.98		6.32
	F Trainer	SL21	97.60		97.60		
	A Winter	SL09	105.60		105.60		3.16
	Cash sales		265.08	39.48		225.60	
			898.28	39.48	633.20	225.60	12.79

(b) **Main ledger**

VAT account

	£			£
		28/4	CRB	39.48

Sales ledger control account

	£			£
		28/4	CRB	633.20
			CRB – discount	12.79

Sales account

	£			£
		28/4	CRB	225.60

Discount allowed account

		£		£
28/4	CRB	12.79		

(c) **Subsidiary ledger**

G Heilbron SL04

	£			£
		28/4	CRB	108.45

L Tessa — SL15

	£			£
		28/4	CRB	110.57
			CRB – discount	3.31

J Dent — SL17

	£			£
		28/4	CRB	210.98
			CRB – discount	6.32

F Trainer — SL21

	£			£
		28/4	CRB	97.60

A Winter — SL09

	£			£
		28/4	CRB	105.60
			CRB – discount	3.16

(Note that the total of the 'Discount' column is not included in the cross-cast total of £1,449.50. The discounts allowed are entered into the cash receipts book on a memorandum basis; the total at the end of each period is posted to the sales ledger control account and to an expense account.)

△ ACTIVITY 25

(a)

Cash receipts book

Date	Narrative	SL Code	Total £	VAT £	Debtors £	Cash sales £	Discount £
20X1							
15/5	McCaul & Partners	M04	147.56		147.56		2.95
	Dunn Assocs	D02	264.08		264.08		
	P Martin	M02	167.45		167.45		
	F Little	L03	265.89		265.89		7.97
	D Raine	R01	158.02		158.02		3.95
	Cash sales		446.50	66.50		380.00	
			1,449.50	66.50	1,003.00	380.00	14.87

(Note that the total of the 'Discount' column is not included in the cross-cast total of £1,449.50. The discounts allowed are entered into the cash receipts book on a memorandum basis; the total at the end of each period is posted to the sales ledger control account and to an expense account.)

KEY TECHNIQUES : **ANSWERS**

(b) **Main ledger**

VAT account

	£			£
		15/5	CRB	66.50

Sales ledger control account

	£			£
		15/5	CRB	1,003.00
		15/5	CRB – discount	14.87

Sales account

	£			£
		15/5	CRB	380.00

Discount allowed

		£		£
15/5	CRB	14.87		

(c) **Subsidiary ledger**

McCaul & Partners

	£			£
		15/5	CRB	147.56
		15/5	CRB – discount	2.95

Dunn Associates

	£			£
		15/5	CRB	264.08

P Martin

	£			£
		15/5	CRB	167.45

F Little

	£			£
		15/5	CRB	265.89
		15/5	CRB – discount	7.97

D Raine

	£			£
		15/5	CRB	158.02
		15/5	CRB – discount	3.95

UNIT 30 : WORKBOOK

Chapter 7
Credit purchases – discounts and VAT

▲ ACTIVITY 26

(a) VAT = £400 × 17.5% = £70.00

(b) VAT = £650 × 17.5% = £113.75

(c) VAT = £425 × $\frac{17.5}{117.5}$ = £63.29

(d) VAT = £77 × $\frac{17.5}{117.5}$ = £11.46

▲ ACTIVITY 27

(a) VAT = £(850 − (3% × 850)) × 17.5% = £144.28

(b) VAT = £(600 − (5% × 600)) × 17.5% = £99.75

(c) VAT = £(325 − (2% × 325)) × 17.5% = £55.73

(d) VAT = £(57 − (4% × 57)) × 17.5% = £9.57

▲ ACTIVITY 28

Calculate the invoice value and amount paid by Z.

	£
Net price	600.00
VAT £(600 − (3% × 600)) × 17.5%	101.85
Invoice value	701.85
Less: Discount 3% × 600	(18.00)
Amount paid	683.85

Purchases

	£		£
PLCA	600.00		

PLCA

	£		£
Bank	683.85	Purchases + VAT	701.85
Discount	18.00		
	701.85		701.85

Bank

	£		£
		PLCA	683.85

KEY TECHNIQUES : ANSWERS

VAT

	£		£
PLCA	101.85		

Discount received

	£		£
		PLCA	18.00

Chapter 8
The purchases day book – main and subsidiary ledgers

▲ ACTIVITY 29

Purchases day book

Date	Invoice No	Code	Supplier	Total	VAT	Fabric	Header Tape	Other
12/4/X1	06738	PL03	Fabric Supplies Ltd	1,097.22	160.62	798.00	138.60	
	0328	PL04	Lillian Fisher	107.74	16.04			91.70
	CN0477	PL05	Headstream & Co	(79.90)	(11.90)	(51.40)	(16.60)	
	07359	PL01	Mainstream Fabrics	330.04	48.52	281.52		
				1,455.10	213.28	1,028.12	122.00	91.70

▲ ACTIVITY 30

Purchases day book

Date	Invoice No	Code	Supplier	Total	VAT	Wood	Bricks/Cement	Consumables
3/5/X1	077401	PL16	Magnum Supplies	493.90	72.30		421.60	
	046193	PL08	A J Broom & Co Ltd	118.47	17.64	85.08		15.75
	47823	PL13	Jenson Ltd	433.74	62.94	284.80	86.00	
				1,046.11	152.88	369.88	507.60	15.75

UNIT 30 : WORKBOOK

ACTIVITY 31

Purchases day book

Date	Invoice No	Code	Supplier	Total	VAT	Wood	Bricks/ Cement	Consum- ables
3/5/X1	CN06113	PL13	Jenson Ltd	30.07	4.36	25.71		
	06132	PL03	Haddow Bros	41.70	6.10	35.60		
	C4163	PL16	Magnum Supplies	45.80	6.70		39.10	
				117.57	17.16	61.31	39.10	–

ACTIVITY 32

Main ledger

Purchases ledger control account

		£			£
19/4	PRDB	245.10	12/4	Balance b/f	12,678.57

VAT account

		£			£
			12/4	Balance b/f	1,023.90
			19/4	PRDB	36.50

Purchases returns – 01 account

		£			£
			12/4	Balance b/f	337.60
			19/4	PRDB	60.40

Purchases returns – 02 account

		£			£
			12/4	Balance b/f	228.59
			19/4	PRDB	23.40

Purchases returns – 03 account

		£			£
			12/4	Balance b/f	889.46
			19/4	PRDB	108.00

Purchases returns – 04 account

		£			£
			12/4	Balance b/f	362.78
			19/4	PRDB	16.80

Subsidiary ledger

F Williams PL06

		£			£
18/4	PRDB C4772	164.50	12/4	Balance b/f	673.47

K Bartlett PL13

		£			£
19/4	PRDB 06638	53.11	12/4	Balance b/f	421.36

J D Withers PL16

		£			£
15/4	PRDB C0179	27.49	12/4	Balance b/f	446.37

△ ACTIVITY 33

Main ledger

Purchases ledger control account

	£			£
		1 May	Balance b/d	3,104.67
		5 May	PDB	1,002.57

VAT account

		£			£
5 May	PDB	149.30	1 May	Balance b/d	723.56

Purchases account

		£		£
1 May	Balance b/d	24,367.48		
5 May	PDB	853.27		

Subsidiary ledger

T Ives PL01

	£			£
		1 May	Balance b/d	332.56
		5 May	PDB 002633	192.98

H Samuels PL02

	£			£
		1 May	Balance b/d	286.90
		3 May	PDB 92544	109.79

L Jameson PL03

	£			£
		1 May	Balance b/d	623.89
		1 May	PDB 36558	393.91

G Rails PL04

	£			£
		1 May	Balance b/d	68.97
		4 May	PDB 03542	180.93

K Davison PL07

	£			£
		1 May	Balance b/d	125.47
		1 May	PDB 102785	124.96

UNIT 30 : WORKBOOK

Chapter 9
The analysed cash payments book

▲ ACTIVITY 34

Cash payments book

Date	Details	Cheque no	Code	Total £	VAT £	Purchases ledger £	Cash purchases £	Other £	Discounts received £
12/3/X1	Homer Ltd	03648	PL12	168.70		168.70			5.06
	Forker & Co	03649	PL07	179.45		179.45			5.38
	Purchases	03650		334.87	49.87		285.00		
	Print Ass.	03651	PL08	190.45		190.45			
	ABG Ltd	03652	PL02	220.67		220.67			6.62
	Purchases	03653		193.87	28.87		165.00		
	G Greg	03654	PL19	67.89		67.89			
				1,355.90	78.74	827.16	450.00	–	17.06

Main ledger

Purchases ledger control account

		£			£
12/3	CPB	827.16	5/3	Balance b/d	4,136.24
12/3	CPB – discount	17.06			

VAT account

		£			£
12/3	CPB	78.74	5/3	Balance b/d	1,372.56

Purchases account

		£			£
5/3	Balance b/d	20,465.88			
12/3	CPB	450.00			

Discounts received account

		£			£
			5/3	Balance b/d	784.56
			12/3	CPB	17.06

KEY TECHNIQUES : ANSWERS

Subsidiary ledger

ABG Ltd PL02

		£			£
12/3	CPB 03652	220.67	5/3	Balance b/d	486.90
12/3	CPB – discount	6.62			

Forker & Co PL07

		£			£
12/3	CPB 03649	179.45	5/3	Balance b/d	503.78
12/3	CPB – discount	5.38			

Print Associates PL08

		£			£
12/3	CPB 03651	190.45	5/3	Balance b/d	229.56

Homer Ltd PL12

		£			£
12/3	CPB 03648	168.70	5/3	Balance b/d	734.90
12/3	CPB – discount	5.06			

G Greg PL19

		£			£
12/3	CPB 03654	67.89	5/3	Balance b/d	67.89

△ ACTIVITY 35

Cash payments book

Date	Details	Cheque no	Code	Total £	VAT £	Purchases ledger £	Cash purchases £	Other £	Discounts received £
20X1									
30/5	J M Bond	200572	PL01	247.56		247.56			
	Magnum Supplies	200573	PL16	662.36		662.36			13.25
	A J Broom	200574	PL08	153.57		153.57			
	Jenson Ltd	200575	PL13	336.57		336.57			6.73
	KKL Traders	200576	PL20	442.78		442.78			8.85
	Purchases	200577		108.66	16.18		92.48		
				1,951.50	16.18	1,842.84	92.48	–	28.83

Main ledger

Purchases ledger control account

		£			£
30 May	CPB	1,842.84	23 May	Balance b/d	5,328.46
30 May	CPB – discount	28.83			

VAT account

		£			£
30 May	CPB	16.18	23 May	Balance b/d	1,365.35

Purchases account

		£			£
23 May	Balance b/d	36,785.90			
30 May	CPB	92.48			

Discounts received account

		£			£
			23 May	Balance b/d	1,573.56
			30 May	CPB	28.83

Subsidiary ledger

J M Bond PL01

		£			£
30 May	CPB 200572	247.56	23 May	Balance b/d	247.56

A J Broom Ltd PL08

		£			£
30 May	CPB 200574	153.57	23 May	Balance b/d	524.36

Jenson Ltd PL13

		£			£
30 May	CPB 200575	336.57	23 May	Balance b/d	512.36
30 May	CPB – discount	6.73			

Magnum Supplies PL16

		£			£
30 May	CPB 200573	662.36	23 May	Balance b/d	675.61
30 May	CPB – discount	13.25			

KKL Traders PL20

		£			£
30 May	CPB 200576	442.78	23 May	Balance b/d	612.46
30 May	CPB – discount	8.85			

Chapter 10
Credit sales: documents

△ ACTIVITY 36

CREDIT NOTE

Credit note to:
H M Music
Tenant House
Perley
TN7 8ER

Keyboard Supplies
Keyboard Supplies
Trench Park Estate
Fieldham Sussex TN21 4AF
Tel: 01829 654545
Fax: 01829 654646

Credit Note no: CN0337
Tax point: 17 April 20X1
VAT reg no: 466 1128 30
Your reference: SL09
Purchase order no:

Code	Description	Quantity	VAT rate %	Unit price £	Amount exclusive of VAT £
B3060	Bento Keyboard	1	17.5	126.00	126.00
					126.00
Trade discount 15 %					18.90
					107.10
VAT at 17.5%					18.74
Total amount					125.84

UNIT 30 : WORKBOOK

ACTIVITY 37

INVOICE

Invoice to:
Musicolor Ltd
23 High Street
Nutford
Sussex TN11 4TZ

Deliver to:
As above

Keyboard Supplies
Trench Park Estate
Fieldham , Sussex TN21 4AF
Tel: 01829 654545
Fax: 01829 654646

Invoice no:	06113
Tax point:	17 April 20X1
VAT reg no:	466 1128 30
Your reference:	SL06
Purchase order no:	04318

Code	Description	Quantity	VAT rate %	Unit price £	Amount exclusive of VAT £
Z4600	Zanni Keyboard	2	17.5	185.00	370.00
A4802	Atol Keyboard	3	17.5	130.00	390.00
					760.00
Trade discount 10 %					76.00
					684.00
VAT at 17.5%					116.10
Total amount payable					800.10

Deduct discount of 3% if paid within 10 days, 30 days net.

INVOICE

Invoice to:
Newford Music
32/34 Main Street
Welland
Sussex TN4 6BD

Deliver to:
As above

Keyboard Supplies
Trench Park Estate
Fieldham Sussex TN21 4AF
Tel: 01829 654545
Fax: 01829 654646

Invoice no:	06114
Tax point:	17 April 20X1
VAT reg no:	466 1128 30
Your reference:	SL18
Purchase order no:	47115

Code	Description	Quantity	VAT rate %	Unit price £	Amount exclusive of VAT £
Z4406	Zanni Keyboard	4	17.5	165.00	660.00
					660.00
Trade discount 20 %					132.00
					528.00
VAT at 17.5%					89.62
Total amount payable					617.62

Deduct discount of 3% if paid within 10 days, 30 days net.

KEY TECHNIQUES : **ANSWERS**

INVOICE

Invoice to:
F T Music Supplies
The Barn
Nutford
Sussex TN11 7AJ

Deliver to:
As above

Keyboard Supplies
Trench Park Estate
Fieldham Sussex TN21 4AF
Tel: 01829 654545
Fax: 01829 654646

Invoice no:	06115
Tax point:	17 April 20X1
VAT reg no:	466 1128 30
Your reference:	SL23
Purchase order no:	71143

Code	Description	Quantity	VAT rate %	Unit price £	Amount exclusive of VAT £
B2010	Bento Keyboard	2	17.5	148.00	296.00
G4706	Garland Keyboard	3	17.5	96.00	288.00
					584.00
Trade discount 15 %					87.60
					496.40
VAT at 17.5%					86.87
Total amount payable					583.27

Chapter 11
The banking system

△ ACTIVITY 38

The following problems exist on the cheques received:

Cheque from K T Lopez – not signed;
Cheque from L Garry – post dated;
Cheque from L Barrett – made out to wrong name;
Cheque from P Ibbott – more than six months old;
Cheque from J Lovell – discrepancy between words and figures.

Chapter 12
Checking receipts

△ ACTIVITY 39

Cheque from BZS Music – settlement discount of £8.64 has been taken – this is valid.

Cheque from Musicolor Ltd – settlement discount of £22.00 has been taken – but is not valid as the cheque has been received after 10 days from the invoice date. However, in the interest of good customer relations, perhaps the discount should be granted but the customer should be informed and reminded of the settlement discount terms.

Cheque from Harmer & Co – settlement discount of £8.82 has been taken – this is valid.

Cheque from Newford Music – settlement discount of £23.76 has been taken – this is not valid as the receipt is too late to claim the discount. Again the discount might be granted in the interest of good customer relations but the customer should be informed and reminded of the settlement discount terms.

Cheque from Trent Music – settlement discount of £13.27 has been taken – however it should have been £11.34 (3% x £378.00). Customer should be informed of the error.

KEY TECHNIQUES : ANSWERS

Chapter 13
Banking receipts

ACTIVITY 40

To be retained by receiving bank

For the credit of _____

Cheques etc for collection to be included in total credit of £903.00 paid in 4/5/20X1.

	£	Brought forward	£	Brought forward	£
K Fisher	135.49				
J Gilman	225.78				
S David	174.67				
L Craig	258.34				
Carried forward	£794.28	Carried forward	£	Total cheques etc	£

Date 4/5/X1

Cashier's stamp and initials

56 - 28 - 48

FINANCIAL BANK PLC
EXETER HIGH STREET

£50 Notes	–	–
£20 Notes	–	–
£10 Notes	20	00
£5 Notes	55	00
£2 Coins	6	00
£1 Coins	15	00
50p	8	50
20p	1	80
Silver	2	10
Bronze	0	32
Total Cash	108	72
Cheques, POs etc	794	28
TOTAL £	903	00

Fee

No Chqs: 4

Paid in by _____

Address/Ref No. _____

UNIT 30 : WORKBOOK

▲ ACTIVITY 41

To be retained by receiving bank

For the credit of _____

Cheques etc for collection to be included in total credit of £1,847.78 paid in 10/4/20X0.

	£			
K Tenterton	258.70	Brought forward	£981.03	Brought forward	£
H Ollie	117.58	C Beale	264.67		
E Edwards	274.51	Credit card vouchers	277.93		
P Trench	330.24				
Carried forward	£981.03	Carried forward	£1,523.63	Total cheques etc	£

Date 10/4/X0

Cashier's stamp and initials

56 - 28 - 48

FINANCIAL BANK PLC
EXETER HIGH STREET

Fee	No Chqs 5	Paid in by _____ Address/Ref No. _____

£50 Notes	–	–
£20 Notes	60	00
£10 Notes	150	00
£5 Notes	85	00
£2 Coins	10	00
£1 Coins	9	00
50p	6	50
20p	2	20
Silver	0	95
Bronze	0	50
Total Cash	324	15
Cheques, POs etc	1,523	63
TOTAL £	1,847	78

Have you imprinted the summary with your Retailer's Card?

Bank processing copy of Summary with your Vouchers in correct order:
1. Summary
2. Sales Vouchers
3. Refund Vouchers

Keep Retailer's copy and Retailer's Duplicate copy
No more than 200 Vouchers to each Summary
Do not use Staples, Pins, Paper Clips

	Items	Amount	
Sales vouchers	4	277	93
Less Refund Vouchers	–	–	–
Date 10 April X0	Total £	277	93

_____
Retailer's Signature

Retailer Summary

Retailer's Copy / Retailer Summary

Complete this summary for every Deposit of Sales Vouchers and enter the **Total** on your normal Current Account paying-in slip

KEY TECHNIQUES : ANSWERS

Please do not pin or staple this voucher as this will affect the machine processing.

All sales vouchers must be deposited within three banking days of the dates shown on them.

If you are submitting more than 26 vouchers please enclose a separate listing.

If a voucher contravenes the terms of the retailer agreement then the amount shown on the voucher may be charged back to your bank account, either direct or via your paying in branch.

Similarly, if the total amount shown on the Retail Voucher Summary does not balance with our total of vouchers, the difference will be credited (or debited) to your bank account.

	£	p
1	59	79
2	69	99
3	58	70
4	89	45
5		
6		
7		
8		
9		
10		
11		
12		
13		
14		
15		
16		
17		
18		
19		
20		
21		
22		
23		
24		
25		
26	277	93

SALES VOUCHERS   TOTAL

	£	p
1		
2		
3		
4		
5		
6		
7		

REFUND VOUCHERS   TOTAL

UNIT 30 : WORKBOOK

ACTIVITY 42

Tasks 1 & 2
Cheques received and remittance advices

NR Charles	No problems.
Proctor & Proctor	No problems.
Terrence James & Co Ltd	No problems.
Sid Pearl	Cheque not signed. Too late for discount. Put cheque to one side.
George Fox	Cheque made out to the wrong person. Slightly post-dated. Put cheque to one side.
JR Berry	No remittance advice (but cheque valid). Pay into bank.

Task 3

123

George Jones Scrapmerchants
34 Coppice Street
Oldham
OL6 3RT

Date   6 / 4 / X1
Customer Arthur Denton
          17 Bury New Road, Bolton BL4 6FG

£   27.55

Received with thanks

124

George Jones Scrapmerchants
34 Coppice Street
Oldham
OL6 3RT

Date   6 / 4 / X1
Customer Steel Associates
          Copper Mill, Copper Street, Oldham OL6 2YJ

£   8.45

Received with thanks

KEY TECHNIQUES : ANSWERS

125

George Jones Scrapmerchants
34 Coppice Street
Oldham
OL6 3RT

Date 6 / 4 / X1
Customer A J Palmer & Co Ltd
89 Store Street, Manchester M17 3SD

£ 11.90

Received with thanks

Task 4
Remittance List

Date 6 April 20X1

Customer	Receipt no	Invoice no	£		Discount allowed	
NR Charles		920	205	96	4	20
Proctor & Proctor		899	253	23	5	17
Terrence James		880	84	94	1	73
JR Berry			66	23		
Foster Bros		822	20	00		
Acme Scrap		865	7	00		
Arthur Denton	123		27	55		
Steel Associates	124		8	45		
A J Palmer	125		11	90		
TOTAL			**685**	**26**	**11**	**10**

Analysis   Cash   47.90
           Cheques   610.36
           Postal order   27.00
                         685.26

UNIT 30 : WORKBOOK

Task 5

For the credit of _George Jones Scrapmerchants_   To be retained by receiving bank
Cheques etc for collection to be included in total credit of £<u>685.26</u> paid in <u>6/4/</u>20X1.

	£	Brought forward	£610.36	Brought forward	£
NR Charles	205.96	Foster Bros	20.00		
Proctor & Proctor	253.23	Acme Scrap	7.00		
Terrence James	84.94				
JR Berry	66.23				
Carried forward	£610.36	Carried forward	£637.36	Total cheques etc	£

Date <u>6 April 20X1</u>
Cashier's stamp and initials

25 - 45 - 67

MIDWESTERN BANK
UNION STREET
OLDHAM

£50 Notes		
£20 Notes		
£10 Notes	30	00
£5 Notes	10	00
£2 Coins		
£1 Coins	6	00
50p	1	00
20p		80
Silver		10
Bronze		
Total Cash	47	90
Cheques, POs etc	637	36
TOTAL £	685	26

Fee | No Chqs 4 | Paid in by _A N Other_
Address/Ref No. _____

◮ ACTIVITY 43

Task 1   Errors

Cheques
J D Fisher   No problems.
G Kwong   No problems.
J Mahal   No problems.
P Fletcher   Amount and words on cheque do not agree.
C Dodgson   No problems.
T Patrick   Order form and cheque are wrong. Should be £315.00.
R Grossman   No problems.
J Reardon   No problems.

Credit card payments
T Danielson   No problems.
A Torquist   No problems.
N Metzger   Card out of date.

KEY TECHNIQUES : ANSWERS

How errors would be dealt with:

(a) Amounts on cheque do not agree — Do not bank payment – return payment and order form to customer.
(b) Order form wrong — Return order form and cheque to customer with request for correct payment of £315.
(c) Credit card out of date — Write to customer asking for a valid credit card.

In all three cases, the order would not be processed or despatched.

Task 2

Monies Received Listing						Date 25/6/X1	
Customer name	Order No	Deposit/ balance	Cheque £	Postal order £	Express £	Global £	Discount allowed £
J D Fisher		B	19.00				
G Kwong		B	7.00				
J Mahal		B	20.00				
C Dodgson		B	20.00				
R Grossman		B	10.00				
J Reardon		B	8.00				
T Danielson		B			19.00		
A Torquist		B			27.00		
Total			84.00		46.00		

UNIT 30 : WORKBOOK

Task 3

To be retained by receiving bank

For the credit of T-S DESIGNS LIMITED

Cheques etc for collection to be included in total credit of £130.00 paid in 25/6/20X1.

	£			Brought forward	£
		Brought forward	£76 00		
J D Fisher	19 00	J Reardon	8 00		
G Kwong	7 00	Express	46 00		
J Mahal	20 00				
C Dodgson	20 00				
R Grossman	10 00				
Carried forward	£76 00	Carried forward	£130 00	Total cheques etc	£

Date 25/6/20X1
Cashier's stamp and initials

45 - 67 - 17

SOUTHERN BANK PLC
SHEPHERD'S BUSH GREEN

£50 Notes		
£20 Notes		
£10 Notes		
£5 Notes		
£2 Coins		
£1 Coins		
50p		
20p		
Silver		
Bronze		
Total Cash	–	
Cheques, POs etc	130	00
TOTAL £	130	00

Fee

No Chqs 6

Credit T-S DESIGNS
Paid in by A N Other
Address/Ref No. _____

KEY TECHNIQUES : ANSWERS

		£	p
Please do not pin or staple this voucher as this will affect the machine processing.	1		
	2	19	00
	3	27	00
All sales vouchers must be deposited within three banking days of the dates shown on them.	4		
	5		
	6		
	7		
If you are submitting more than 26 vouchers please enclose a separate listing.	8		
	9		
	10		
If a voucher contravenes the terms of the retailer agreement then the amount shown on the voucher may be charged back to your bank account, either direct or via your paying in branch.	11		
	12		
	13		
	14		
	15		
	16		
Similarly, if the total amount shown on the Retail Voucher Summary does not balance with our total of vouchers, the difference will be credited (or debited) to your bank account.	17		
	18		
	19		
	20		
	21		
	22		
	23		
	24		
	25		
	26		
SALES VOUCHERS TOTAL		46	00
		£	p
	1		
	2		
	3		
	4		
	5		
	6		
	7		
REFUND VOUCHERS			

EXPRESS

PLEASE WRIE FIRMLY WITH A BALLPOINT PEN

RETAIL VOUCHER SUMMARY

RETAILER NAME

T-S DESIGNS

VOUCHERS ARE ACCEPTED SUBJECT TO VERIFICATION AND TO TERMS AND CONDITIONS OF THE MERCHANT AGREEMENT

KEEP COPIES 1 & 2 AND REMIT COPIES 3 & 4 WITH YOUR SALES VOUCHERS

DAY MONTH YEAR		RETAILER NUMBER	
2 5 0 6 X 1			
DESCRIPTION		Amount	
NO OF VOUCHERS			
SALES VOUCHERS	2	46	00
REFUND VOUCHERS			

AUTHORISATION CODE	TOTAL POUNDS PENCE
	46 : 00

RETAILER COPY

PLEASE COMPLETE THIS SUMMARY QUOTING YOUR CURRENT RETAILER NUMBER

RETAILER COPY

Chapter 14
Debtors' statements

△ ACTIVITY 44

FARMHOUSE PICKLES LTD

To: Grant & Co

225 School Lane
Weymouth
Dorset
WE36 5NR
Tel: 0261 480444
Fax: 0261 480555
Date: 30 April 20X1

STATEMENT

Date	Transaction	Debit £	Credit £	Balance £
1 April	Opening balance			337.69
4 April	Inv 32656	150.58		488.27
12 April	Credit 0335		38.70	449.57
18 April	Inv 32671	179.52		629.09
20 April	Payment		330.94	298.15
20 April	Discount		6.75	291.40
24 April	Credit 0346		17.65	273.75
25 April	Inv 32689	94.36		368.11

May we remind you that our credit terms are 30 days

KAPLAN PUBLISHING

UNIT 30 : WORKBOOK

FARMHOUSE PICKLES LTD

To: Mitchell Partners

225 School Lane
Weymouth
Dorset
WE36 5NR
Tel: 0261 480444
Fax: 0261 480555
Date: 30 April 20X1

STATEMENT

Date	Transaction	Debit £	Credit £	Balance £
1 April	Opening balance			180.46
7 April	Inv 32662	441.57		622.03
12 April	Credit 0344		66.89	555.14
20 April	Inv 32669	274.57		829.71
21 April	Payment		613.58	216.13
21 April	Discount		8.45	207.68

May we remind you that our credit terms are 30 days

△ ACTIVITY 45

Task 1 No errors noted in journal entry form.

Task 2 and Task 6

Main ledger

Account name   Sales ledger control   Account no   01 06 10 00

23/11/X1	b/f	3,705.63	27/11/X1	Cash	118.08
30/11/X1	Journal 3347	21,018.39	29/11/X1	Cash	118.08
			30/11/X1	Journal 3348	466.18

Account name   Sales – Product 01   Account no   03 70 10 01

23/11/X1	b/f	34,875.94
30/11/X1	Journal 3347	1,395.78

KEY TECHNIQUES : **ANSWERS**

Account name	Sales – Product 02	Account no	03 70 10 02
		23/11/X1 b/f	175,311.50
		30/11/X1 Journal 3347	7,666.82

Account name	Sales – Product 03	Account no	03 70 10 03
		23/11/X1 b/f	123,844.73
		30/11/X1 Journal 3347	5,557.46

Account name	Sales – Product 04	Account no	03 70 10 04
		23/11/X1 b/f	78,914.90
		30/11/X1 Journal 3347	3,267.93

Account name	VAT control		Account no	02 08 90 00
30/11/X1	Journal 3348	69.42	23/11/X1 b/f	20,935.86
			30/11/X1 Journal 3347	3,130.40

Account name	Sales returns – Product 01		Account no 04 60 10 01
23/11/X1	b/f	3,105.89	

Account name	Sales returns – Product 02		Account no 04 60 10 02
23/11/X1	b/f	15,222.75	
30/11/X1	Journal 3348	111.16	

Account name	Sales returns – Product 03		Account no 04 60 10 03
23/11/X1	b/f	10,413.67	
30/11/X1	Journal 3348	123.80	

Account name	Sales returns – Product 04		Account no 04 60 10 04
23/11/X1	b/f	6,116.70	
30/11/X1	Journal 3348	161.80	

KAPLAN PUBLISHING

Task 3 and Task 7

SUBSIDIARY (SALES) LEDGER ACCOUNTS

Customer name: Arnold Toys
Customer address: 57 Gray Street Bath BA1 2NT
Telephone: 01225 633112
Account number: A2

Dr   Cr

Date	Transaction	£		Date	Transaction	£	
19/11	Invoice 2195	118	08	20/11	CR 2198	323	60
20/11	Invoice 2198	2,201	95		c/f	1,996	43
		2,320	03			2,320	03
23/11	b/f	1,996	43	27/11	Cash	118	08
27/11	Invoice 2208	456	19	29/11	Cash	118	08

Customer name: Gerald Blythe & Sons
Customer address: 121 St John's Road Cambridge CB2 3AH
Telephone: 01223 461922
Account number: B2

Dr   Cr

Date	Transaction	£		Date	Transaction	£	
12/11	Invoice 2186	325	11	20/11	Cash	325	11
22/11	Invoice 2203	119	80		c/f	119	80
		444	91			444	91
23/11	b/f	119	80				
30/11	Invoice 2214	629	68	26/11	CN C461	190	11

SUBSIDIARY (SALES) LEDGER ACCOUNTS

Customer name	Daisychains		Account number		D2	
Customer address	111 George Street Crawley RH10 1HL					
Telephone	01293 811566					

Dr / Cr

Date	Transaction	£		Date	Transaction	£	
13/9	Invoice 2103	3,115	11				
27/9	Invoice 2122	211	55		c/f	3,326	66
		3,326	66			3,326	66
28/9	b/f	3,326	66	19/10	Cash	3,115	11 ✓
16/10	Invoice 2150	501	30		c/f	712	85
		3,827	96			3,827	96
19/10	b/f	712	85				
23/10	Invoice 2157	871	07		c/f	1,583	92
		1,583	92			1,583	92
26/10	b/f	1,583	92				
26/11	Invoice 2205	1,661	63				
28/11	Invoice 2211	2,057	17				

Customer name	Gameboard Ltd		Account number		G4	
Customer address	15 Park Street Woking GU21 1BY					
Telephone	01483 757442					

Dr / Cr

Date	Transaction	£		Date	Transaction	£	
2/11	b/f	3	09	8/11	Cr	3	09
14/11	Invoice 2187	115	83	16/11	CONTRA	86	94
					c/f	28	89
		115	83			115	83
16/11	b/f	28	89	20/11	Cash	28	89
29/11	Invoice 2212	2,657	24				

UNIT 30 : WORKBOOK

SUBSIDIARY (SALES) LEDGER ACCOUNTS

Customer name	Highlight Ltd		Account number		H3
Customer address	10 Station Road St Albans AL4 3EH				
Telephone	01727 46737				

Dr   Cr

Date	Transaction	£		Date	Transaction	£	
2/11	Invoice 2173	202	95	14/9	b/f	33	75
					c/f	169	20
		202	95			202	95
2/11	b/f	169	20	16/11	Cash	169	20
14/11	Invoice 2185	311	87		c/f	311	87
		481	07			481	07
16/11	b/f	311	87	22/11	Cash	311	87
27/11	Invoice 2209	260	98	30/11	CN C462	47	70

Customer name	Jubilee Games & Toys		Account number		J2
Customer address	3 Bourne Avenue Bracknell RG12 1AR				
Telephone	01344 678222				

Dr   Cr

Date	Transaction	£		Date	Transaction	£	
23/10	Invoice 2159	86	90	13/11	Cash	73	20
26/11	Invoice 2206	4,325	30				

Customer name	Lighthouse Products		Account number		L1
Customer address	135 Chapel Road Windsor S14 1UL				
Telephone	01753 828688				

Dr   Cr

Date	Transaction	£		Date	Transaction	£	
13/11	Invoice 2188	326	11	20/11	CONTRA	44	22
	c/f	44	22	21/11	Cash	326	11
		370	33			370	33
28/11	Invoice 2210	7,069	34	23/11	b/f	44	22
				30/11	CN C463	228	37

KEY TECHNIQUES : **ANSWERS**

Customer name	Mirabelle Leisure		Account number		M3	
Customer address	19 Masons Hill Brighton BN1 8RT					
Telephone	01273 207146					

Dr   Cr

Date	Transaction	£		Date	Transaction	£	
14/11	Invoice 2189	411	38				
15/11	Invoice 2190	83	91		c/f	495	29
		495	29			495	29
16/11	b/f	495	29	20/11	Cash	459	29
					c/f	36	00
		495	29			495	29
23/11	b/f	36	00				
27/11	Invoice 2207	954	04				
29/11	Invoice 2213	946	82				

Task 4

Date	Code	Customer	CN	Total £	01 £	02 £	03 £	04 £	VAT £
26/11/X1	B2	Gerald Blythe	C461	190.11				161.80	28.31
30/11/X1	H3	Highlight Ltd	C462	47.70			40.60		7.10
30/11/X1	L1	Lighthouse Products	C463	228.37		111.16	83.20		34.01
				466.18	–	111.16	123.80	161.80	69.42

Task 5

JOURNAL	SALES DAY BOOK POSTINGS		NO 3348
Prepared by		Week ending	30/11/X1
Authorised by			
Account		Debit	Credit
Sales ledger control			466.18
Sales returns product 01		–	
Sales returns product 02		111.16	
Sales returns product 03		123.80	
Sales returns product 04		161.80	
VAT		69.42	
TOTALS		466.18	466.18

UNIT 30 : WORKBOOK

Task 8

TOYBOX GAMES LTD
125 Finchley Way Bristol BS1 4PL Tel: 01272 200299

STATEMENT OF ACCOUNT

Customer name Daisychains **Customer account no** D2
Customer address 111 George Street Crawley RH10 1HL

Statement date

Date	Transaction	Dr £	Dr p	Cr £	Cr p	Balance £	Balance p
31/10/X1	Balance brought forward	1,583	92			1,583	92
26/11/X1	Invoice 2205	1,661	63			3,245	55
28/11/X1	Invoice 2211	2,057	17			5,302	72
						5,302	72

TOYBOX GAMES LTD
125 Finchley Way Bristol BS1 4PL Tel: 01272 200299

STATEMENT OF ACCOUNT

Customer name Jubilee Games & Toy **Customer account no** J2
Customer address 3 Bourne Avenue Bracknell RG12 1AR

Statement date

Date	Transaction	Dr £	Dr p	Cr £	Cr p	Balance £	Balance p
31/10/X1	Balance brought forward	86	90			86	90
13/11/X1	Cash			73	20	13	70
26/11/X1	Invoice 2206	4,325	30			4,339	00
						4,339	00

Chapter 15
Accounting for sales – summary

△ ACTIVITY 46 △△△△

Task 1

Sales invoices

39117	missing
39118	clerical error on Peters' total
39120	discount omitted

The corrected invoices are shown on the pages which follow.

KEY TECHNIQUES : ANSWERS

SALES INVOICE
ELLIOTT BROOK ASSOCIATES

39118

Address
25 Eaton Terrace
Eastbourne BN16 3RS
VAT Reg No 544 2900 17

Telephone 01323 866755
Fax 01323 995655
Tax point 16 May 20X0

Hire of staff
FAO The Manager
Kenmare Hotel
73 East Sands Way
Eastbourne
Client code KEN 11

Name	Start	Finish	Hours	Grade	Rate £	Total excl VAT £
Price	10/5/X0	13/5/X0	12	D	3.00	36.00
Haines	11/5/X0	13/5/X0	16	C	4.00	64.00
Peters	7/5/X0	12/5/X0	30	B	6.25	187.50
						287.50
			Discount			0
						287.50
			VAT at 17.5%			50.31
						337.81 : £337.81

SALES INVOICE
ELLIOTT BROOK ASSOCIATES

39120

Address
25 Eaton Terrace
Eastbourne BN16 3RS
VAT Reg No 544 2900 17

Telephone 01323 866755
Fax 01323 995655
Tax point 16 May 20X0

Hire of staff
FAO Services Manager
Royal Hotel
Royal View
Eastbourne
Client code ROY 05

Name	Start	Finish	Hours	Grade	Rate £	Total excl VAT £
Clarke	7/5/X0	8/5/X0	15	A	7.50	112.50
Hartley	9/5/X0	13/5/X0	40	A	7.50	300.00
						412.50
			Discount			41.25
						371.25
			VAT at 17.5%			64.96
						436.21 : £436.21

Task 2

SALES DAY BOOK

DATE	CLIENT	INVOICE	NET	VAT	GROSS
16/5/X0	IMPERIAL	39114	270.00	47.25	317.25
	ROSETREE	39115	196.75	34.43	231.18
	WEST BAY	39116	179.25	31.37	210.62
		39117			
	KENMARE	39118	287.50	50.31	337.81
	SEAVIEW	39119	180.00	31.50	211.50
	ROYAL HOTEL	39120	371.25	64.96	436.21
	CROWN AND ANCHOR	39121	30.00	5.25	35.25
16/5/X0	TOTAL		1,514.75	265.07	1,779.82

Task 3
Credit notes

12234   missing
12235   duplicate

Task 4

CREDIT NOTES DAY BOOK

DATE	CLIENT	CREDIT NO	NET £	VAT £	GROSS £
16/5/X0	ROYAL	12233	12.90	2.26	15.16
		12234			
	Duplicate	12235			
	SANDRINGHAM	12236	45.89	8.03	53.92
16/5/X0	TOTAL		58.79	10.29	69.08

ACTIVITY 47

Main ledger

Purchases ledger control account

	£		£
26 April SDB	643.89		

Sales account

	£		£
		26 April SDB	548.01

VAT account

	£		£
		26 April SDB	95.88

Subsidiary ledger

J T Howard   SL15

	£		£
22 April SDB 4671	138.93		

F Parker   SL07

	£		£
22 April SDB 4672	99.07		

Harlow Ltd   SL02

	£		£
23 April SDB 4673	125.10		

Edmunds & Co   SL13

	£		£
24 April SDB 4674	167.75		

Peters & Co   SL09

	£		£
26 April SDB 4675	113.04		

UNIT 30 : WORKBOOK

ACTIVITY 48

Sales day book

Date	Invoice No	Customer name	Code	Total £	VAT £	01 £	02 £	03 £
20X0								
6/9	04771	Harold Ellis	H03	93.77	13.96	15.68		64.13
7/9	04772	P Pilot	P01	134.67	20.05		114.62	
	04773	R Tracy	T02	83.30	12.40	23.22	30.80	16.88
8/9	C0612	Harold Ellis	H03	(15.51)	(2.31)			(13.20)
9/9	04774	Planet Inc	P04	165.34	24.62		64.82	75.90
10/9	04775	Harold Ellis	H03	47.23	7.03	23.80	16.40	
	C0613	C Calver	C01	(17.17)	(2.55)	(8.20)		(6.42)
				491.63	73.20	54.50	226.64	137.29

Main ledger

Purchases ledger control account

		£			£
10/9	SDB	491.63			

Sales – 01

	£			£
		10/9	SDB	54.50

Sales – 02

	£			£
		10/9	SDB	226.64

Sales – 03

	£			£
		10/9	SDB	137.29

VAT account

	£			£
		10/9	SDB	73.20

Subsidiary ledger

Harold Ellis H03

		£			£
6/9	SDB 04771	93.77	8/9	SDB C0612	15.51
10/9	SDB 04775	47.23			

P Pilot P01

		£		£
7/9	SDB 04772	134.67		

R Tracy T02

		£		£
7/9	SDB 04773	83.30		

Planet Inc P04

		£		£
9/9	SDB 04774	165.34		

C Calver C01

	£			£
		10/9	SDB C0613	17.17

UNIT 30 : WORKBOOK

▲ ACTIVITY 49

Task 1

To be retained by receiving bank

For the credit of Paperbox Ltd

Cheques etc for collection to be included in total credit of £2,489.87 paid in 19/2/20X0.

	£				
		Brought forward	£1,099.70	Brought forward	£1,876.81
N J Peal	291.60	Pearce & Fellows	659.18	R F Wholesalers Ltd	539.50
Stationery Supplies	245.30	Abraham Matthews Ltd	117.93	Credit Card Voucher	73.56
Candle Company Ltd	562.80				
Carried forward	£1,099.70	Carried forward	£1,876.81	Total cheques etc	£2,489.87

Date 19/02/X0

Cashier's stamp and initials

56 - 28 - 48

FINANCIAL BANK PLC
GREENOCK

£50 Notes		
£20 Notes		
£10 Notes		
£5 Notes		
£2 Coins		
£1 Coins		
50p		
20p		
Silver		
Bronze		
Total Cash		
Cheques, POs etc	2489	87
TOTAL £	2489	87

Fee | No Chqs 6 | Paid in by _____ Address/Ref No. _____

Have you imprinted the summary with your Retailer's Card?

Bank processing copy of Summary with your Vouchers in correct order:
1 Summary
2 Sales Vouchers
3 Refund Vouchers

Keep Retailer's copy and Retailer's Duplicate copy

No more than 200 Vouchers to each Summary

Do not use Staples, Pins, Paper Clips

	Items	Amount	
Sales vouchers	4	73	56
Less Refund Vouchers	–	–	–
Date 19/02/X0	Total £	73	:56

Retailer's Copy

Retailer Summary

Retailer's Signature _____

Complete this summary for every Deposit of Sales Vouchers and enter the **Total** on your normal Current Account paying-in slip

KEY TECHNIQUES : ANSWERS

			£	p
Please do not pin or staple this voucher as this will affect the machine processing.		1	22	60
		2	5	83
		3	26	18
All sales vouchers must be deposited within three banking days of the dates shown on them.		4	18	95
		5		
		6		
		7		
If you are submitting more than 26 vouchers please enclose a separate listing.		8		
		9		
		10		
If a voucher contravenes the terms of the retailer agreement then the amount shown on the voucher may be charged back to your bank account, either direct or via your paying in branch.		11		
		12		
		13		
		14		
		15		
		16		
Similarly, if the total amount shown on the Retail Voucher Summary does not balance with our total of vouchers, the difference will be credited (or debited) to your bank account.		17		
		18		
		19		
		20		
		21		
		22		
		23		
		24		
		25		
		26	73	56
SALES VOUCHERS	TOTAL			

		£	p
	1		
	2		
	3		
	4		
	5		
	6		
	7		
REFUND VOUCHERS	TOTAL		

Note re VAT calculations

When recording mail order (cash) sales, the VAT element must be accounted for as this is the first time these sales have been recorded.

Example
KB Smith

$£22.60 \times \dfrac{17.5}{117.5} = £3.36$

UNIT 30 : WORKBOOK

Task 2

Cash Book Receipts

Date	Narrative	Paying-in slip no	Total	Debtors	Mail Order Sales	Other	VAT	Discount allowed
19/2/X0	N J Peal		291.60	291.60				
	Stationery Supplies		245.30	245.30				5.01
	Candle Company Ltd		562.80	562.80				4.95
	Pearce & Fellows		659.18	659.18				13.45
	Abraham Matthews Ltd		117.93	117.93				
	K B Smith		22.60		19.24		3.36	
	R Jones		5.83		4.97		0.86	
	C Bastok		26.18		22.29		3.89	
	J Rirolli		18.95		16.13		2.82	
	R F Wholesalers Ltd (Rent)		539.50			539.50		
	Totals		2,489.87	1,876.81	62.63	539.50	10.93	23.41

Task 3

Journal no. 106
Date 19/2/X0
Prepared by A N Other

Code	Account	Debit		Credit	
	Bank	2,489	87		
	Sales mail order			62	63
	Trade debtors			1,876	81
	VAT control account			10	93
	Rent			539	50
	Discounts allowed	23	41		
	Trade debtors			23	41
Total		2,513	28	2,513	28

Chapter 16
Credit purchases: documents

△ ACTIVITY 50

Credit note from J M Bond & Co

The trade discount deducted should have been £6.16. Therefore, the total amount of credit is wrong.

△ ACTIVITY 51

Invoice from A J Broom & Company Ltd

Seven joist hangers were invoiced and delivered but only five were ordered.

Invoice from Jenson Ltd

The VAT calculation is incorrect – the amount should be £99.37.

Invoice from Haddow Bros

12 sheets were invoiced and ordered but only 10 were delivered.

UNIT 30 : WORKBOOK

Chapter 17
Making payments

▲ ACTIVITY 52

REMITTANCE ADVICE

To:
Building Contract Supplies
Unit 15 Royal Estate
Manchester
M13 2EF

Nethan Builders
Brecon House, Stamford Road
Manchester M16 4PL

Tel: 0161 521 6411
Fax: 0161 530 6412
VAT Reg no: 471 3860 42
Date: 18 May 20X1

Date	Invoice no	Amount £	Discount taken £	Paid £
18 May 20X1	07742	199.47	2.55	196.92

Total paid £ 196.92

Cheque no 200550

REMITTANCE ADVICE

To:
Jenson Ltd
30 Longfield Park
Kingsway
M45 2TP

Nethan Builders
Brecon House, Stamford Road
Manchester M16 4PL

Tel: 0161 521 6411
Fax: 0161 530 6412
VAT Reg no: 471 3860 42
Date: 18 May 20X1

Date	Invoice no	Amount £	Discount taken £	Paid £
18 May 20X1	47811	180.46	-	180.46

Total paid £ 180.46

Cheque no 200551

REMITTANCE ADVICE

To:
Magnum Supplies
140/150 Park Estate
Manchester
M20 6EG

Nethan Builders
Brecon House, Stamford Road
Manchester M16 4PL

Tel: 0161 521 6411
Fax: 0161 530 6412
VAT Reg no: 471 3860 42
Date: 18 May 20X1

Date	Invoice no	Amount £	Discount taken £	Paid £
18 May 20X1	077422	740.85	12.65	728.20

Total paid £ 728.20

Cheque no 200552

REMITTANCE ADVICE

To:
Haddow Bros
The White House
Standing Way
Manchester M13 6FH

Nethan Builders
Brecon House, Stamford Road
Manchester M16 4PL

Tel: 0161 521 6411
Fax: 0161 530 6412
VAT Reg no: 471 3860 42
Date: 18 May 20X1

Date	Invoice no	Amount £	Discount taken £	Paid £
18 May 20X1	G33940	500.46	–	500.46

Total paid £ 500.46

Cheque no 200553

UNIT 30 : WORKBOOK

NATIONAL BANK PLC
18 Coventry Road
Manchester
M13 2TU

19-14-60
18 May 20 X1

Pay   Building Contract Supplies   or order

One hundred and ninety six pounds   £ 196.92

and 92 pence----------------------------

Account payee

20050   19-14-60   50731247   **NETHAN BUILDERS**

NATIONAL BANK PLC
18 Coventry Road
Manchester
M13 2TU

19-14-60
18 May 20 X1

Pay   Jenson Ltd   or order

One hundred and eighty pounds   £ 180.46

and 46 pence---------------------------

Account payee

200551   19-14-60   50731247   **NETHAN BUILDERS**

NATIONAL BANK PLC
18 Coventry Road
Manchester
M13 2TU

19-14-60
18 May 20 X1

Pay   Magnum Supplies   or order

Seven hundred and twenty eight   £ 728.20

pounds and 20 pence ---------------------

Account payee

200552   19-14-60   50731247   **NETHAN BUILDERS**

KEY TECHNIQUES : **ANSWERS**

```
NATIONAL BANK PLC                                    19-14-60
18 Coventry Road
Manchester                                    18 May    20  X1
M13 2TU

  Pay     Haddow Bros                                     or order

  Five hundred pounds and                              £ 500.46

  46 pence -----------------------

                              Account payee

  200553        19-14-60         50731247        NETHAN BUILDERS
```

Chapter 18
Payroll procedures

△ ACTIVITY 53

Wages control account

	£		£
Net pay	118,212	Gross pay	167,384
PAYE	35,129	Employer's NIC	20,086
Employee's NIC	14,043		
Employer's NIC	20,086		
	187,470		187,470

△ ACTIVITY 54

	£
Gross pay	368.70
Less: PAYE	(46.45)
NIC	(23.96)
Net pay	298.29

KAPLAN PUBLISHING

UNIT 30 : WORKBOOK

ACTIVITY 55

Gross wages control account

		£			£
31 May	Net pay – Bank	4,087	31 May	Gross – wages expense	5,050
	PAYE – HMRC	635	31 May	Emp'ers NIC – wages exp	425
	Emp'ees NIC – HMRC	328			
	Empl'ers NIC – HMRC	425			
		5,475			5,475

Wages expense account

		£			£
30 Apr	Balance b/d	23,446			
31 May	Gross – wages control	5,050			
	Emp'ers NIC – control	425	31 May	Balance c/d	28,921
		28,921			28,921
31 May	Balance b/d	28,921			

HM Revenue and Customs account

		£			£
19 May	CPB	760	30 Apr	Balance b/d	760
			31 May	PAYE – wages control	635
				Emp'ees NIC – control	328
31 May	Balance c/d	1,388		Emp'ers NIC – control	425
		2,148			2,148
			31 May	Balance b/d	1,388

ACTIVITY 56

TASK 1

Cash Book Payments

Date	Narrative	Cheque no	Total	Creditors	Salaries	Other	VAT
24/4/X1	Fowler & Kenworthy Ltd	2374	17,678.67	17,678.67			
	Vinegar Supply Co Ltd	75	1,657.99	1,657.99			
	Western Farmers Ltd	76	34,766.45	34,766.45			
	Fish Supply Group plc	77	14,365.00	14,365.00			
	General Grain Supply Co Ltd	78	2,334.45	2,334.45			
	Tamar Flour Millers Ltd	79	1,766.38	1,766.38			
	Angus Meat Suppliers plc	80	5,443.12	5,443.12			
	Hobbs and Davies Ltd	81	773.56	773.56			
	Jersey Foods Ltd	82	3,716.33	3,716.33			
	Flour Products Ltd	83	12,674.99	12,674.99			
	D I Ltd	84	543.92	543.92			
	Finer Products Ltd	85	23,894.34	23,894.34			
	Greengates Ltd	86	9,333.25	9,333.25			
	Catering Supplies Ltd	87	112.32	112.32			
	Plastic Products Ltd	88	6,833.28	6,833.28			
	Simpson Foods Ltd	89	346.60	346.60			
	Paper Bag Company Ltd	90	10,004.43	10,004.43			
	United Food Producers Ltd	91	9,567.76	9,567.76			
	TY Foods Ltd	92	17,334.78	17,334.78			
	Bell Distribution Int Ltd	93	3,885.38	3,885.38			
	Winter & White Ltd	94	267.56	267.56			
	Dairy Produce Co. Ltd	95	245.87	245.87			
	Ghanwani Foods Ltd	96	844.20	844.20			
	Cross & Fordingham Ltd	97	18,794.95	18,794.95			
	T & P Importers Ltd	98	10,339.27	10,339.27			
	Golden Grains Ltd	99	5,680.11	5,680.11			
	Imperial Foods plc	2400	605.02	605.02			
	L Freeborough	01	76.83		76.83		
28/4/X1	Kennedy Property	SO	6,547.45			6,547.45 (rent)	
24/4/X1	Security Insurance	DD	546.90			546.90 (insurance)	
27/4/X1	English Telecomm	DD	378.65			322.26 (tel)	56.39
25/4/X1	Salaries Dept 01	BACS	23,564.22		23,564.22		
	Dept 02	BACS	12,453.64		12,453.64		
	Dept 03	BACS	35,555.25		35,555.25		
	Dept 04	BACS	3,630.66		3,630.66		
			296,563.58	213,809.98	75,280.60	7,416.61	56.39

UNIT 30 : WORKBOOK

TASK 2

	Journal no	78
	Date	4/5/20X1
	Authorised	Patricia Konig

	Dr	Cr
Dr Purchases ledger control account	213,809.98	
Salaries expense account	75,280.60	
Rent account	6,547.45	
Insurance account	546.90	
Telephone account	322.26	
VAT account	56.39	
Bank account		296,563.58
Cr		
Reason Posting of cash book payments.	296,563.58	296,563.58

TASK 3

Purchases ledger control account

			£				£
30/4/X1	CPB		213,809.98	23/4/X1	Balance b/f		346,589.45

Salaries expense account

			£		£
23/4/X1	Balance b/f		250,437.36		
30/4/X1	CPB		75,280.60		

Rent account

			£		£
23/4/X1	Balance b/f		7,235.46		
30/4/X1	CPB		6,547.45		

Insurance account

			£		£
23/4/X1	Balance b/f		478.69		
30/4/X1	CPB		546.90		

Telephone account

			£		£
23/4/X1	Balance b/f		412.56		
30/4/X1	CPB		322.26		

VAT account

			£				£
30/4/X1	CPB		56.39	23/4/X1	Balance b/f		20,376.43

KEY TECHNIQUES : ANSWERS

TASK 4

Fowler & Kenworthy Ltd — 2374

		£			£
30/4/X1	CPB	17,678.67	23/4/X1	Balance b/f	23,475.68

Hobbs and Davies Ltd — 2381

		£			£
30/4/X1	CPB	773.56	23/4/X1	Balance b/f	1,043.50

Paper Bag Company Ltd — 2390

		£			£
30/4/X1	CPB	10,004.43	23/4/X1	Balance b/f	10,004.43

T & P Importers Ltd — 2398

		£			£
30/4/X1	CPB	10,339.27	23/4/X1	Balance b/f	15,364.89

TASK 5

Salaries expense account

		£			£
23/4/X1	Balance b/f	250,437.36			
30/4/X1	Gross – salaries control	93,053.89			
30/4/X1	Employer's NIC	7,816.53			

Gross salaries control account

		£			£
30/4/X1	Net – Bank	75,280.60	30/4/X1	Gross – expense	93,053.89
30/4/X1	PAYE	11,724.79	30/4/X1	Employer's NIC	7,816.53
30/4/X1	Employee's NIC	6,048.50			
30/4/X1	Employer's NIC	7,816.53			

HMRC account

		£			£
			12/4/X1	Balance b/f	18,584.34
			30/4/X1	PAYE	11,724.79
			30/4/X1	Employee's NIC	6,048.50
			30/4/X1	Employer's NIC	7,816.53

UNIT 30 : WORKBOOK

Chapter 19
Accounting for purchases – summary

△ ACTIVITY 57

Purchases day book

Date	Invoice no	Code	Supplier	Total	VAT	Paint	Wallpaper	Other
22/3/X1	047992	PL03	Mortimer & Co	180.97	26.37		112.00	42.60
	61624	PL06	F L Decor Supplies	64.29	9.57		54.72	
	05531	PL08	Specialist Paint Ltd	219.11	32.21	98.40		88.50
				464.37	68.15	98.40	166.72	131.10

△ ACTIVITY 58

JOURNAL ENTRY	No: 1254	
Prepared by: A N Other		
Authorised by:		
Date: 12/3/X1		
Narrative: To post the purchase day book to the main ledger		
Account	*Debit*	*Credit*
VAT	184.77	
Purchases – 01	310.76	
Purchases – 02	156.09	
Purchases – 03	245.66	
Purchases – 04	343.43	
Purchases ledger control		1,240.71
TOTALS	1,240.71	1,240.71

Subsidiary ledger

ABG Ltd — PL02

			£			£
12/3	PDB CN477		48.31	5/3	Balance b/d	486.90
				10/3	PDB 016127	292.58

Forker & Co — PL07

			£			£
10/3	PDB C4366		23.73	5/3	Balance b/d	503.78
				8/3	PDB 11675	207.24

KEY TECHNIQUES : **ANSWERS**

Print Associates — PL08

	£			£
		5/3	Balance b/d	229.56
		9/3	PDB 46251	230.04

Homer Ltd — PL12

	£			£
		5/3	Balance b/d	734.90
		8/3	PDB 06121	223.87
		11/3	PDB 06132	189.33

G Greg — PL19

	£			£
		5/3	Balance b/d	67.89
		11/3	PDB 77918	169.69

△ ACTIVITY 59

Main ledger

Purchases ledger control account

		£			£
			17/2	Balance b/d	2,357.57
			24/2	PDB	942.08

VAT account

		£			£
24/2	PDB	140.30	17/2	Balance b/d	662.47

Purchases – 01 account

		£		£
17/2	Balance b/d	14,275.09		
24/2	PDB	222.05		

Purchases – 02 account

		£		£
17/2	Balance b/d	12,574.26		
24/2	PDB	179.04		

Purchases – 03 account

		£		£
17/2	Balance b/d	29,384.74		
24/2	PDB	302.55		

Purchases – 04 account

		£		£
17/2	Balance b/d	9,274.36		
24/2	PDB	98.14		

UNIT 30 : WORKBOOK

Subsidiary ledger

P & F Davis & Co — PL03

		£			£
			17/2	Balance b/d	368.36
			21/2	PDB 46120	166.54
			24/2	PDB 46122	189.23

Clooney & Partner — PL06

		£			£
			17/2	Balance b/d	226.48
			22/2	PDB 46121	230.58

S Doorman — PL07

		£			£
23/2	PDB CN463	21.51	17/2	Balance b/d	218.47
			20/2	PDB 46119	189.53

Fred Janitor — PL11

		£			£
23/2	PDB CN462	30.99	17/2	Balance b/d	111.45
			20/2	PDB 46118	218.70

△ ACTIVITY 60

Date	Details	Cheque no	Code	Total £	VAT £	Purchases ledger £	Cash purchases £	Other £	Discounts received £
8 May	G Rails	001221	PL04	177.56		177.56			4.43
	L Jameson	001222	PL03	257.68		257.68			7.73
	Purchases	001223		216.43	32.23		184.20		
	K Davison	001224	PL07	167.89		167.89			
	T Ives	001225	PL01	289.06		289.06			5.79
	Purchases	001226		263.78	39.28		224.50		
	H Samuels	001227	PL02	124.36		124.36			
				1,496.76	71.51	1,016.55	408.70	–	17.95

KEY TECHNIQUES : ANSWERS

JOURNAL ENTRY		No: 1468	
Prepared by: A N Other			
Authorised by:			
Date: 8 May 20X1			
Narrative: To post the cash payments book for week ending 8 May 20X1			
Account		Debit	Credit
Purchases ledger control		1,016.55	
VAT		71.51	
Purchases		408.70	
Bank			1,496.76
Purchases ledger control		17.95	
Discount received			17.95
TOTALS		1,514.71	1,514.71

Subsidiary ledger

T Ives — PL01

		£			£
8 May	CPB 001225	289.06	1 May	Balance b/d	332.56
8 May	CPB – discount	5.79			

H Samuels — PL02

		£			£
8 May	CPB 001227	124.36	1 May	Balance b/d	286.90

L Jameson — PL03

		£			£
8 May	CPB 001222	257.68	1 May	Balance b/d	623.89
8 May	CPB – discount	7.73			

G Rails — PL04

		£			£
8 May	CPB 001221	177.56	1 May	Balance b/d	181.99
8 May	CPB – discount	4.43			

K Davison — PL07

		£			£
8 May	CPB 001224	167.89	1 May	Balance b/d	167.89

KAPLAN PUBLISHING

UNIT 30 : WORKBOOK

Chapter 20
Petty cash systems

▲ ACTIVITY 61

Petty cash book											
Receipts			Payments								
Date	Narrative	Total £	Date	Narrative	Voucher no	Total £	Postage £	Staff welfare £	Stationery £	Travel expenses £	VAT £
5/1/X1	Bal b/d	150.00	12/1/X1	Postage	03526	13.68	13.68				
				Staff welfare	03527	25.00		25.00			
				Stationery	03528	14.80			12.60		2.20
				Taxi fare	03529	12.00				10.21	1.79
				Staff welfare	03530	6.40		6.40			
				Postage	03531	12.57	12.57				
				Rail fare	03532	6.80				6.80	
				Stationery	03533	7.99			6.80		1.19
				Taxi fare	03534	18.80				16.00	2.80
						118.04	26.25	31.40	19.40	33.01	7.98

CHEQUE REQUISITION FORM
CHEQUE DETAILS
Date .... 12/1/X1 ....
Payee .... Cash ....
Amount £ .... 118.04 ....
Reason .... To restore petty cash ....
Invoice no. (attached/to follow) ...... - ....
Receipt (attached/to follow) .... - ....
Required by (Print) ...... PETTY CASHIER ....
(Signature ..... Petty Cashier ....
Authorised by: ....

Main ledger accounts

Postage account

		£		£
5 Jan	Balance b/d	248.68		
12 Jan	PCB	26.25		

Staff welfare account

		£			£
5 Jan	Balance b/d	225.47			
12 Jan	PCB	31.40			

Stationery account

		£			£
5 Jan	Balance b/d	176.57			
12 Jan	PCB	19.40			

Travel expenses account

		£			£
5 Jan	Balance b/d	160.90			
12 Jan	PCB	33.01			

VAT account

		£			£
12 Jan	PCB	7.98	5 Jan	Balance b/d	2,385.78

△ ACTIVITY 62

Voucher total

	£
02634	13.73
02635	8.91
02636	10.57
02637	3.21
02638	11.30
02639	14.66
	62.38

UNIT 30 : WORKBOOK

Cash total

			£
£10 note	1		10.00
£5 note	2		10.00
£2 coin	3		6.00
£1 coin	7		7.00
50p coin	5		2.50
20p coin	4		0.80
10p coin	1		0.10
5p coin	2		0.10
2p coin	3		0.06
1p coin	6		0.06
			36.62

Reconciliation of cash and vouchers at 22 May 20X1

	£
Voucher total	62.38
Cash total	36.62
	99.00

The reconciliation shows that there is £1 missing. More cash has been paid out of the petty cash box than is supported by the petty cash vouchers. This could be due to a number of reasons:

· A petty cash claim was made out for, say, £11.30 but mistakenly the amount given to the employee was £12.30.
· An employee borrowed £1 from the petty cash box for business expenses and this has not been recorded on a petty cash voucher.
· £1 has been stolen from the petty cash box.

△ ACTIVITY 63

Claimed by	Amount	Comment
J Athersych	£7.04	Valid
J Athersych	£4.85	Valid – less than £5
F Rivers	£12.80	Valid – authorised by department head
M Patterson	£6.60	Cannot be paid – no receipt
D R Ray	£42.80	Cannot be paid – more than £30
J Athersych	£3.70	Valid – less than £5
D R Ray	£12.50	Cannot be paid – not authorised by department head
M Patterson	£19.50	Valid
M T Noble	£17.46	Valid
J Norman	£7.60	Cannot be paid – not authorised by department head

ACTIVITY 64

Petty cash book

Receipts			Payments								
Date	Narrative	Total £	Date	Narrative	Voucher no	Total £	Postage £	Tea and coffee £	Stationery £	Travel expenses £	VAT £
	Bal b/d	100.00	30/4/X1	Coffee/milk	2534	4.68		4.68			
				Postage	2535	13.26	13.26				
				Stationery	2536	10.27			8.74		1.53
				Taxi fare	2537	15.00				12.77	2.23
				Postage	2538	6.75	6.75				
				Train fare	2539	7.40				7.40	
				Stationery	2540	3.86			3.29		0.57
						61.22	20.01	4.68	12.03	20.17	4.33

Main ledger accounts

Postage account

		£			£
23 Apr	Balance b/d	231.67			
30 Apr	PCB	20.01			

Stationery account

		£			£
23 Apr	Balance b/d	334.78			
30 Apr	PCB	12.03			

Tea and coffee account

		£			£
23 Apr	Balance b/d	55.36			
30 Apr	PCB	4.68			

Travel expenses account

		£			£
23 Apr	Balance b/d	579.03			
30 Apr	PCB	20.17			

VAT account

		£			£
30 Apr	PCB	4.33	23 Apr	Balance b/d	967.44

UNIT 30 : WORKBOOK

ACTIVITY 65

TASK 1
Petty cash vouchers which cannot be paid
25/11	Flowers	Receipt required
26/11	VAT book	Authorisation missing
27/11	Rail tickets	Exceeds £100.00 Requires authorisation by MD
30/11	Window cleaner	Uncertainty over coding

TASK 2
The balance of petty cash brought forward can be calculated from the main ledger account or can be assumed to be £100 because the company uses an imprest system.

PETTY CASH BOOK

Date	Voucher number	£	£ 01 Sales	£ 02 Production	£ 03 Buying	£ 04 Finance	£ VAT	Code
30/11/X1	335	13 71			12 21		1 50	0323
	336	3 68				3 68		0424
	337	12 99	12 99					0122
	338	6 78	6 48				0 30	0123
	339	3 51		3 51				0223
	340	6 51				6 51		0423
Totals		47 18	19 47	3 51	12 21	10 19	1 80	

346

TASK 3

JOURNAL	PETTY CASH EXPENDITURE		No 3346	
Prepared by A N Other		**Week ending** 30/11/X1		
Authorised by				

Department	Expense	Account code	Debit	Credit
Sales / marketing	Entertainment	01 20		
	Education	21		
	Travelling	22	12.99	
	Welfare	23	6.48	
	Stationery/Post	24		
Production	Entertainment	02 20		
	Education	21		
	Travelling	22		
	Welfare	23	3.51	
	Stationery/Post	24		
Buying	Entertainment	03 20		
	Education	21		
	Travelling	22		
	Welfare	23	12.21	
	Stationery/Post	24		
Finance	Entertainment	04 20		
	Education	21		
	Travelling	22		
	Welfare	23	6.51	
	Stationery/Post	24	3.68	
VAT			1.80	
Petty cash				47.18
TOTALS			47.18	47.18

UNIT 30 : WORKBOOK

Chapter 21
Bank reconciliations

△ ACTIVITY 66

Cash receipts book

Date	Narrative	Total £	VAT £	Debtors £	Other £	Discount £
20X1						
7/3	Paying in slip 0062	1,112.60 ✓	78.80	583.52	450.28	23.60
8/3	Paying in slip 0063	1,047.80 ✓	60.24	643.34	344.22	30.01
9/3	Paying in slip 0064	1,287.64 ✓	71.20	809.59	406.85	34.20
10/3	Paying in slip 0065	987.80	49.90	652.76	285.14	18.03
11/3	Paying in slip 0066	1,127.94	51.84	779.88	296.22	23.12
	BGC – L Fernley	406.90		406.90		
	Bank interest	6.83			6.83	
		5,977.51	311.98	3,875.99	1,789.54	128.96

Cash payments book

Date	Details	Cheque No	Code	Total £	VAT £	Creditors £	Cash purchases £	Other £	Discounts received £
20X1									
7/3	P Barn	012379	PL06	383.21 ✓		383.21			
	Purchases	012380	ML	268.33 ✓	39.96		228.37		
	R Trevor	012381	PL12	496.80 ✓		496.80			6.30
8/3	F Nunn	012382	PL07	218.32		218.32			
	F Taylor	012383	PL09	467.28 ✓		467.28			9.34
	C Cook	012384	PL10	301.40 ✓		301.40			
9/3	L White	012385	PL17	222.61		222.61			
	Purchases	012386	ML	269.40 ✓	40.12		229.28		
	T Finn	012387	PL02	148.60 ✓		148.60			
10/3	S Penn	012388	PL16	489.23		489.23			7.41
11/3	P Price	012389	PL20	299.99		299.99			
	Purchases	012390	ML	264.49	39.39		225.10		
	Loan Finance	SO	ML	200.00				200.00	
				4,029.66	119.47	3,027.44	682.75	200.00	23.05

… KEY TECHNIQUES : ANSWERS

FINANCIAL BANK plc CONFIDENTIAL

You can bank on us!

10 Yorkshire Street   Account   CURRENT   Sheet 00614
Headingley
Leeds LS1 1QT   Account name   T R FABER LTD
Telephone: 0113 633061
Statement date   11 March 20X1   Account Number   27943316

Date	Details	Withdrawals (£)	Deposits (£)	Balance (£)
7/3	Balance from sheet 00613			860.40
	Bank giro credit L Fernley		406.90	1,267.30
9/3	Cheque 012380	268.33 ✓		
	Cheque 012381	496.80 ✓		
	Credit 0062		1,112.60 ✓	1,614.77
10/3	Cheque 012383	467.28 ✓		
	Cheque 012384	301.40 ✓		
	Credit 0063		1,047.80 ✓	
	SO - Loan Finance	200.00		1,693.89
11/3	Cheque 012379	383.21 ✓		
	Cheque 012386	269.40 ✓		
	Cheque 012387	148.60 ✓		
	Credit 0064		1,287.64 ✓	
	Bank interest		6.83	2,187.15

SO Standing order   DD Direct debit   CP Card purchase
AC Automated cash   OD Overdrawn   TR Transfer

Balance on the cash book

	£
Opening balance	860.40
Add: receipts	5,977.51
Less: payments	(4,029.66)
Closing balance	2,808.25

The amended closing balance on the cash book is £2,808.25 whilst the balance shown on the bank statement is £2,187.15. The difference is due to:

- paying-in slips 0065 and 0066 have not yet cleared the banking system;
- cheque numbers 012382, 012385, 012388, 012389 and 012390 have not yet cleared the banking system.

UNIT 30 : WORKBOOK

▲ ACTIVITY 67

Cash book

Receipts		£	Payments		£
16/4	Donald & Co	225.47 ✓	16/4	Balance b/d	310.45
17/4	Harper Ltd	305.68 ✓	17/4	Cheque 03621	204.56
	Fisler Partners	104.67 ✓	18/4	Cheque 03622	150.46 ✓
18/4	Denver Ltd	279.57 ✓	19/4	Cheque 03623	100.80
19/4	Gerald Bros	310.45 ✓		Cheque 03624	158.67 ✓
20/4	Johnson & Co	97.68 ✓	20/4	Cheque 03625	224.67
			20/4	Balance c/d	173.91
		1,323.52			1,323.52

There are three unticked items on the bank statement:

- direct debit £183.60 to the District Council;
- cheque number 03621 £240.56 – this has been entered into the cash book as £204.56;
- bank interest £3.64.

Cheques 03623 and 03625 are unticked items in the cash book but these are payments that have not yet cleared through the banking system.

EXPRESS BANK   CONFIDENTIAL

You can bank on us!

High Street
Fenbury
TL4 6JY
Telephone: 0169 422130

Account   CURRENT   Sheet 0213

Account name   P L DERBY LTD

Statement date 20 April 20X1   Account Number 40429107

Date	Details	Withdrawals (£)	Deposits (£)	Balance (£)
16/4	Balance from sheet 0212			310.45 OD
17/4	DD - District Council	183.60		494.05 OD
18/4	Credit		225.47 ✓	268.58 OD
19/4	Credit		104.67 ✓	
	Cheque 03621	240.56		
	Bank interest	3.64		408.11 OD
20/4	Credit		305.68 ✓	
	Credit		279.57 ✓	
	Cheque 03622	150.46 ✓		
	Cheque 03624	158.67 ✓		131.99 OD

SO Standing order   DD Direct debit   CP Card purchase
AC Automated cash   OD Overdrawn   TR Transfer

KEY TECHNIQUES : ANSWERS

△ ACTIVITY 68

Graham

Task (a)

Cash account

	£		£
Brought forward	204	Sundry accounts	
Interest on deposit account	18	Standing orders	35
		Bank charges	14
		Carried forward	173
	222		222
Brought forward	173		

Task (b)

BANK RECONCILIATION STATEMENT AT 31 MARCH 20X3

	£
Balance per bank statement	2,618
Add Uncleared lodgements	723
	3,341
Less Unpresented cheques	(3,168)
Balance per cash account	173

△ ACTIVITY 69

BANK RECONCILIATION STATEMENT AS AT 30 JUNE 20X1

	£	£
Balance per bank statement		(1,160.25) O/D
Outstanding lodgements:		
30 June		6,910.25
		5,750.00
Unpresented cheques:		
121	538.00	
122	212.00	
		(750.00)
Balance per cash book (7,100.45 + 17,111.55 − 19,212.00)		£5,000.00

UNIT 30 : WORKBOOK

ACTIVITY 70

BANK RECONCILIATION STATEMENT – 31 DECEMBER 20X8

	£
Balance per the cash book	2,381.99
Less items not yet credited	(4,744.66)
	(2,362.67)
Add items not yet debited (800 + 1,436.32 + 9,968.35)	12,204.67
Balance per bank statement	9,842.00

ACTIVITY 71

TASK 1

Cash book receipts

Date	Narrative	Paying-in slip	Total	Debtors	Mail order	VAT control	Discount allowed
26/6	Trade debtors	598	15,685.23 ✓	15,685.23			
	Mail order (Chq/PO)	599	386.29 ✓		328.76	57.53	
	Mail order (CC)	600	189.80		76.43	13.37	
27/6	Trade debtors	601	6,650.28 ✓	6,650.28			
	Mail order	602	115.98 ✓		98.71	17.27	
	Megastores plc	CHAPS	11,755.25 ✓	11,755.25			204.17
28/6	Trade debtors	603	12,223.81 ✓	12,223.81			
	Mail order	604	609.22 ✓		518.49	90.73	
29/6	Trade debtors	605	5,395.40	5,395.40			
	Mail order	606	98.60		83.91	14.69	
30/6	Trade debtors	607	2,641.68	2,641.68			
	Mail Order/shop	608	249.59		212.43	37.16	
29/6	Freeman Foods Group	CHAPS	14,776.04 ✓	14,776.04			256.64
30/6	Totals		70,777.17	69,127.69	1,318.73	230.75	460.81

At this stage you may notice that the cash book totals do not cross-cast – there is a difference of £100. This error should be highlighted when you compare the cash book and the bank statement.

KEY TECHNIQUES : ANSWERS

Cash book payments

Date	Narrative	Cheque	Total	Creditors	Salaries	Other	VAT control	Discount received
26/6	Blackwood Foodstuffs	389	325.99✓	325.99				
	Bruning & Soler	390	683.85✓	683.85				
	Dehlavi Kosmetatos	391	2,112.16✓	2,112.16				
	Environmentally Friendly Co Ltd	392	705.77	705.77				
	Greig Handling (Import)	393	1,253.98✓	1,253.98				
	Halpern Freedman	394	338.11✓	338.11				
	Kobo Design Studio	395	500.00✓	500.00				
	Rayner Food Co	396	375.22	375.22				
	Year 2000 Produce Co	397	1,100.68	1,100.68				
27/6	HM Revenue & Customs	398	23,599.28				23,599.28	
28/6	Salaries - Bank Giro	400	48,995.63		48,995.63			
30/6	Arthur Chong Ltd	401	235.55	235.55				
	Dwyer & Co (Import)	402	469.55	469.55				23.48
	Earthworld Ltd	403	449.28	449.28				22.46
	English Electricity	DD	159.78✓			135.98	23.80	
	English Telecom	DD	224.47✓			191.04	33.43	
Totals			81,529.30	8,550.14	48,995.63	327.02	23,656.51	45.94

Balance on the cash account

	£
Opening balance	84,579.77
Cash book receipts total	70,777.17
Cash book payments total	(81,529.30)
Cash book balance	73,827.64

TASK 2

Main ledger accounts

Sales ledger control account

			£				£
24/6	Balance b/d		312,465.99	30/6	Cash book receipts		69,127.69
				30/6	Cash book receipts – discount		460.81

Mail order sales account

	£			£
		24/6	Balance b/d	26,578.46
		30/6	Cash book receipts	1,318.73

VAT control account

		£			£
30/6	Cash book payments	23,656.51	24/6	Balance b/d	29,375.32
			30/6	Cash book receipts	230.75

Discount allowed account

		£		£
24/6	Balance b/d	4,627.56		
30/6	Cash book receipts	460.81		

Purchases ledger control account

		£			£
30/6	Cash book payments	8,550.14	24/6	Balance b/d	25,476.34
30/6	Cash book payments - discount	45.94			

Salaries account

		£		£
24/6	Balance b/d	105,374.36		
30/6	Cash book payments	48,995.63		

Electricity account

		£		£
24/6	Balance b/d	1,496.57		
30/6	Cash book payments	135.98		

Telephone account

		£		£
24/6	Balance b/d	967.47		
30/6	Cash book payments	191.04		

Discount received account

	£			£
		24/6	Balance b/d	336.58
		30/6	Cash book payments	45.94

KEY TECHNIQUES : **ANSWERS**

TASK 3

FINANCIAL BANK plc   CONFIDENTIAL

You can bank on us!

467 HIGH STREET   Account   CURRENT   Sheet 455
TAUNTON
TA1 9WE   Account name   NATURAL PRODUCTS LIMITED
Telephone:
01832 722098

20X1   Statement date   30 JUNE 20X1   Account Number   34786695

Date	Details	Withdrawals (£)	Deposits (£)	Balance (£)
27 JUN	Balance from sheet 454			11,305.11
27 JUN	MEGASTORES PLC CHAPS		11,755.25 ✓	
	COUNTER CREDIT 591		13,604.01	
	COUNTER CREDIT 592		112.13	
	374	127.09		
	376	5,955.80		
	ENGLISH ELECTRIC DD	159.78 ✓		30,533.83
28 JUN	COUNTER CREDIT 593		11,655.24	
	COUNTER CREDIT 594		683.11	
	COUNTER CREDIT 595		112.19	
	372	87.93		
	389	325.99 ✓		
	ENGLISH TELECOM DD	224.47 ✓		42,345.98
29 JUN	COUNTER CREDIT 596		325.11	
	COUNTER CREDIT 597		60,331.90	
	391	2,112.16 ✓		
	382	331.80		
	FREEMAN FOODS GRP CHAPS		14,776.04 ✓	
	COUNTER CREDIT 598		15,685.23 ✓	
	COUNTER CREDIT 599		386.29 ✓	
	COUNTER CREDIT 600		89.80	
	394	338.11 ✓		
	395	500.00 ✓		
	386	441.09		
	388	111.94		130,105.25
30 JUN	COUNTER CREDIT 601		6,650.28 ✓	
	COUNTER CREDIT 602		115.98 ✓	
	381	117.54		
	384	3,785.60		
	387	785.11		
	390	683.85 ✓		
	393	1,253.98 ✓		
	399	175.10		
	COUNTER CREDIT 603		12,223.81 ✓	
	COUNTER CREDIT 604		609.22 ✓	142,903.36

key SO Standing order   DD Direct debit   CP Card purchase
     AC Automated cash   OD Overdrawn
     CHAPS Clearing House Automated Payments System
     BACS Bankers Automated Clearing Service

UNIT 30 : WORKBOOK

TASK 4

MEMORANDUM

To: Caroline Everly
From: A N Other
Subject: Comparison of bankstatement and cashbook
Date: 6 July 20X1

I am enclosing the cash book and bank statement.

When comparing the cash book and the bank statement as at 30 June 20X1 the following errors in the cashbook were noted:

Receipt 600 was recorded in the total column of the cash receipts book as £189.80 instead of £89.80. The analysis was recorded as £(76.43 +13.37) = £89.80.

Cheque number 399 for £175.10 was omitted from the cash book.

TASK 5

Amended cash book balance

	£
Balance per Task 1	73,827.64
Receipt adjustment	(100.00)
Payment omitted	(175.10)
Amended balance	73,552.54

Chapter 22
Ledger balances and control accounts

△ ACTIVITY 72   △△△△

(a) Subsidiary ledger – sales ledger

N Pevsner

	£		£
b/f	5,700	c/f	5,850
Sales	150		
	5,850		5,850
b/f	5,850		

R Hackney

	£		£
b/f	5,823	Cash	5,700
Sales	5,280	Bad debt	123
		c/f	5,280
	11,103		11,103
b/f	5,280		

Prince of Wales Hotel

	£		£
b/f	5,826	Cash	5,826
Sales	4,995	c/f	4,995
	10,821		10,821
b/f	4,995		

Subsidiary ledger – purchases ledger

E Lutyens

	£		£
Cash	2,700	b/f	5,481
c/f	5,631	Purchases	2,850
	8,331		8,331
		b/f	5,631

M Hutchinson

	£		£
Cash	150	b/f	5,553
c/f	7,458	Purchases	2,055
	7,608		7,608
		b/f	7,458

H Falkner

	£		£
Cash	2,469	b/f	5,559
c/f	6,450	Purchases	3,360
	8,919		8,919
		b/f	6,450

(b)

Sales ledger control account

	£		£
b/f	17,349	Cash	11,526
Sales	10,425	Bad debts expense written off – R Hackney	123
		c/f	16,125
	27,774		27,774
b/f	16,125		

Purchases ledger control account

	£		£
Cash	5,319	b/f	16,593
c/f	19,539	Purchases	8,265
	24,858		24,858
		b/f	19,539

(c)

Bad debts expense

	£		£
Sales ledger control account (written-off – Hackney)	123		

(d)

List of debtors	£	List of creditors	£
N Pevsner	5,850	E Lutyens	5,631
R Hackney	5,280	M Hutchinson	7,458
Prince of Wales Hotel	4,995	H Falkner	6,450
	16,125		19,539

△ ACTIVITY 73

(a)

Purchases ledger control account

	£		£
Cash paid	47,028	b/f	5,926
Purchases returns account	202	Purchases (total from PDB)	47,713
Discounts received account	867		
Sales ledger control account (contra)	75		
c/f (bal fig)	5,467		
	53,639		53,639

KEY TECHNIQUES : ANSWERS

(b) **Sales ledger control account**

	£		£
b/f	10,268	Bank account	69,872
Sales (total from SDB)	71,504	Bad debts account	96
		Sales returns account (total from SRDB)	358
		Discounts allowed (total from discount column in CB)	1,435
		Purchases ledger control account (contra)	75
		c/f (bal fig)	9,936
	81,772		81,772

ACTIVITY 74

(a) **Purchases ledger control account**

	£		£
Cash (2)	1,800	Draft bal b/f	97,186
Contra – sales ledger (3)	1,386	Purchases day book undercast (1)	6,000
Ball c/f	100,000		
	103,186		103,186
		Adjusted bal b/f	100,000

(b) **Reconciliation with list of balances**

	£
Total per list of balances	96,238
Debit balance extracted as a credit (4) (2 x 40)	(80)
Balance omitted (5)	3,842
Adjusted balance per control account	100,000

ACTIVITY 75

(a) **Sales ledger control account**

		£			£
30 Sep	b/f	3,825	30 Sep	Bad debts account (2)	400
				Purchases ledger control account (4)	70
				Discount allowed (5)	140
				c/f	3,215
		3,825			3,825
1 Oct	b/f	3,215			

KAPLAN PUBLISHING

UNIT 30 : WORKBOOK

(b) **List of sales ledger balances**

	£
Original total	3,362
Add: Debit balances previously omitted (1)	103
	3,465
Less: Item posted twice to Sparrow's account (3)	(250)
Amended total agreeing with balance on sales ledger control account	3,215

△ ACTIVITY 76

(a)

JOURNAL ENTRY	Number:	
Prepared by: A N Other		
Authorised by:		
Date:		
Narrative: To write off bad debt		
Account	Debit	Credit
Bad debts expense	800.00	
Sales ledger control		800.00
TOTALS	800.00	800.00

(b)

JOURNAL ENTRY	Number:	
Prepared by: A N Other		
Authorised by:		
Date:		
Narrative: To enter contra entry		
Account	Debit	Credit
Purchases ledger control	240.00	
Sales ledger control		240.00
TOTALS	240.00	240.00

(c)

JOURNAL ENTRY	Number:	
Prepared by: A N Other		
Authorised by:		
Date:		
Narrative: To correct undercast of discount allowed		
Account	Debit	Credit
Discount allowed	100.00	
Sales ledger control		100.00
TOTALS	100.00	100.00

△ ACTIVITY 77

(a)

JOURNAL ENTRY	Number:	
Prepared by: A N Other		
Authorised by:		
Date:		
Narrative: To correct overcast of purchases day book		
Account	Debit	Credit
Purchases ledger control	1,000.00	
Purchases		1,000.00
TOTALS	1,000.00	1,000.00

(b)

JOURNAL ENTRY	Number:	
Prepared by: A N Other		
Authorised by:		
Date:		
Narrative: To correct posting of discount received		
Account	Debit	Credit
Purchases ledger control	9.00	
Discount received		9.00
TOTALS	9.00	9.00

(c)

JOURNAL ENTRY	Number:	
Prepared by: A N Other		
Authorised by:		
Date:		
Narrative:		
To enter contra in main ledger		
Account	Debit	Credit
Purchases ledger control	300.00	
Sales ledger control		300.00
TOTALS	300.00	300.00

Chapter 23
Drafting an initial trial balance

△ ACTIVITY 78

Trial balance at 31 May 20X1

	£	£
Purchases	385,800	
Creditors		32,000
Computer	8,000	
Motor car	19,200	
Discount received		3,850
Telephone	4,320	
Sales returns	6,720	
Wages	141,440	
VAT		7,200
Drawings	60,000	
Discount allowed	6,400	
Rent and rates	26,200	
Debtors	53,500	
Motor expenses	7,700	
Sales		642,080
Stock	38,880	
Inland Revenue		3,800
Purchases returns		2,560
Electricity	6,080	
Bank	1,920	
Capital		74,670
	766,160	766,160

ACTIVITY 79

Capital account

		£			£
			1 Mar	Bank	12,000

Bank account

		£			£
1 Mar	Capital	12,000	2 Mar	Motor car	4,500
7 Mar	Sales	3,000	2 Mar	Purchases	2,400
20 Mar	Sales	2,100	14 Mar	Rent	600
26 Mar	Debtors	3,800	18 Mar	Stationery	200
			25 Mar	Creditors	3,100
			28 Mar	Drawings	1,600
			31 Mar	Balance c/d	8,500
		20,900			20,900
1 Apr	Balance b/d	8,500			

Motor car account

		£			£
2 Mar	Bank	4,500			

Purchases account

		£			£
2 Mar	Bank	2,400			
4 Mar	Creditors	2,500			
12 Mar	Creditors	4,100	31 Mar	Balance c/d	9,000
		9,000			9,000
1 Apr	Balance b/d	9,000			

Creditors' account

		£			£
25 Mar	Bank	3,100	4 Mar	Purchases	2,500
31 Mar	Balance c/d	3,500	12 Mar	Purchases	4,100
		6,600			6,600
			1 Apr	Balance b/d	3,500

Sales account

		£			£
31 Mar	Balance c/d	13,200	7 Mar	Bank	3,000
			10 Mar	Debtors	4,600
			15 Mar	Debtors	3,500
			20 Mar	Bank	2,100
		13,200			13,200
			1 Apr	Balance b/d	13,200

Debtors' account

		£			£
10 Mar	Sales	4,600	26 Mar	Bank	3,800
15 Mar	Sales	3,500	31 Mar	Balance c/d	4,300
		8,100			8,100
1 Apr	Balance b/d	4,300			

Rent account

		£			£
14 Mar	Bank	600			

Stationery account

		£			£
18 Mar	Bank	200			

Drawings account

		£			£
28 Mar	Bank	1,600			

Trial balance at 31 March

	£	£
Capital		12,000
Bank	8,500	
Motor car	4,500	
Purchases	9,000	
Creditors		3,500
Sales		13,200
Debtors	4,300	
Rent	600	
Stationery	200	
Drawings	1,600	
	28,700	28,700

KEY TECHNIQUES : **ANSWERS**

△ ACTIVITY 80

Trial balance at 30 June 20X1

	£	£
Debtors	33,440	
Bank	1,200	
Sales		401,300
Stock	24,300	
Wages	88,400	
Telephone	2,700	
Motor car	12,000	
VAT		7,000
Electricity	3,800	
Rent	16,400	
Purchases	241,180	
Purchases returns		1,600
Sales returns	4,200	
Office equipment	5,000	
Capital		49,160
Motor expenses	4,840	
Discounts allowed	4,010	
Discounts received		2,410
Creditors		20,000
Drawings	40,000	
	481,470	481,470

△ ACTIVITY 81

TASKS 1 TO 3
Main ledger

Sales ledger control account

Date	Details	Amount £	Date	Details	Amount £
Dec 1	Balance b/d	537,483	Dec 1	Sales returns DB	167
	Sales DB	24,587		Bank	1,755
	Bank	1,000		Discounts	45
			Dec 1	Balance c/d	561,103
		563,070			563,070
Dec 2	Balance b/d	561,103			

Purchases ledger control account

Date	Details	Amount £	Date	Details	Amount £
Dec 1	Purchases returns DB	32	Dec 1	Balance b/d	404,546
	Bank (4,388+10,565)	14,953		Purchases DB	29,310
	Discounts	112			
Dec 1	Balance c/d	418,759			
		433,856			433,856
			Dec 2	Balance b/d	418,759

Equipment

Date	Details	Amount £	Date	Details	Amount £
Dec 1	Balance b/d	4,182	Dec 1	Balance c/d	5,008
	Bank (970 – 144)	826			
		5,008			5,008
Dec 2	Balance b/d	5,008			

Heating and lighting

Date	Details	Amount £	Date	Details	Amount £
Dec 1	Balance b/d	1,728	Dec 1	Balance c/d	2,244
	Purchases DB	516			
		2,244			2,244
Dec 2	Balance b/d	2,244			

Purchases

Date	Details	Amount £	Date	Details	Amount £
Dec 1	Balance b/d	2,432,679	Dec 1	Balance c/d	2,457,304
	Purchases DB	24,429			
	Bank (230 – 34)	196			
		2,457,304			2,457,304
Dec 2	Balance b/d	2,457,304			

VAT

Date	Details	Amount £	Date	Details	Amount £
Dec 1	Purchases DB	4,365	Dec 1	Balance b/d	63,217
	Sales returns DB	25		Sales DB	3,662
	Bank	193		Purchases returns DB	5
Dec 1	Balance c/d	62,301			
		66,884			66,884
			Dec 2	Balance b/d	62,301

Subsidiary (sales) ledger

Classic Music

Date	Details	Amount £	Date	Details	Amount £
Dec 1	Balance b/d	16,742	Dec 1	Sales returns DB	167
	Sales DB	1,978		Bank	1,755
	Bank	1,000		Discount allowed	45
			Dec 1	Balance c/d	17,753
		19,720			19,720
Dec 2	Balance b/d	17,753			

Subsidiary (purchases) ledger

Atlantic Imports Ltd

Date	Details	Amount £	Date	Details	Amount £
Dec 1	Purchases returns DB	32	Dec 1	Balance b/d	43,607
	Bank	4,388		Purchases DB	12,528
	Discount received	112			
Dec 1	Balance c/d	51,603			
		56,135			56,135
			Dec 2	Balance b/d	51,603

TASK 4
List of updated balances

	Debit balances £	Credit balances £
Customers:		
Hit Records Ltd (10,841 + 4,279)	15,120	
Smiths & Co (18,198 + 6,023)	24,221	
Classic Music	17,753	
Other customers (491,702 + 12,307)	504,009	
Suppliers:		
HMI Ltd (82,719 + 10,524)		93,243
Atlantic Imports Ltd		51,603
Southern Electric (NIL + 606)		606
Other suppliers (278,220 + 5,652 – 10,565)		273,307
Purchases	2,457,304	
Sales (3,284,782 + 20,925)		3,305,707
Sales returns (10,973 + 142)	11,115	
Purchases returns (9,817 + 27)		9,844
Heating and lighting	2,244	
Equipment	5,008	
Equipment repairs (166 + 102 – 15)	253	
Bank charges (82 + 67)	149	
VAT		62,301
Bank		1,075
Discount allowed (11,420 + 45)	11,465	
Discount received (8,516 + 112)		8,628
Other debit balances	1,368,815	
Other credit balances		611,142
Totals	4,417,456	4,417,456

MOCK SIMULATION 1
ANSWERS

UNIT 30 : WORKBOOK

PART ONE

TASK 1

INVOICE NO: 1325

BRAMALL TOYS LTD
BLADES PARADE, BURSLEM ROAD, SHEFFIELD S2 4SV
Telephone: 0114 273 5895

To: Hutchison Ltd
Nicholson Centre
Ramley   Northants RY3 4AY

Date / tax point   21 November 20X1
Customer Order No   4260

Quantity	Description	Item Code	Unit Price £	Trade discount £	Total amount £
10	Cot mobile	P182	6.70	16.75	50.25
5	Compact keyboard	S546	15.20	19.00	57.00

Total goods	107.25
VAT @ 17½%	18.76
Total Due	126.01

Terms: net, 30 days

VAT registration number 643 782 692

INVOICE NO: 1326

BRAMALL TOYS LTD
BLADES PARADE, BURSLEM ROAD, SHEFFIELD S2 4SV
Telephone: 0114 273 5895

To: Walker plc
Walker House
Ardrees Avenue
Twycroft BN3 7PS

Date / tax point   21 November 20X1
Customer Order No   3178

Quantity	Description	Item Code	Unit Price £	Trade discount £	Total amount £
12	Activity centre	P121	10.50	31.50	94.50
20	Stencil set	S529	5.80	29.00	87.00

Total goods	181.50
VAT @ 17½%	31.76
Total Due	213.26

Terms: net, 30 days

VAT registration number 643 782 692

MOCK SIMULATION 1 : **ANSWERS**

INVOICE   NO: 1327

BRAMALL TOYS LTD
BLADES PARADE, BURSLEM ROAD, SHEFFIELD S2 4SV
Telephone: 0114 273 5895

To: Hodges & Co
108 Wyndale Road
Brooking
Herts BK12 1ER

Date / tax point   21 November 20X1
Customer Order No   909

Quantity	Description	Item Code	Unit Price £	Trade discount £	Total amount £
15	Pop Up Farm	P322	6.50	29.25	68.25

Total goods	68.25
VAT @ 17½%	11.94
Total Due	80.19

Terms: net, 30 days   VAT registration number 643 782 692

INVOICE   NO: 1328

BRAMALL TOYS LTD
BLADES PARADE, BURSLEM ROAD, SHEFFIELD S2 4SV
Telephone: 0114 273 5895

To: Whitehouse Stores Ltd
Unit 8
Hockley Trading Est
Hammerfold LR2 8DT

Date / tax point   21 November 20X1
Customer Order No   463

Quantity	Description	Item Code	Unit Price £	Trade discount £	Total amount £
2	Tree House	S571	85.60	51.36	119.84
30	Bubble Ball	P189	3.10	27.90	65.10

Total goods	184.94
VAT @ 17½%	32.36
Total Due	217.30

Terms: net, 30 days   VAT registration number 643 782 692

KAPLAN PUBLISHING

INVOICE — NO: 1329

BRAMALL TOYS LTD
BLADES PARADE, BURSLEM ROAD, SHEFFIELD S2 4SV
Telephone: 0114 273 5895

To: Walker plc
Walker House
Ardrees Avenue
Twycroft BN3 7PS

Date / tax point   21 November 20X1
Customer Order No   3192

Quantity	Description	Item Code	Unit Price £	Trade discount £	Total amount £
10	Toddler Truck	P335	12.60	31.50	94.50
5	Magnetic Easel	S520	28.30	35.38	106.12

Total goods	200.62
VAT @ 17½%	35.10
Total Due	235.72

Terms: net, 30 days   VAT registration number 643 782 692

INVOICE — NO: 1330

BRAMALL TOYS LTD
BLADES PARADE, BURSLEM ROAD, SHEFFIELD S2 4SV
Telephone: 0114 273 5895

To: White & Veart
216 Breech Street
Holyfield   M32 5FG

Date / tax point   21 November 20X1
Customer Order No   284

Quantity	Description	Item Code	Unit Price £	Trade discount £	Total amount £
20	Plastic Garage	P370	7.25	50.75	94.25
4	Trampoline	S558	31.50	44.10	81.90

Total goods	176.15
VAT @ 17½%	30.82
Total Due	206.97

Terms: net, 30 days   VAT registration number 643 782 692

MOCK SIMULATION 1 : **ANSWERS**

INVOICE NO: 1331

BRAMALL TOYS LTD
BLADES PARADE, BURSLEM ROAD, SHEFFIELD S2 4SV
Telephone: 0114 273 5895

To: Blake Ltd
34 Exley Road
Triverton TN2 6WY

Date / tax point 21 November 20X1
Customer Order No 392

Quantity	Description	Item Code	Unit Price £	Trade discount £	Total amount £
50	Painting Overall	S522	2.50	37.50	87.50
20	Chime Bear	P094	4.25	25.50	59.50

Total goods	147.00
VAT @ 17½%	25.72
Total Due	172.72

Terms: net, 30 days

VAT registration number 643 782 692

INVOICE NO: 1332

BRAMALL TOYS LTD
BLADES PARADE, BURSLEM ROAD, SHEFFIELD S2 4SV
Telephone: 0114 273 5895

To: Angell Flo Ltd
75 Britholme Street
Slough
Berks SL3 3MN

Date / tax point 21 November 20X1
Customer Order No 1603

Quantity	Description	Item Code	Unit Price £	Trade discount £	Total amount £
10	Trike	P309	8.75	30.63	56.87
10	Activity Centre	P121	10.50	36.75	68.25

Total goods	125.12
VAT @ 17½%	21.89
Total Due	147.01

Terms: net, 30 days

VAT registration number 643 782 692

KAPLAN PUBLISHING

UNIT 30 : WORKBOOK

TASK 2

CREDIT NOTE   **NO: 513**

BRAMALL TOYS LTD
BLADES PARADE, BURSLEM ROAD, SHEFFIELD S2 4SV
Telephone: 0114 273 5895

To: Hodges & Co
108 Wyndale Road
Brooking Herts BK12 1ER

Date / tax point   21 November 20X1

Quantity	Description	Item Code	Unit Price £	Trade discount £	Total amount £
2	Activity Centre	P121	10.50	6.30	14.70

REASON FOR CREDIT
Returned goods

Total goods	14.70
VAT @ 17½%	2.57
Total Credit Due	17.27

VAT registration number 643 782 692

CREDIT NOTE   **NO: 514**

BRAMALL TOYS LTD
BLADES PARADE, BURSLEM ROAD, SHEFFIELD S2 4SV
Telephone: 0114 273 5895

To: Blake Ltd
34 Exley Road
Triverton TN2 6WY

Date / tax point   21 November 20X1

Quantity	Description	Item Code	Unit Price £	Trade discount £	Total amount £
1	Magnetic Easel	S520	28.30	8.49	19.81

REASON FOR CREDIT
Returned goods

Total goods	19.81
VAT @ 17½%	3.46
Total Credit Due	23.27

VAT registration number 643 782 692

MOCK SIMULATION 1 : **ANSWERS**

CREDIT NOTE   NO: 515
BRAMALL TOYS LTD
BLADES PARADE, BURSLEM ROAD, SHEFFIELD S2 4SV
Telephone: 0114 273 5895

To: Angell Flo Ltd
75 Britholme Street
Slough
Berks SL3 3MN

Date / tax point   21 November 20X1

Quantity	Description	Item Code	Unit Price £	Trade discount £	Total amount £
3	Toddler Truck	P335	12.60	13.23	24.57

REASON FOR CREDIT
Returned goods

Total goods	24.57
VAT @ 17½%	4.29
Total Credit Due	28.86

VAT registration number 643 782 692

CREDIT NOTE   NO:
BRAMALL TOYS LTD
BLADES PARADE, BURSLEM ROAD, SHEFFIELD S2 4SV
Telephone: 0114 273 5895

To:

Date / tax point

Quantity	Description	Item Code	Unit Price £	Trade discount £	Total amount £

REASON FOR CREDIT

Total goods	
VAT @ 17½%	
Total Credit Due	

VAT registration number 643 782 692

UNIT 30 : WORKBOOK

Details of goods returned note	Action
Customer White & Veart **Date of Return** 21 November X1	The item code and item description do not match. Check with signature on goods returned note to find out which it is, and with records to check what had been supplied to the customer previously.

TASK 3

SALES DAY BOOK

SDB 73

Date 20X1	Invoice	Customer	Total £	VAT £	Pre-school toys £	School-age toys £
17 Nov	1318	Bigston Ltd	243.75	36.30	114.70	92.75
17 Nov	1319	Dalglish Ltd	490.62	73.07	204.65	212.90
18 Nov	1320	Hodges & Co	411.60	61.30	28.90	321.40
19 Nov	1321	Whitehouse Stores Ltd	631.38	94.03	346.75	190.60
19 Nov	1322	Blake Ltd	340.69	50.74	187.50	102.45
19 Nov	1323	Walker plc	519.87	77.42	301.55	140.90
20 Nov	1324	Angell Flo Ltd	182.88	27.23	55.60	100.05
21 Nov	1325	Hutchison Ltd	126.01	18.76	50.25	57.00
21 Nov	1326	Walker plc	213.26	31.76	94.50	87.00
21 Nov	1327	Hodges & Co	80.19	11.94	68.25	
21 Nov	1328	Whitehouse Stores Ltd	217.30	32.36	65.10	119.84
21 Nov	1329	Walker plc	235.72	35.10	94.50	106.12
21 Nov	1330	White & Veart	206.97	30.82	94.25	81.90
21 Nov	1331	Blake Ltd	172.72	25.72	59.50	87.50
21 Nov	1332	Angell Flo Ltd	147.01	21.89	125.12	
21 Nov		Total	4,219.97	628.44	1,891.12	1,700.41

SALES RETURNS DAY BOOK

SRDB 17

Date 20X1	Credit Note	Customer	Total £	VAT £	Pre-school toys £	School-age toys £
17 Nov	510	Whitehouse Stores Ltd	54.40	8.10	46.30	
19 Nov	511	Walker plc	67.91	10.11		57.80
20 Nov	512	Hutchison Ltd	71.85	10.70	42.20	18.95
21 Nov	513	Hodges & Co	17.27	2.57	14.70	
21 Nov	514	Blake Ltd	23.27	3.46		19.81
21 Nov	515	Angell Flo Ltd	28.86	4.29	24.57	
21 Nov		Total	263.56	39.23	127.77	96.56

UNIT 30 : WORKBOOK

PART TWO

TASK 4

Document number	Action
1	Approve sale. Ensure cheque card number written on back of cheque.
2	Sale not approved – card has expired. Customer may have new card on him to use – if not ask for payment by other means, i.e. cash/credit card.
3	Approve sale. Ensure cheque card number written on back of cheque.
4	Approve sale. Ensure cheque card number written on back of cheque.
5	Sale not approved – card does not have same account number. Ask customer for correct card, or payment by other means, i.e. cash/credit card.
6	Approve sale. Ensure cheque card number written on back of cheque.
7	Sale approved.
8	Sale approved.
9	Sale not approved – credit card slip not signed. Ask customer to sign the slip.
10	Sale approved.

MOCK SIMULATION 1 : **ANSWERS**

TASK 5

Bank Giro Credit

Date 21/11/X1

Credit Bramall Toys Ltd

	£	p
£50 Notes	100	00
£20 Notes	380	00
£10 Notes	150	00
£5 Notes	55	00
£2, £1	22	00
50p	7	50
20p	2	80
10p, 5p	2	80
2p, 1p		44
Total cash	720	54
Cheques, etc see over	589	72
£	1,310	26

Date 21/11/X1
Cashier's stamp and initials

Code no 25 - 46 - 70

Bank   Wadworth Bank Ltd

Branch Chambers Street, Scarborough

Credit   Bramall Toys Ltd

Account no 21758391

No of cheques 11

Paid in by A Student

	£	p
£50 Notes	100	00
£20 Notes	380	00
£10 Notes	150	00
£5 Notes	55	00
£2, £1	22	00
50p	7	50
20p	2	80
10p, 5p	2	80
2p, 1p		44
Total cash	720	54
Cheques, etc see over	589	72
£	1,310	26

Cheques, etc

	£	p		£	p
			Brought forward £	355	19
D Page	31	76	Credit Card Voucher	234	53
L Thew	19	05			
C Boardman	33	75			
K Martin	48	09			
G Kelly	72	11			
S Hicks	18	82			
I Ironside	28	30			
J Rockett	22	65			
L Harper	10	67			
N Trebble	15	55			
O Heald	54	44			
Carried forward £	355	19	Carried over £	589	72

Counterfoil Carried over £

UNIT 30 : WORKBOOK

TASK 5, CONTINUED

HAVE YOU IMPRINTED THE SUMMARY WITH YOUR RETAILER'S CARD?

BANK Processing (White) copy of Summary with your vouchers in correct order:
1. SUMMARY
2. SALES VOUCHERS
3. REFUND VOUCHERS

KEEP Retailer's copies (Blue & Yellow)
NO MORE THAN 200 Vouchers to each Summary.
DO NOT USE Staples, Pins, Paper Clips

	ITEMS	AMOUNT
SALES VOUCHERS (LISTED OVERLEAF)	8	234 53
LESS REFUND VOUCHERS		
DATE 21.11.X1	TOTAL £	234 53

SUMMARY – RETAILER'S COPY

WADSWORTH BANK   BANKING SUMMARY

A Student
RETAILER'S SIGNATURE

Complete this summary for every deposit of sales vouchers and enter the total on your normal current account paying-in slip

	£	p
1	33	14
2	19	75
3	35	90
4	24	23
5	18	99
6	75	28
7	14	58
8	12	66
9		
10		
11		
12		
13		
14		
15		
16		
17		
18		
19		
20		
Total	234	53

DO NOT TICK OR MAKE ANY MARKS OUTSIDE THE LISTING AREA

Carried overleaf

MOCK SIMULATION 1 : ANSWERS

TASK 6

Cash Book Receipts						41
Date	Narrative	Total	Debtors	Cash Sales	VAT	Discount allowed
18 Nov	Hutchison Ltd	152.81	152.81			
18 Nov	White & Veart	526.74	526.74			
19 Nov	Bigston Ltd	82.53	82.53			
19 Nov	Walker plc	272.19	272.19			
17 Nov	Cash Sales	1,146.73		975.94	170.79	
18 Nov	Cash Sales	1,225.78		1,043.22	182.56	
19 Nov	Cash Sales	1,234.05		1,050.26	183.79	
20 Nov	Cash Sales	900.14		766.08	134.06	
21 Nov	Cash Sales	1,310.26		1,115.12	195.14	
		6,851.23	1,034.27	4,950.62	866.34	

PART THREE
TASKS 7 AND 8

SUBSIDIARY (SALES) LEDGER ACCOUNTS

Account: Angell Flo Ltd

Debit   Credit

Date 20X1	Details	Amount £	Date 20X1	Details	Amount £
14 Nov	Balance b/f	691.29	21 Nov	Cr Note 515	28.86
20 Nov	Sales – Inv 1324	182.88			
21 Nov	Sales – Inv 1332	147.01			

Account:　　Bigston Ltd

Debit			Credit		
Date 20X1	Details	Amount £	Date 20X1	Details	Amount £
14 Nov	Balance b/f	274.04	19 Nov	Bank CBR 41	82.53
17 Nov	Sales – Inv 1318	243.75			

Account:　　Blake Ltd

Debit			Credit		
Date 20X1	Details	Amount £	Date 20X1	Details	Amount £
14 Nov	Balance b/f	577.03	21 Nov	Cr Note 514	23.27
19 Nov	Sales – Inv 1322	340.69			
21 Nov	Sales – Inv 1331	172.72			

Account:　　Dalglish Ltd

Debit			Credit		
Date 20X1	Details	Amount £	Date 20X1	Details	Amount £
14 Nov	Balance b/f	1,521.11			
17 Nov	Sales – Inv No 1319	490.62			

Account:　　Hodges & Co

Debit			Credit		
Date 20X1	Details	Amount £	Date 20X1	Details	Amount £
14 Nov	Balance b/f	546.62	21 Nov	Cr Note 513	17.27
18 Nov	Sales – Inv No 1320	411.60			
21 Nov	Sales – Inv No 1327	80.19			

MOCK SIMULATION 1 : ANSWERS

Account: Hutchison Ltd

Debit / Credit

Date 20X1	Details	Amount £	Date 20X1	Details	Amount £
14 Nov	Balance b/f	426.89	18 Nov	Bank CBR 41	152.81
21 Nov	Sales – Inv No 1325	126.01	20 Nov	Cr Note 512	71.85

Account: Walker plc

Debit / Credit

Date 20X1	Details	Amount £	Date 20X1	Details	Amount £
14 Nov	Balance b/f	522.74	19 Nov	Bank CBR 41	272.19
19 Nov	Sales – Inv No 1323	519.87	19 Nov	Cr Note 511	67.91
21 Nov	Sales – Inv No 1326	213.26			
21 Nov	Sales – Inv No 1329	235.72			

Account: White & Veart

Debit / Credit

Date 20X1	Details	Amount £	Date 20X1	Details	Amount £
14 Nov	Balance b/f	926.38	18 Nov	Bank CBR 41	526.74
21 Nov	Sales – Inv No 1330	206.97			

Account: Whitehouse Stores Ltd

Debit / Credit

Date 20X1	Details	Amount £	Date 20X1	Details	Amount £
14 Nov	Balance b/f	641.56	17 Nov	Cr Note 510	54.40
19 Nov	Sales – Inv No 1321	631.38			
21 Nov	Sales – Inv No 1328	217.30			

UNIT 30 : WORKBOOK

TASK 9

MAIN LEDGER ACCOUNTS

Account: Sales ledger control

Debit | | | Credit | | |

Date 20X1	Details	Amount £	Date 20X1	Details	Amount £
14 Nov	Balance b/f	14,890.75	21 Nov	Bank CBR 41	1,034.27
21 Nov	Sales Day Book	4,219.97	21 Nov	Sales Returns Day Book	263.56

Account: VAT

Debit | | | Credit | | |

Date 20X1	Details	Amount £	Date 20X1	Details	Amount £
21 Nov	Sales Returns Day Book	39.23	14 Nov	Balance b/f	2,533.40
			21 Nov	Sales Day Book	628.44
			21 Nov	Bank CBR 41	866.34

Account: Sales: pre-school toys

Debit | | | Credit | | |

Date 20X1	Details	Amount £	Date 20X1	Details	Amount £
			14 Nov	Balance b/f	52,147.60
			21 Nov	Sales Day Book	1,891.12
			21 Nov	Bank CBR 41	4,950.62

Account: Sales returns: pre-school toys

Debit | | | Credit | | |

Date 20X1	Details	Amount £	Date 20X1	Details	Amount £
14 Nov	Balance b/f	2,430.91			
21 Nov	Sales Returns Day Book	127.77			

MOCK SIMULATION 1 : **ANSWERS**

Account: Sales: school-age toys

Debit | | | Credit | |

Date 20X1	Details	Amount £	Date 20X1	Details	Amount £
			14 Nov	Balance b/f Sales	37,182.58
			21 Nov	Day Book	1,700.41

Account: Sales returns: school-age toys

Debit | | | Credit | |

Date 20X1	Details	Amount £	Date 20X1	Details	Amount £
14 Nov	Balance b/f Sales	1,724.49			
21 Nov	Returns Day Book	96.56			

MOCK SIMULATION 2
ANSWERS

UNIT 30 : WORKBOOK

PART ONE

TASK 1

Petty Cash Voucher

Folio _____
Date _____

For what required	AMOUNT	
	£	p
Stationery	11	10
	11	10

Signature   *Adam Haynes*
Passed by

Petty Cash Voucher

Folio   175
Date   7/11/X1

For what required	AMOUNT	
	£	p
Stationery	6	95
	6	95

Signature   *Adam Haynes*
Passed by   A Student

Petty Cash Voucher

Folio _____
Date _____

For what required	AMOUNT	
	£	p
Stationery	4	94
	4	94

Signature   *Adam Haynes*
Passed by

Petty Cash Voucher

Folio   176
Date   7/11/X1

For what required	AMOUNT	
	£	p
Stationery	7	33
	7	33

Signature   *Adam Haynes*
Passed by   A Student

MOCK SIMULATION 2 : **ANSWERS**

Petty Cash Voucher		
Folio		
Date		
For what required	AMOUNT £	p
Stationery	15	35
	15	35
Signature *Adam Haynes*		
Passed by		

Petty Cash Voucher		
Folio		
Date		
For what required	AMOUNT £	p
Stationery	12	35
	12	35
Signature *Jane Hawkins*		
Passed by		

Petty Cash Voucher		
Folio 177		
Date 7/11/X1		
For what required	AMOUNT £	p
Stamps	5	25
	5	25
Signature *Jane Hawkins*		
Passed by A Student		

Petty Cash Voucher		
Folio 178		
Date 7/11/X1		
For what required	AMOUNT £	p
Stamps	3	94
	3	94
Signature *Jane Hawkins*		
Passed by A Student		

Petty Cash Voucher		
Folio 179		
Date 7/11/X1		
For what required	AMOUNT £	p
Stamps	0	76
	0	76
Signature *Jane Hawkins*		
Passed by A Student		

Petty Cash Voucher		
Folio 180		
Date 7/11/X1		
For what required	AMOUNT £	p
Taxi fare (meeting with auditors)	5	20
	5	20
Signature *Gillian Russell*		
Passed by A Student		

KAPLAN PUBLISHING

UNIT 30 : WORKBOOK

Petty Cash Voucher

Folio _____181_____

Date _____7/11/X1_____

For what required	AMOUNT	
	£	p
Taxi fare (meeting with supplier)	6	10
	6	10

Signature   *Ben Thornley*

Passed by   A Student

TASK 1, CONTINUED

**MEMORANDUM OF DISCREPANCIES
FOR LETTER TO GILLIAN RUSSELL**

Details of claim	Action
Stationery Supplies Receipt 3 Nov X1 Adam Haynes Total £15.35	Above my limit for authorisation. G Russell to authorise.
Petty Cash Voucher From Adam Haynes for stationery £4.94	No corresponding receipt to process. Wait for relevant receipt
Stamps from Jane Hawkins £12.35	Above my limit for authorisation. G Russell to authorise.
Stationery from Adam Haynes £11.10	Above my limit for authorisation. G Russell to authorise.

MOCK SIMULATION 2 : **ANSWERS**

TASK 2

PETTY CASH BOOK								PCB22
Receipts £	Date 20X1	Details	Voucher	Total £	VAT £	Travel £	Stationery £	Postage £
100.00	31-Oct	Balance b/d						
	7.11.X1	Stationery Supp	175	6.95	1.03		5.92	
	7.11.X1	Stationery Supp	176	7.33	1.09		6.24	
	7.11.X1	Stamps	177	5.25				5.25
	7.11.X1	Stamps	178	3.94				3.94
	7.11.X1	Stamps	179	0.76				0.76
	7.11.X1	Taxi	180	5.20	0.77	4.43		
	7.11.X1	Taxi	181	6.10	0.91	5.19		
				35.53	3.80	9.62	12.16	9.95
35.53	7.11.X1	Cash to restore						
	7.11.X1	Bal c/f		100.00				

TASK 3

PETTY CASH BOX

```
              £
£10  x  4  =  40.00
£5   x  3  =  15.00
£1   x  6  =   6.00
50p  x  3  =   1.50
20p  x  4  =    .80
10p  x  9  =    .90
2p   x  8  =    .16
1p   x 11  =    .11
              ─────
Total        £64.47
              ─────
```

UNIT 30 : WORKBOOK

RECONCILIATION OF PETTY CASH

Petty Cash Book

	£
Opening balance of imprest	100.00
Payments	(35.53)
Closing balance	64.47
Cash counted	64.47

PART TWO

TASK 4

REMITTANCE ADVICE

From: Seamer Retail Limited
37 Cain Road
Scarborough
YO12 4HF

To: Baxley Limited
Station Road
Horsford
TV12 3EW

Date: 7 Nov X1

Details	Amount £	p
Invoice No 4132 dated 26/10/X1		
Goods	1,788	56
VAT	309	86
Cheque no 305082 enclosed	2,098	42

In case of query, please contact   A Student / G Russell

Date
7/11/X1

Payee
Baxley
Limited

£2098.42

305082

WADSWORTH BANK PLC
Chambers Street, Scarborough,
YO12 3NZ

25–46–70

7 November 20 X1

Pay Baxley Limited

Two thousand and ninety-eight pounds

and 42p only

£ 2098.42

For Seamer Retail Ltd

305082   25 - 46 - 70   21758391

MOCK SIMULATION 2 : ANSWERS

REMITTANCE ADVICE

From: Seamer Retail Limited
 37 Cain Road
 Scarborough
 YO12 4HF

To: Harborne Limited
 12 Barton Street
 Apton
 AN3 4RT

Date: 7 Nov X1

Details	Amount £	p
Invoice No 2541 dated 7/10/X1		
Goods	2,076	22
VAT	363	33
Cheque no 305083 enclosed	2,439	55

In case of query, please contact A Student / G Russell

Date 7/11/X1

Payee Harbourne Limited

£2439.55

305083

WADSWORTH BANK PLC
Chambers Street, Scarborough,
YO12 3NZ

25–46–70

7 November 20 X1

Pay Harborne Limited

Two thousand four hundred and thirty-nine pounds and 55p only

£ 2439.55

For Seamer Retail Ltd

305083   25 - 46 - 70   21758391

UNIT 30 : WORKBOOK

REMITTANCE ADVICE

From: Seamer Retail Limited
37 Cain Road
Scarborough
YO12 4HF

To: Hurley Limited
241 Steels Avenue
Picton
SR5 9TY

Date: 7 Nov X1

Details		Amount £	p
Invoice No 1008 dated 1/10/X1			
	Goods	300	17
	VAT	52	52
Cheque no 305084 enclosed		352	69

In case of query, please contact A Student / G Russell

Date
7/11/X1

Payee
Hurley
Limited

£352.69

305084

WADSWORTH BANK PLC
Chambers Street, Scarborough,
YO12 3NZ

25–46–70

7 November 20 X1

Pay Hurley Limited

Three hundred and fifty-two pounds

and 69p only

£ 352.69

For Seamer Retail Ltd

305084   25 - 46 - 70   21758391

MOCK SIMULATION 2 : **ANSWERS**

REMITTANCE ADVICE

From:	Seamer Retail Limited
	37 Cain Road
	Scarborough
	YO12 4HF

To:	Allen and Banks
	49 Exley Road
	Traxham
	TM5 1UJ

Date: 7 Nov X1

Details		Amount	
		£	p
Invoice No 1673 dated 27/10/X1	Goods	654	08
	Discount	(9	81)
	VAT	112	74
Cheque no 305085 enclosed		757	01

In case of query, please contact *A Student / G Russell*

Date 7/11/X1	**WADSWORTH BANK PLC**		25–46–70
	Chambers Street, Scarborough, YO12 3NZ		7 November 20 X1
Payee Allen and Banks			
	Pay *Allen and Banks*		
Discount taken £9.81	*Seven hundred and fifty seven pounds and 01p*		£ *757.01*
			For Seamer Retail Ltd
£757.01			
305085	305085 25 - 46 - 70 21758391		

KAPLAN PUBLISHING

UNIT 30 : WORKBOOK

REMITTANCE ADVICE

From: **Seamer Retail Limited
37 Cain Road
Scarborough
YO12 4HF**

To: **Wallace Limited
101-105 Knighton Road
Brixley
BY2 3FR**

Date: **7 Nov X1**

Details	Amount	
	£	p
Invoice No 4321 dated 10/10/X1		
Goods	102	66
VAT	17	96
Cheque 305086 enclosed	120	62

In case of query, please contact   *A Student* / *G Russell*

Date
7/11/X1

Payee
Wallace
Limited

£120.62

305086

WADSWORTH BANK PLC
Chambers Street, Scarborough,
YO12 3NZ

25–46–70

7 November 20 X1

Pay   *Wallace Limited*   or order

One hundred and twenty pounds and 62p only   £ 120.62

For Seamer Retail Ltd

305086   25 - 46 - 70   21758391

MOCK SIMULATION 2 : **ANSWERS**

TASK 5

CASH BOOK PAYMENTS

CPB 53

Date 20X1	Payee/details	Cheque no	Total £	VAT £	Creditors £	Discount Received £	Sundry £
7 Nov	Petty Cash	305081	35.53				35.53
7 Nov	Baxley Ltd Inv 4132	305082	2,098.42		2,098.42		
7 Nov	Harborne Ltd Inv 2541	305083	2,439.55		2,439.55		
7 Nov	Hurley Ltd Inv 1008	305084	352.69		352.69		
7 Nov	Allen & Banks Inv 1673	305085	757.01		757.01	9.81	
7 Nov	Wallace Ltd Inv 4321	305086	120.62		120.62		
			5,803.82		5,768.29	9.81	35.53

TASK 6

MAIN LEDGER

Account: Postage

Debit			Credit		
Date 20X1	Details	Amount £	Date 20X1	Details	Amount £
31-Oct	Bal b/f	213.76			
7 Nov	Petty Cash Book	9.95			

Account: Stationery

Debit			Credit		
Date 20X1	Details	Amount £	Date 20X1	Details	Amount £
31-Oct	Bal b/f	543.09			
7 Nov	Petty Cash Book	12.16			

397

Account: Travel

Debit			Credit		
Date 20X1	Details	Amount £	Date 20X1	Details	Amount £
31-Oct	Bal b/f	513.88			
7 Nov	Petty Cash Book	9.62			

Account: Purchase ledger control

Debit			Credit		
Date 20X1	Details	Amount £	Date 20X1	Details	Amount £
7 Nov	Bank	5,768.29	31-Oct	Bal b/f	28,996.21
7 Nov	Discount received	9.81			

Account: VAT

Debit			Credit		
Date 20X1	Details	Amount £	Date 20X1	Details	Amount £
7 Nov	Petty Cash Book	3.80	31-Oct	Bal b/f	2,499.04

Account: Cash sales

Debit			Credit		
Date 20X1	Details	Amount £	Date 20X1	Details	Amount £
			31-Oct	Bal b/f	51,235.99

MOCK SIMULATION 2 : **ANSWERS**

Account: Discount received

Debit			Credit		
Date 20X1	Details	Amount £	Date 20X1	Details	Amount £
			31-Oct	Bal b/f	147.39
			7- Nov	Purchase ledger control	9.81

SUBSIDIARY (PURCHASES) LEDGER

Account: Allen and Banks

Debit			Credit		
Date 20X1	Details	Amount £	Date 20X1	Details	Amount £
7 Nov 7 Nov	Bank Discount received	757.01 9.81	31-Oct	Bal b/f	1,152.90

Account: Baxley Limited

Debit			Credit		
Date 20X1	Details	Amount £	Date 20X1	Details	Amount £
7 Nov	Bank	2,098.42	31-Oct	Bal b/f	3,012.75

Account: Harborne Limited

Debit			Credit		
Date 20X1	Details	Amount £	Date 20X1	Details	Amount £
7 Nov	Bank	2,439.55	31- Oct	Bal b/f	3,225.67

KAPLAN PUBLISHING

UNIT 30 : WORKBOOK

Account: Hurley Limited

Debit			Credit		
Date 20X1	Details	Amount £	Date 20X1	Details	Amount £
7 Nov	Bank	352.69	31-Oct	Bal b/f	961.44

Account: Wallace Limited

Debit			Credit		
Date 20X1	Details	Amount £	Date 20X1	Details	Amount £
7 Nov	Bank	120.62	31-Oct	Bal b/f	546.08

PART THREE

TASK 7

MEMO

To: Gillian Russell
From: A Student
Subject: Week ending 7 Nov 20X1 Discrepancies
Date: 7 Nov 20X1

The following discrepancies were found in the course of dealing with the Petty Cash:

Petty Cash claim from Adam Haynes for £4.94 for stationery was not processed as there was no corresponding receipt.

There were three vouchers/receipts which are awaiting your authorisation before processing.

A Student

MOCK SIMULATION 3
ANSWERS

UNIT 30 : WORKBOOK

PART ONE

TASKS 1, 2 and 3

SUBSIDIARY (PURCHASES) LEDGER

Hadley Turf Supplies

Date 20X1	Details	Amount £	Date 20X1	Details	Amount £
1 June	Purchases returns DB	517	1 June	Balance b/d	12,500
1 June	Balance c/d	14,521	1 June	Purchases DB	2,538
		15,038			15,038
			2 June	Balance b/d	14,521

Blackwood Nurseries

Date 20X1	Details	Amount £	Date 20X1	Details	Amount £
1 June	Purchases returns DB	705	1 June	Balance b/d	8,260
1 June	Balance c/d	9,388	1 June	Purchases DB	1,598
			1 June	Journal	235
		10,093			10,093
			2 June	Balance b/d	9,388

Lawnmower Repair Shop

Date 20X1	Details	Amount £	Date 20X1	Details	Amount £
1 June	Journal	235	1 June	Balance b/d	970
1 June	Balance c/d	5,435	1 June	Purchases DB	4,700
		5,670			5,670
			2 June	Balance b/d	5,435

Western Electricity

Date 20X1	Details	Amount £	Date 20X1	Details	Amount £
1 June	Balance c/d	510	1 June	Balance b/d	40
			1 June	Purchases DB	470
		510			510
			2 June	Balance b/d	510

MOCK SIMULATION 3 : **ANSWERS**

Other suppliers

Date 20X1	Details	Amount £	Date 20X1	Details	Amount £
			1 June	Balance b/d	10,000

MAIN LEDGER

Purchases

Date 20X1	Details	Amount £	Date 20X1	Details	Amount £
1 June	Balance b/d	88,039	1 June	Balance c/d	95,559
1 June	Purchases DB	7,520			
		95,559			95,559
2 June	Balance b/d	95,559			

Purchases returns

Date 20X1	Details	Amount £	Date 20X1	Details	Amount £
1 June	Balance c/d	2,040	1 June	Balance b/d	1,000
			1 June	Purchases returns DB	1,040
		2,040			2,040
			2 June	Balance b/d	2,040

Purchases (Creditors) ledger control

Date 20X1	Details	Amount £	Date 20X1	Details	Amount £
1 June	Purchases returns DB	1,222	1 June	Balance b/d	32,109
1 June	Balance c/d	40,193	1 June	Purchases DB	9,306
		41,415			41,415
			2 June	Balance b/d	40,193

KAPLAN PUBLISHING

Sales

Date 20X1	Details	Amount £	Date 20X1	Details	Amount £
1 June	Balance c/d	185,570	1 June	Balance b/d	180,770
			1 June	SDB	4,800
		185,570			185,570
			2 June	Balance b/d	185,570

Sales (Debtors) ledger control

Date 20X1	Details	Amount £	Date 20X1	Details	Amount £
1 June	Balance b/d	66,468	1 June	Balance c/d	72,108
1 June	SDB	5,640			
		72,108			72,108
2 June	Balance b/d	72,108			

Heat and light

Date 20X1	Details	Amount £	Date 20X1	Details	Amount £
1 June	Balance b/d	566	1 June	Balance c/d	966
1 June	Purchases DB	400			
		966			966
2 June	Balance b/d	966			

VAT

Date 20X1	Details	Amount £	Date 20X1	Details	Amount £
1 June	Purchases DB	1,386	1 June	Balance b/d	8,078
1 June	Balance c/d	7,714	1 June	SDB	840
			1 June	Purchases returns DB	182
		9,100			9,100
			2 June	Balance b/d	7,714

TASK 4

Reconciliation of Purchases ledger control account at 1 June 20X1.

List of creditors

Name	Amount £
Hadley Turf Supplies	14,521
Blackwood Nurseries	9,388
Lawnmower Repair Shop	5,435
Western Electricity	510
Other suppliers	10,000
Total	39,854
Adjustments	
Add (b) Hadley invoice	163
Revised total	40,017
Balance per control account	40,193
Adjustments	
Less (a) overcast PDB	(200)
Add (c) credit note entered twice in PRDB	24
Revised total	40,017

TASK 5

Western Bank plc
Bradbury Way
Swinford LE1 8OU

Gregson Garden Services Limited
Account 86759485

STATEMENT OF ACCOUNT

Date 20X1	Details	Debit £	Credit £	Balance £
26 May	Balance b/f			8,070C ✓
27 May	Cheque 111987	4,760 ✓		3,310C
28 May	Bank Giro Credit: Carter & Son		7,000 ✓	10,310C
28 May	Cheque 111988	2,198 ✓		8,112C
31 May	Bank charges	55 ✓		8,057C
31 May	Direct Debit: Contract Cleaning	235 ✓		7,822C
31 May	Credit		1,880 ✓	9,702C

D = Debit C = Credit

Cash Book

20X1		£	20X1		£
20 May	Balance b/d	8,070 ✓	21 May	Patio Pavers	4,760 ✓
26 May	B Bradley	1,880 ✓	22 May	L Briggs	2,198 ✓
31 May	Park Maintenance	2,170	31 May	T Brown	1,500
28 May	Carter & Son BGC	7,000 ✓	31 May	Bank Charges	55 ✓
			31 May	Contract Cleaning DD	235 ✓
			31 May	Balance c/d	10,372
		19,120			19,120
1 June	Balance b/d	10,372			

PART 2

TASK 6

VAT

		£			£
June	– Purchases	3,592	June	– Balance b/d	4,110
	– Sales returns	19		– Sales	801
	– Balance c/d	1,304		– Purchases returns	4
		4,915			4,915

TASK 7

Sales ledger control account

		£			£
June	– Balance b/d	78,852	June	– Sales returns	126
	– Sales	5,380		– Bank	2,012
				– Bad debt	3,678
				– Balance c/d	78,416
		84,232			84,232

TASK 8

Sportsworld Ltd

		£			£
June	– Balance b/d	3,523	June	– Sales returns	126
	– Sales	2,191		– Bank	1,485
				– Balance c/d	4,103
		5,714			5,714

Royal Sports Ltd

		£			£
June	– Bank	7,991	June	– Balance b/d	24,236
	– Balance c/d	32,155		– Purchases	15,910
		40,146			40,146

UNIT 30 : WORKBOOK

TASK 9

List of updated balances at the end of the day

	Debit balances £	Credit balances £
Customers:		
Barnes Department Stores (W1)	11,191	
Sportsworld Ltd (Task 8)	4,103	
Birmingham Sports (W2)	5,779	
Hi-sport (W3)	7,128	
Keysports (W4)	Nil	
Suppliers:		
Royal Sports Ltd (Task 8)		32,155
Leisurewear UK Ltd (W5)		48,978
Sales (W6)		357,450
Purchases (W7)	208,817	
Sales returns (W8)	2,273	
Purchases returns (W9)		1,867
Bank (W10)		16,047
VAT (Task 6)		1,304
Bad debts (W11)	3,678	
Other debit balances	486,775	
Other credit balances		271,943
Totals	729,744	729,744

WORKINGS

W1   **Barnes Department Stores**

	£		£
Opening balance	10,629	Closing balance	11,191
Invoice	562		
	11,191		11,191

W2   **Birmingham Sports**

	£		£
Opening balance	4,890	Closing balance	5,779
Invoice	889		
	5,779		5,779

MOCK SIMULATION 3 : **ANSWERS**

W3

Hi-sport

	£		£
Opening balance	5,917	Bank	527
Invoice	1,738	Closing balance	7,128
	7,655		7,655

W4

Keysports

	£		£
Opening balance	3,678	Bad debt	3,678

W5

Leisurewear UK Ltd

	£		£
Purchase returns	28	Opening balance	40,802
Closing balance	48,978	Purchases	8,204
	49,006		49,006

W6

Sales

	£		£
Closing balance	357,450	Opening balance	352,871
		Invoices	4,579
	357,450		357,450

W7

Purchases

	£		£
Opening balance	188,295	Closing balance	208,817
Invoices received	20,522		
	208,817		208,817

W8

Sales returns

	£		£
Opening balance	2,166	Closing balance	2,273
Invoices received	107		
	2,273		2,273

W9

Purchases returns

	£		£
Closing balance	1,867	Opening balance	1,843
		Credit note	24
	1,867		1,867

KAPLAN PUBLISHING

UNIT 30 : WORKBOOK

W10

Bank

	£		£
Receipts	2,012	Opening balance	10,068
Closing balance	16,047	Payments	7,991
	18,059		18,059

W11

Bad debts

	£		£
Bad debt write off	3,678		

SPECIMEN EXAM PAPER ANSWERS

UNIT 30 : WORKBOOK

SECTION 1

Task 1.1 – Debit

Task 1.2

Account name	Amount £	Debit/Credit
Office equipment	3,500	Debit
Sales	321,650	Credit
Sales returns	15,800	Debit
Sales ledger control	112,636	Debit
Discount allowed	750	Debit
Motor expenses	1,225	Debit
Rent and rates	3,600	Debit

Task 1.3

a)

Account name	Amount £	Debit/Credit
Creations Limited	2,115	Debit
Jackson and Company	9,870	Debit
Loxley Limited	3,055	Debit
PTT Limited	7,050	Debit

b)

Account name	Amount £	Debit/Credit
Sales ledger control	22,090	Debit
Sales	18,800	Credit
VAT	3,290	Credit

Task 1.4

a)

Account name	Amount £	Debit/Credit
Creations Limited	4,700	Credit
Loxley Limited	423	Credit

b)

Account name	Amount £	Debit/Credit
Sales returns	4,360	Debit
VAT	763	Debit
Sales ledger control	5,123	Credit

SPECIMEN EXAMINATION : ANSWERS

Task 1.5

a)

Account name	Amount £	Debit/Credit
Lee Limited	3,525	Credit
Ball and McGee	1,410	Credit
Horner and Company	12,690	Credit
H&H Ltd	4,700	Credit

b)

Account name	Amount £	Debit/Credit
Purchases	19,000	Debit
VAT	3,325	Debit
Purchases ledger control	22,325	Credit

Task 1.6

Subsidiary (sales) ledger

Account name	Amount £	Debit/Credit
Jackson and Company	3,650	Credit
Jackson and Company	100	Credit

Subsidiary (purchases) ledger

Account name	Amount £	Debit/Credit
Croxford Ltd	2,000	Debit

Main ledger

Account name	Amount £	Debit/Credit
Motor expenses	350	Debit
Rent and rates	1,200	Debit
Office equipment	3,250	Debit
Purchases ledger control	2,000	Debit
Sales ledger control	3,650	Credit
Sales ledger control	100	Credit

Task 1.7

Hotel expenses

Date 2005	Details	Amount £	Date 2005	Details	Amount £
01 June	Balance b/f	3,000			
26 June	Bank	595	30 June	Balance c/d	3,595
	Total	3,595		Total	3,595
1 July	Balance b/d	3,595			

Loan from bank

Date 2005	Details	Amount £	Date 2005	Details	Amount £
18 June	Bank	700	1 June	Balance b/f	15,000
30 June	Balance c/d	14,300			
	Total	15,000		Total	15,000
			1 July	Balance b/d	14,300

Task 1.8

a)

Account name	Amount £	Debit/Credit
Motor expenses	70	Debit
Miscellaneous expenses	70	Credit

b)

Account name	Amount £	Debit/Credit
Purchases ledger control	4,500	Debit
Purchases	4,500	Credit

c)

Account name	Amount £	Debit/Credit
Bad debts	200	Debit
VAT	35	Debit
Sales ledger control	235	Credit

SPECIMEN EXAMINATION : **ANSWERS**

Task 1.9

Account name	Amount £	Debit/Credit
Rent	10	Debit
Suspense	75	Debit
Heat and light	85	Credit

Task 1.10

Account name	Amount £	Debit £	Credit £
Motor vehicles		5,200	
Office equipment		8,750	
Stock		17,000	
Cash at bank		5,040	
Petty cash control		60	
Sales ledger control		125,853	
Purchases ledger control			56,713
VAT owing to H M Revenue & Customs			13,990
Loan from bank			14,300
Capital			32,373
Sales			340,450
Sales returns		20,160	
Purchases		206,511	
Purchases returns			862
Discount received			248
Discount allowed		850	
Wages		50,425	
Heat and light		963	
Motor expenses		1,645	
Rent and rates		4,810	
Travel expenses		1,650	
Hotel expenses		3,595	
Telephone		1,006	
Accountancy fees		2,530	
Bad debts written off		200	
Miscellaneous expenses		2,688	
Totals		458,936	458,936

UNIT 30 : WORKBOOK

SECTION 2

Task 2.1

a) iii)

	£
Invoice total	210.87
Less: discount (180 x 2%)	(3.60)
	207.27

b)
  ii) To offer a lower price to an organisation within the same trade

c)
  i) Those placing large orders

Task 2.2

i) The Garden Warehouse are entitled to a refund from HM Customs and Excise

Task 2.3

ii) 02 June   Acceptance is valid from when it is posted.

Task 2.4

a)
  WB50
  or
  WR50
  or
  PL50

b)
  iii) Subsidiary (purchases) ledger

Task 2.5

a) The trial balance will balance

b) The trial balance will balance

c) The trial balance will balance

d) The trial balance will not balance

SPECIMEN EXAMINATION : **ANSWERS**

Task 2.6

6 months

Task 2.7

Debit   Purchases ledger control account
Credit   Sales ledger control account

Task 2.8

Total of net wages paid to employees
Total of trade union fee deductions

Task 2.9

Transaction	Capital or Revenue
Purchase of office stationery	Revenue
Annual decoration of offices	Revenue
Purchase of a delivery van	Capital
Purchase of fuel for the delivery van	Revenue

Task 2.10

Amount required to restore imprest system = payments made
= £10 + 5 + 30
= £45

Task 2.11

Goods must be worth the price asked

Task 2.12

a) VAT on sales = £122,000 × 0.175 = £21,350

b) VAT on purchases = £9,870 × 17.5/117.5 = £1,470

c) Balance on VAT account = £21,350 – 1,470 = £19,880

d) Payable to HM Customs and Excise

Task 2.13

The maximum amount allowed to be outstanding at any one time.

KAPLAN PUBLISHING

UNIT 30 : WORKBOOK

Task 2.14

a)

Account name	Amount £	Debit/Credit
Bank (800 x 1.175)	940	Debit
Sales	800	Credit
VAT	140	Credit

b)

Date 1 July 2005	MBC Bank plc Worcester	£50 notes	
		£20 notes	40.00
	Account The Garden Warehouse	£10 notes	40.00
		£5 notes	40.00
No. of items 1	**Paid in by** Marian Walker	£2 coin	
		£1 coin	
		Other coin	
		Total cash	120.00
		Cheques, POs	940.00
	49-20-40 39287594 78	£	1,060.00

Task 2.15

Delivery note

Task 2.16

To accompany a cheque in payment of an account	Remittance advice
To list unpaid invoices and ask for payment each month	Statement of account
To correct an overcharge on an invoice issued	Credit note

Task 2.17

a)

		Debit/Credit
Balance of creditors at 1 June 2005	£53,386	Credit
Goods bought on credit	£20,500	Credit
Money paid to credit suppliers	£16,193	Debit
Discounts received	£380	Debit
Goods returned to credit suppliers	£600	Debit

SPECIMEN EXAMINATION : **ANSWERS**

b)

Cr   £56,713

c)

	£
Gardens Unlimited	15,620
P Lower	1,695
L Brown	23,000
White Brothers	16,200
Hoe and Dig	578
	57,093

	£
Purchase ledger control account balance as at 30 June 2005	56,713
Total of subsidiary (purchases) ledger accounts as at 30 June 2005	57,093
Difference	380

d)

ii) Discounts received have been omitted from the subsidiary (purchases) ledger.

The subsidiary ledger total is £380 higher than that of the control account therefore as the discounts received total £380 it is likely that they have only been posted to the control account in the main ledger.

Task 2.18

MIDDLE BANK plc
12 High Street, Droitwich, WR15 7LW

To: The Garden Warehouse   Account No: 867287234   24 June 2005

STATEMENT OF ACCOUNT

Date 2005	Details	Paid out £	Paid in £	Balance £	Tick
1 June	Balance b/f			15,619 C	x
6 June	Cheque 008301	2,650		12,969 C	x
8 June	Cheque 008302	1,986		10,983 C	x
10 June	Bank Giro Credit A Parker		550	11,533 C	x
10 June	Bank Giro Credit L Westwood		6,140	17,673 C	x
13 June	Cheque 008303	8,432		9,241 C	x
15 June	Direct Debit Droitwich CC	100		9,141 C	
20 June	Direct Debit Cranston Insurance	250		8,891 C	
22 June	Overdraft facility fee	50		8,841 C	
22 June	Bank charges	16		8,825 C	
22 June	Bank interest		26	8,851 C	

D = Debit C = Credit

CASH BOOK

Date 2005	Details	Tick	Bank £	Date 2005	Cheque Number	Details	Tick	Bank £
1 June	Balance b/f	x	15,619	1 June	008301	Portman Brothers	x	2,650
10 June	A Parker	x	550	1 June	008302	Tether & Tie	x	1,986
10 June	L Westwood	x	6,140	6 June	008303	D Price	x	8,432
15 June	CCC Ltd		1,260	6 June	008304	Mundon Ltd		1,407
22 June	B Williams		142	22 June	008305	Hackett Ltd		350
22 June	Bank interest		26	15 June		Droitwich CC		100
				20 June		Cranston Ins		250
				22 June		Overdraft facility fee		50
				22 June		Bank charges		16
				28 June		Balance c/d		8,496
			23,737					23,737
29 June	Balance b/d		8,496					

Bank reconciliation statement as at 28 June 2005		
Balance per bank statement		£8,851
Add:		
	Name: CCC Limited	£1,260
	Name: B Williams	£ 142
Total to add		£1,402
Less:		
	Name: Mundon Limited	£1,407
	Name: Hackett Limited	£ 350
Total to subtract		£1,757
Balance as per cash book		£8,496

Task 2.19

The Garden Warehouse
2a Lower Parade
Droitwich
Worcestershire, WR16 8IS
VAT Registration No. 387 2987 00

TGL Limited
The Avenue
Broadway
West Midlands
B84 3LD

Invoice No: 853

Your order number: 290

Date: 1 July 2005

Quantity	Description	Product code	Net £	VAT £	Total £
500	Heavy duty gardening forks	F60	6,000	1,029	7,029

2% settlement discount for payment within 7 days

Note: VAT calculation £6,000 x 98% x 17.5% = £1,029

Task 2.20

> **The Garden Warehouse**
> **2a Lower Parade**
> **Droitwich**
> **Worcestershire, WR16 81S**
>
> Swindon Spades
> 18 High Street
> Swindon
> FR3 1JH
>
> 1 July 2005
>
> Dear Sir
>
> Overdue account
>
> I wish to draw your attention to our invoice number 110 for £3,525 dated 16 January 2005.
>
> This amount is now considerably overdue and we require payment by return.
>
> Yours faithfully
>
>
> Marian Walker